A Feast for Lawyers

A FEAST FOR

SOL STEIN

LAWYERS
INSIDE
CHAPTER 11:
An Exposé

M. Evans and Company, Inc.   *New York*

Library of Congress Cataloging-in-Publication Data
Stein, Sol.
   A feast for lawyers : inside Chapter 11—an expose / Sol Stein.
      p. cm.
   Includes bibliographical references.
   ISBN 0-87131-589-0
      1. Corporate reorganizations—United States.   2. Bankruptcy-
-United States.   I. Title.
KF1544.S74   1989   89-23721
346.73'06626—dc20
[347.3066626]

Copyright © 1989 by The Colophon Corporation

M. Evans and Company, Inc.
216 East 49 Street
New York, New York 10017

Design by Ben Kann

Manufactured in the United States of America

9 8 7 6 5 4 3 2 1

This book is dedicated to Leslie Fiedler, Elia Kazan, Daniel Miller, Thomas Reeves, Budd Schulberg, Joanna Woolfolk, and the many other friends, authors, agents, and foreign publishers whose writings and work got trapped in the economic folly of the Chapter 11 law.

By the same author

"I've got no control over my own life."
>—Roxanne, in "L. A. Law" when
>faced with bankruptcy in an
>episode aired April 28, 1988

"It has been said that we talk around cruelty because we don't want to talk about it. And when we are forced to confront it, we call it sadism. By turning the conversation to the pathological condition we deny its relevance to us. In other words, what is most unacceptable about cruelty is not that it exists but that, in the words of the political philosopher Judith Shklar, it is an 'ordinary vice': something that, although horrible, is expectable, something our neighbor could very well do."
>—Sherry Turkle,
>Associate Professor of Sociology,
>M.I.T., in a front page review of
>*By Silence Betrayed,*
>*The New York Times Book Review*

"A casual attitude toward human hurt and pain is the surest sign of educational failure. It is also the beginning of the end of a free society."
>—Norman Cousins, *Human Options*

"It is from the level of calamities not that of everyday life that we learn impressive and useful lessons."
>—William Makepeace Thackeray

"Bearing witness matters because it rights the balance of power."
>—Leigh Hafrey, in a review of Lawrence
>Thornton's *Imagining Argentina,* in *The*
>*New York Times Book Review*

I am indebted to those individuals who tried to save Stein and Day from the depredations of Chapter 11:

Joshua J. Angel

William Hammett
President, The Manhattan Institute for Policy Research

Terence Herzog

Oliver Janney
former President, the River Road Association

John Kelly
Vice President, Marboro Books

Werner M. Linz
Chairman, The Crossroad/Continuum Publishing Group

Francis Pandolfi
then President, Lifeboat Associates

Don Reiman
architect and former member of
the Briarcliff Manor Planning Board

Holly von Bernuth
then President, the River Road Association

Those who sought to entomb Stein and Day are
acknowledged elsewhere in this book

Contents

Foreword

I am a survivor of a part of the judicial system that each year processes many thousands of human beings in a manner and with a purpose that is not known to their fellow citizens. Nor is what happens known to the preponderance of lawyers who may send clients into the rehabilitation camps without knowing what really goes on there.

In that system, reorganization does not mean reorganization. Equity does not mean fairness. Equal justice under law is a banner on the Supreme Court building that is openly held in contempt.

My responsibility to testify comes from understanding that to tell is to teach, and to report is the obligation of a writer.

Despite the proven pain, humiliation, coercion, and corruption that are part of the Chapter 11 process, there are no armies or citizen undergrounds trying to overthrow the perpetrators. The sad fact is that Chapter 11 is run by an arm of the United States Government, and its keepers are not aberrant aliens but officers of the court.

I feel called on to testify because so far no one who has been inside the Chapter 11 experience has written a cautionary tale for others.

A number of people didn't want to see this book published because they make handsome livings from what goes on behind closed doors in the world of Chapter 11. I know some of their faces, where and how they work, and, in some cases, who pulls their strings. Many of them are members of a highly paid class of individuals who don't want anyone who's been inside Chapter 11 to report what he's seen. And like some not so salubrious organizations that profit from the misery of others, they threaten to exact severe penalties from those who dare to talk.

The public owes a debt of gratitude, as I do, to the businessmen and -women who have allowed me to use information from their cases, and their private lives as they were affected by those cases, knowing that I was writing this book. A generation of executives may prove to be grateful, as I am, to two of their number, Thomas Towey of Neptune World Wide Moving and Storage, Inc. and Samuel Metzger of Chipwich, Inc., both of whom guided their companies through the rapids of Chapter 11 so that their businesses might emerge alive at the other end.

One comes to think of Chapter 11 as a hospital—albeit one that the reader of this book will sense sometimes resembles a madhouse rather than a place of healing; if the bankruptcy courts were truly hospitals for business, they might be shut down as a public danger because such a small percentage of their patients emerge at all. Fewer than a third of the cases that come through the doors of Chapter 11 leave it alive. Some experts contend that the odds are from five-to-one to ten-to-one that a company won't make it. The smaller the company, the less its chance of surviving the cauldron. And "small" usually means under $10 million in revenue a year, which covers the great majority of companies that file.

The Bankruptcy Division of the Administrative Office of the United States Courts in Washington, D.C., compiles from each of the 284 United States bankruptcy courts information concerning the amount, duration, and success of bankruptcy filings. The chief of that division, Frank Szczebak, one of the most cooperative of men, was unable to say what percentage of companies entering Chapter 11 are able to reorganize successfully. But one thing all the people in the bankruptcy business agree on is that the percentage of success is pitifully small. The appalling price of that success is described here.

It would be remiss of me to shed light on the dark workings of Chapter 11 and not examine alternative practices from which business stands a better chance of cure. In 1988, Christopher Beard, publisher of *Turnarounds & Workouts: News for People Tracking Distressed Businesses*, introduced me to an occupation I didn't know existed, and which no bankruptcy lawyer had ever told me about. These people are sometimes called consultants, which means little, or crisis managers, which is much more descriptive of what they do. They are also called turnaround specialists and turnaround managers, and what they all do is work with companies on the brink of insolvency to try to help them avoid the necessity of filing under Chapter 11 of the Bankruptcy Code or being pushed into an involuntary Chapter 7. Their client companies are almost always very sick when they are called in. How these turnaround specialists try to save their clients is described in their own voices in this book.

I talked at length with seven such healers, headquartered in different parts of the United States: David Ferrari, president of the Argus Management Corporation of Natick, Massachusetts; Kenneth E. Glass of Canton, Ohio, whose practice covers all forty-eight contiguous states; Daniel M. Morris, president of Morris Anderson & Associates of Glenview, Illinois, whose practice is also national; Gilbert C. Osnos, head of Bresanti, Galef, & Osnos of New York; Ronald F. Stengel of R.F. Stengel & Co., Inc. of Wayne, Pennsylvania; and two who specialize in the smaller companies that often find it difficult to secure professional help of quality, Malcolm Moses of Melville, New York, and Adam Radzik, president of R & E Business Consultants of West Orange, New Jersey. They and their colleagues constitute a countervailing force to the abhorrent underside of the bankruptcy trade.

The bankruptcy bar itself is sharply divided between a minority of ethical professionals scattered around the United States, several of whom I interviewed for this book, and a majority whose methods, techniques, habits, routines, ploys, angles, ethics, and destructive practices are detailed in these pages.

A singular act of courage was demonstrated by Joshua J. Angel, a bankruptcy lawyer who is always identifiable in or out of the courtroom by his trademark, a bright red tie. Angel specializes in getting companies *out* of Chapter 11 successfully and, if at all possible, quickly. He encouraged me to write a novel with Chapter 11 as a central theme. I decided that on the subject of bankruptcy, truth was stranger than fiction, and that reality is what I have set down in this book.

The examples and incidents depicted here come from all over the country and all kinds of industries. My most striking discovery was the similarity of the effects on both the people and the businesses involved. To contain what I discovered within the compass of a single book, I have focused in depth on three companies that saw their destinies worked out in the same courtroom and under the eye of the same judge, who also sat over perhaps the most publicized Chapter 11 case of our century, that of Texaco. But the Texaco case, bits of which I witnessed firsthand, is not at all typical. Nor can it be said that the cases of Neptune and Chipwich are typical because both companies were successful in making it out of Chapter 11, and that happens only in a minority of cases.

And so, with two of the three cases examined in the greatest detail being success stories, this book might be said to be skewed on the side of optimism. But both of those cases were handled by the same lawyer, and the irony is that the third case would have been had the company I headed not been prevented from hiring him. The reader of this cautionary tale may eventually come to the conclusion that the skill of the advocate may matter as much or more than the merits of a case.[1]

---

1. This simply proves once again that life imitates art. A novel of mine called *The Magician*, published by the Delacorte Press in 1971, was based on the prescient theme that the skill of the advocate is what

A large part of this book necessarily stems from my firsthand experience as chief executive officer of a book publishing company that was compelled to file under Chapter 11. In business and the law there is no such thing as a "scientific" control group, but the fact that this case took place in the same courtroom and with the same judge as the two successful cases reported here provides some revealing comparisons.

This book sets out to do five things: first, to expose Chapter 11 from the inside, something that has never been done before; second, to illumine an area of legal practice that has contributed perhaps more than its share to the precipitous decline of the reputation of a once great profession; third, to provide the entrepreneurs and executives of both healthy and troubled companies with practical insights on how to better protect themselves against sudden developments that may leave no time to take preventive action; fourth, to bear witness to a process that in the vast majority of cases, especially those involving medium-sized and small businesses, has become a base parody of equity and the law's intent; and fifth, to suggest the means by which some of the worst abominations of these practices might be changed.

Sol Stein
Scarborough, New York
May 18, 1989

---

counts. *The Magician* was chosen by the Book-of-the-Month Club and widely taught in American schools. In a further irony, the book was selling in its second million when its publication was abruptly halted by two of Stein and Day's creditors in its Chapter 11 case, causing very large school orders to be returned unfilled.

CHAPTER 1

Ten Lies About Chapter 11

"We French lie to others. Americans lie to themselves."
— Eva Hoffman, quoting a Frenchman in *Lost in Translation*

EACH year many thousands of companies find themselves in a squeeze in which they cannot keep up with the demands of their creditors. Or they cannot cope with a business-busting court decision. This happens to companies large and small all over the United States, sometimes quite suddenly. The chief executives of these companies may decide to—or be forced to—seek protection from their creditors by filing a petition in Chapter 11 under the Bankruptcy Reform Act of 1978 so that they can reorganize their businesses. Where do they go to find out what to do?

The assumption is that they can go to the lawyer who ordinarily advises them and he will do so wisely. Wrong! *Most lawyers in commercial or criminal practice know little or nothing about the subject of commercial insolvency, let alone the intricacies of operating under the bankruptcy laws.* The honest ones will admit it. So will the accountants who do not understand how a balance sheet changes drastically the moment a company files.

The corporate lawyers and litigators I talked to said without exception that they needed to know what happens inside Chapter 11 as much any businessman would because the world of Chapter 11 is for them, too, a foreign country without a good map.

The chances are that whatever lawyer a businessman usually relies on for advice will have to pass that executive on to a specialist in bankruptcy law who is willing to handle a debtor. There's the rub, for many of the attorneys who specialize in this field are a breed unto themselves, who may give advice that is likely to be of greater benefit to themselves than to the businessman or his company.

In many jurisdictions bankruptcy specialists constitute a smallish clan whose members work with each other in case after case. The "teams" of lawyers in every bankruptcy case change, but in the same court the identical players show up time after time. I've seen a bankruptcy lawyer play musical chairs with his "colleagues" and stand up to announce his participation in three separate cases in the same courtroom in one morning.

Where does the bankruptcy lawyer's loyalty lie? The codes of ethics of numerous bar associations say in the strongest terms that the lawyer's loyalty must be to his client. Guess again.

It is generally acknowledged that a high proportion of matrimonial lawyers are skilled at making matters worse. Their adversarial training, it is said, tends to exacerbate existing tensions. It is also commonly thought that lawyers specializing in personal injury work on a contingency basis, so-called "ambulance chasers," are at the bottom rung of the law. The fact is that anyone who lives through Chapter 11 will tell you that compared to some bankruptcy lawyers, ambulance chasers are pretty good guys because they may make the injury sound worse than it is but they don't actually make it worse. They are content to collect a third or so of the money their clients are awarded. Bankruptcy specialists can thrive on keeping their clients sick for a long time and when representing a debtor can collect substantial fees while their clients lose money. That's a serious charge that is among the many that will be proven in this book. Mind you, there is a considerable range of both morality and competence in the bankruptcy field, just as there are exceptions to every category of human behavior, and you'll meet some of them in these pages. But that doesn't mean you can hire one of the exceptional practitioners, which brings us to:

Lie Number 1. *You can hire a lawyer of your choice.*

Not true. Many lawyers who specialize in bankruptcy will work only for institutional creditors, such as banks and insurance companies, because these creditors will pay their monthly bills as they are incurred.

The debtor company, however, once enmeshed in Chapter 11, is not permitted to pay anybody anything—including its lawyers—without the approval of the secured creditors and the court. This presumes, of course, that the debtor's liquid assets are collateralized, as is usually the case. At best, a debtor's legal bills will be allowed to be paid at stated intervals by the court—provided the creditors do not object. The attorney for the debtor will therefore require a sizable retainer before taking the client on. But companies in need of protection, particularly the smaller companies that make up the majority of filings, don't necessarily have a lot of ready cash. And if they do have the cash and it comes from receivables, or from any other source that a bank or other creditor is claiming as collateral, their use of the money to engage a lawyer may be contested in court.

Most law firms require a retainer under any circumstances. After all, it is better for the money to sit in their account, earning interest for them, than to sit in your account earning interest for you—or, God forbid, be used for operating the business. Moreover, a law firm, like the government, likes to collect money that it already has under its control. It's harder to argue about the charges on a bill you've prepaid.

Bankruptcy lawyers who handle debtors have an additional reason for wanting the retainer up front. The process locks the lawyer in because he cannot leave the case without the permission of the court.[1] It also takes a lot of the performance criteria out of the normal lawyer-client relationship. If the client doesn't like the way the case is being handled, he usually has to learn to live with it. The chances of a debtor getting a new lawyer are remote, since the debtor will need the permission of the creditors and the court to use any company money for a second retainer. The creditors' lawyers certainly do not want to see the debtor company ditch a poorly performing lawyer for a possibly more formidable opponent.

And so in the case of the thousands of medium- and smaller-sized companies that make up the majority of Chapter 11 filings, there is a built-in disparity between the lawyers a creditor can hire and the lawyer the debtor can hire. The secured creditors' lawyers get paid as they go—the creditors expect to recoup their legal expenses from the debtor company—while the debtor's lawyer frequently has to wait till the end of the case to get anything above the retainer although his fees and expenses become "administrative costs of the estate."

Let's see what happened when three very different-sized companies went about getting bankruptcy lawyers to represent them: huge Texaco, mid-sized Neptune World Wide Moving and Storage, and the relatively small company that bore my name and my wife's name for twenty-six years, Stein and Day Publishers. These three Chapter 11 companies found their destinies being worked out in the same courtroom and before the same judge, with the biggest and the smallest often back-to-back on the same day.

Cash-rich Texaco had no trouble hiring whatever law firm it wanted as long as that firm didn't already have a client on retainer that was a party to the Texaco case. The

---

1. However, the court can grant such permission if a lawyer isn't making enough money out of a case, even if it leaves a debtor without counsel, and may do so without even reading the debtor's papers opposing the attorney's abandonment of the case. See Chapter 15.

informed business reader will know that firms with deep pockets sometimes pay a retainer to a law firm with a tough reputation in order to prevent their being hired by one of their enemies.

Neptune World Wide Moving got lucky and found an ideal lawyer. They were able to hire Joshua Angel, head of Angel & Frankel, P.C., the second largest bankruptcy law firm in New York that handles debtors. Angel says he won't take on clients unless he is convinced he can help get them back on their feet and eventually out of Chapter 11 as a going concern. Thomas Towey, CEO of Neptune, says of Angel, "Josh was our captain, our pilot. I canonized him immediately." Neptune got successfully out of Chapter 11 in just a little over two years, a remarkably short time for a process that most bankruptcy lawyers seek to stretch out as long as their time clocks tick.

The irony is that through a prospective new investor Stein and Day found that same lawyer, Joshua Angel, who studied our case and was convinced that Stein and Day could be brought out of Chapter 11 into a future as profitable as it was in the past. Moreover, Angel wasn't concerned that Stein and Day could not pay a retainer; he was satisfied to have his compensation be a piece of the action at the end of the line. I'd have been pleased to have him as one of our forty-three shareholders. But Stein and Day wasn't permitted to hire him by the bank that was a secured creditor!

Some months earlier, the bank, Michigan National, had wanted to get an opinion about its paperwork in the Stein and Day case from a New York law firm. They sought out, wouldn't you guess, Angel & Frankel. They consulted Mr. Frankel, who declined to give them a written opinion with regard to their papers. Though he didn't undertake to work for them, Michigan National later prevented Stein and Day from hiring Mr. Frankel's senior partner on the grounds that the law firm would have a conflict of interest.

There seemed to be a simple solution. Stein and Day told the bank it would recognize in writing the legitimacy of its then claims so that it would be impossible for the publishing company to oppose them. The bank still wouldn't let Stein and Day hire Angel & Frankel. Why? Was it because Angel and Frankel were both smart and knowledgeable about bankruptcy law and the bank didn't want Stein and Day to have representation of that quality? Did they want to force the publishing company to take whomever it could get instead of whomever it wanted? As a result of the bank's conflict-of-interest claim, many millions of dollars that would have been recovered from the use of the company's assets under Angel's skilled guidance were forever lost by creditors, the majority of whom were authors and shareholders.

Texaco and Stein and Day pled their Chapter 11 cases in the very same courtroom in White Plains, New York. Texaco, as I've noted, had lots of cash, and they hired whomever they wanted. The lawyers on all sides in the Texaco case put in for fees of $71 million for their year's work.[2] Stein and Day had to settle for a one-man operation who was outclassed, out-thought, and out-fought from day one, and who wasn't at all surprised when he was fired two months later.

Meanwhile Stein and Day was trying mightily to get the bank to let it hire Josh Angel. When the bank made that impossible, Stein and Day finally found a small law firm in an adjacent county that also thought the publishing company a good risk and was willing to work without a retainer. They had been recommended by the head of another publishing company that was in Chapter 11. The trustee for that firm was Harvey Barr, the lead partner in the small law firm. A few weeks later Barr as trustee, fired the publisher who had recommended him. The gods were on vacation that week, and the tea leaves augured disaster.

---

2. One of the law firms in the Texaco case was awarded only 3 percent of the amount they billed, presumably because the judge thought they had overcharged for their services or billed for work that wasn't necessary.

The desperation a CEO can feel in trying to hire the bankruptcy lawyer of his choice is typified by the case of the head of a prestigious east coast firm that had no financial difficulty until a partner in one of its projects fled the scene, leaving behind a fiscal morass. This CEO, whose main business was still thriving, found the one project dragging him into the quicksand of insolvency and he was suddenly forced to seek the "protection" of Chapter 11. He immediately set out to hire the best bankruptcy lawyer he could get and found out that all the good ones were already working for the project's creditors! The result, according to this successful CEO, was more than a year and a half of absolute hell.

If you wouldn't ask to marry somebody on a first date, why hire a bankruptcy lawyer under the same conditions? The truthful answer is that you may have to because all the other local candidates are taken. And you can't go too far afield to find someone because you need a lawyer who's had some experience in the court that has jurisdiction. That's why so many times in Chapter 11, if you're unprepared and under the gun, you're a nominee for a shotgun wedding with a lawyer you know too little about, or whom circumstances forced you to choose from a slate of exactly one candidate.

Lie Number 2. *If your company's problem is that it has insufficient cash to pay its suppliers and creditors, or it cannot pay a large judgment, it will be protected under Chapter 11's automatic stay and be allowed to reorganize.*

That is consummate nonsense. The fact is that your company won't have a chance to reorganize unless it has unencumbered funds or new funding and rational creditors willing to work together to realize the maximum potential from the restoration of normal operations. Also, it must have the services of one of the minority of ethical bankruptcy lawyers with savvy.

I'm not talking about Texaco. When Texaco filed in April of 1987, it had uncollateralized assets and a bevy of operating companies that were not in bankruptcy, so cash flow was not a great problem.

I'm not talking about Eastern Airlines. When Eastern Airlines filed in March of 1989, Frank Lorenzo had been building up a cash war chest for a year in preparation for D-Day.

And I'm not talking about a company like Neptune World Wide Moving, which had no fewer than thirty affiliated companies. Thomas Towey, the hero of Neptune's case who is today its CEO, fought to keep the affiliated companies out of Chapter 11, and that move helped Neptune survive.

But companies of Texaco's or Eastern's size and cash reserves or with Neptune's number of outside affiliates are in a tiny minority. Moreover, the domino effect of a large bankruptcy can affect helpless smaller firms. For instance, within two weeks of Eastern's filing, several tour operators who had sold tour packages that included Eastern flights had to file for protection also.

The fact is that most companies filing for protection under Chapter 11 do so because they cannot pay their bills and their creditors are threatening them. Or because they are under some sudden severe financial pressure. Companies in that kind of squeeze are usually using every cent of cash flow they can get their hands on to stave off creditors and keep functioning. Yet to survive Chapter 11 it is essential for a company to have squirreled away enough cash for two purposes.

First, as we've seen, there is the retainer. Even if a company has a good relationship with a large law firm that has its own effective bankruptcy counsel, the law firm will still require an additional large retainer. After all, the company is about to enter an arena in which the debtor's counsel doesn't get paid regularly, and that sets up a potential conflict-of-interest situation. If payment to the debtor's counsel can be blocked by a secured creditor asserting his right to be paid before the law firm gets its fees, there is a big temptation for the debtor's lawyer to find himself "cooperating" with the secured creditor—not for the client's sake, but in order to grease the way for his fees to be paid. A company can count on its bankruptcy counsel's full loyalty if that company will continue to pay his fees. That means a big war chest of unencumbered funds.

One temptation that besets a lot of executives in closely held companies is to use their own instead of the company's money for a retainer, which is a real no-no. What's important to recognize is that it's a mighty temptation for someone who has lived life as a CEO to solve a financial problem out of his own resources. After all, surely he will get it back . . .

Wrong. For one, the executive lending the money may never see it again. Two, there's a chance that executive will have to hire another lawyer to represent his personal interests as they may differ from the debtor company's interests (believe me, I've been there), and he will then be in the peculiar position of having paid with his own money the lawyer who may be opposing him in court.

A second and even greater need is a source of money for operating the business that isn't controlled by the secured creditors. If you do not have it, the secured creditors will be determining how the company is to be run and even whether it is to continue operating or be liquidated.

Attorney Brian Loftus of Chicago's Winston & Strawn has one absolute for the company that faces Chapter 11. "Stop paying creditors and start piling up cash."

Wait a minute, you say, what about your receivables that you've always used to create more receivables? Those receivables are frequently assigned as collateral to the creditor who is first in line, the bank. It isn't your cash flow. You do not have any cash flow. And therefore you need the creditors' permission to use that money. Every penny. It's called cash collateral, and, as you will learn later in this book, that's a prime source of strife.

It sounds crazy, but what a company needs to operate in Chapter 11 is a source of money that isn't considered by any of its creditors to be part of their security. If the company doesn't have operating money squirreled away, or agreed to in advance by its secured creditors, its managers have to be prepared for a never-ending war for cash collateral if they want to stay in whatever business they're in.

When a company is in Chapter 11 it is rarely referred to as a company. While it is presumably very much alive and looking to reorganize under the protection of the law, its assets are considered like the assets of the dead, an estate. Those of us professionally involved with language know how often the jargon of a field is a giveaway of real meaning. In this case it's a dead giveaway of the law's lie. In the language used by the others, your business is dead—or may become so after its assets are sold off for the benefit of creditors and their legal entourage. Moreover, assets sold while a company is in Chapter 11, with rare exceptions, usually bring subnormal prices or salvage value because the company is no longer perceived as a going concern.

While the law says a company has the right to reorganize its business in Chapter 11, hostile secured creditors can force it into a liquidation mode, even if it means the loss of many millions to the other creditors—and to themselves. There is evidence in the case histories in this book of gunslingers who spray their gunfire every which way. When these cowboys of the law let loose, the company, the majority of its creditors, and a lot of innocent bystanders get hurt, though the gunslingers sometimes end up shooting their clients in the foot (and getting rich in the process).

Many physicians have trouble with euthanasia, apart from its illegality. Banks and their lawyers do not have trouble with business euthanasia. When they pull the plug, it's not to stop the pain of the patient but to collect their money faster. And if that means killing a living business by turning a Chapter 11 case into a forced liquidation, they do not give a damn about who else gets critically hurt in the process. The same is true of malicious trade creditors who become obsessed with hurting the debtor rather than getting their money back.

Part of the racket of Chapter 11 as it is practiced in some

jurisdictions is to exploit the company's management. Its key people are forced to work under humiliating conditions, often for less pay, under the pretext that the company has the opportunity to reorganize, while the real thrust of the 11 case is to liquidate the assets at the lowest possible cost. That means retaining the management, if competent, to realize the best price for the assets rather than converting the case to a Chapter 7, where the liquidation is done by a trustee. That is usually more time consuming and expensive (the trustee gets paid at hourly fees comparable to what a lawyer gets; many trustees are lawyers). The trustee is required to liquidate the assets promptly and so cannot be bothered by the niceties of selling assets individually. He hires auctioneers to get rid of assets en masse if feasible.

If a company's management hasn't been advised to put together a war chest, that company's Chapter 11 could turn out to be a Chapter 7 liquidation in disguise. I know, because mine was.

Lie Number 3. *Filing under Chapter 11 will protect you from your creditors.*

What the law says is that all debts are frozen. But in practice that doesn't keep the creditors from making the life of the company's management far more miserable than it was before the filing.

The heads of companies interviewed for this book, men and women in very different industries who have lived through Chapter 11, almost all said their lives became hell, especially during the first year and a half. The CEOs I talked to were by and large pretty tough business people running companies that had been successful. Entrepreneurs in particular learn to take it. But none of them expected the kind of man-made, orchestrated humiliation that is part of the Chapter 11 game. This isn't the hell of owing money; most of them had some of that before they filed. It is the hell of losing control not only over their businesses but their lives.

Neptune's chief executive, Tom Towey, put it this way: "You're a molecule under a magnifying glass. The creditors think you're not honorable. Three generations of one family owned Neptune. In a family-owned business, the creditors are especially suspicious of the family members. They think you're trying to take out assets.

"Filing is a traumatic moment," Towey continued. "The connotation to everyone else is immediate doom. The shock is terrible, the stigma of disgrace is worse. It's one thing to be caught in a fire, another not to know where the escape door is.

"It can be even more humiliating in your life outside Chapter 11. People drop you. At the association [of companies in the same business], nobody spoke to me. Nobody wants to touch you in case it rubs off. Chapter 11 is like a disease that comes out of the closet." Towey, a tall, lean man, lost twenty-five pounds in the first few weeks.

Neptune's rank-and-file employees suffered, too. The Chase Manhattan Bank seized Neptune's payroll account, and Towey had to get a court order to release it. Thereafter, every payday when employees would go into the local Chase branch where Neptune had its account to cash their checks, they would find those checks were looked on with suspicion. The amount of attention tellers had to give to every Neptune check presented for cashing added to their work burden. Some of the tellers became unpleasant. Nobody likes standing in line at a bank and then getting a glare across the counter as if you were laundering money instead of just cashing a paycheck.

Towey's tale is no different from what I heard time and again from executives who'd been through the experience. If anyone in my presence dares to call that "protection from creditors," they'd better say it in a language I do not understand.

For the person in charge of the Chapter 11 company, the secured creditors cause the most problems. A second level of suspicion and harassment comes from the heavies on the Committee of Unsecured Creditors. And even the so-called "little people," the garbage collectors, the fire alarm maintenance people, local suppliers of every kind of necessary service can make demands for payment that cannot legally be met, refuse indispensable services, and suddenly become like red ants to an executive with all four limbs tied down on an anthill.

The intention of the law is good. It prevents some creditors from being paid while others are not. It particularly prevents some creditors from being *fully* paid and thus diminishes the percentage of debt that will be paid to the unsecured creditors. It also prevents people of bad character from doing some "insider trading" of their own for the benefit of themselves or someone else. In fact, the law says that transactions during the three-month period prior to the Chapter 11 filing can be undone, meaning if any debt was paid, the court can make the recipient pay it back to the estate. And if the transactions involve payment to insiders, such as management and owners, the period is extended to one year prior to filing.

That's all to the good except for the fact that these strictures make it very difficult to cope with reality. A significant percentage of the small suppliers who are owed money and weren't paid before the company filed will insist on being paid or they will deny the debtor an essential service. "Pay me out of your own pocket," they will say.

If the "little people" who provide essential goods and services were not paid before filing, they cannot be paid what they are owed after filing. Some will say they'll continue to supply the Chapter 11 company on a COD basis, *but only if it pays what it owes.* However, the law says that if the debtor repays a creditor without a court order, the debtor is committing a criminal act. The supplier doesn't want to hear about that. He doesn't understand and he doesn't care. "I won't even talk to you until you pay me what you owe me." Some threaten to sue or actually do so. And the general practitioners they hire do not know bankruptcy law. Every suit has to be defended. The company then has the cost of dealing with all that accumulated ignorance.

Tom Towey of Neptune says the easiest course to take is "Nobody gets paid." But even that proves to be unworkable.

The chief secured creditor will be clamoring for the company's fire insurance to be paid on a current basis. He doesn't want to see his collateral going up in smoke. The fire insurance company bases its rates on the fire alarm system in use. What if it isn't functioning and the firm that does the maintenance won't service it until the prepetition claim is paid? Some attorneys will advise their clients to pay all the small suppliers before filing because the cumulative amount owed them is not worth the expense and trouble of dealing with each one of them after filing. Others will counsel in a whisper to let the garbage man double up on payments till he's caught up. And a lawyer worth his keep will warn his client to pay up American Express and any other outstanding company credit-card obligations before filing. Ideally, one ought to take care of all those "little things," but if you file on a few days notice during which you're fighting big fires, how many chief executives can be expected to think about the kind of problems that unpaid "little" bills will generate in their immediate future?

The domino effect of those unpaid small debts can present management with headaches no amount of aspirin will cure.

Lie Number 4. *Your company will enjoy its constitutional right of due process under law.*

The Fifth Amendment to the Constitution of the United States is not a piece of obfuscating legal jargon. It says in quite precise English that no person shall "be deprived of life, liberty, or *property* [italics added], without due process of law." This has been interpreted to mean that when the government would deprive someone of his property or liberty, its procedures must be fair. This requires that notice and a fair hearing be accorded *prior to a deprivation.*

The reader will learn in the course of this book that in Chapter 11 an all-powerful bankruptcy judge can deprive a company, its creditors, and its shareholders of due process by hearing a motion and *not one word of response to that motion;* that a judge will decide a motion in favor of a bankruptcy attorney without even reading papers of the attorney's client in opposition to that motion; that "procedural fairness" is sometimes based on a judge's prior opinions of certain law firms and certain lawyers rather than on the merits of a case. The reader will learn how a judge's threats can cause a debtor to sign false statements against his will. And the reader will also learn exactly how a company can be denied its constitutional right to due process even to the extent of killing the "person" of a perfectly viable corporation.

It was Justice Felix Frankfurter who characterized due process as "representing a profound attitude of fairness between man and man, and more particularly between the individual and government." Justice Frankfurter, of course, was never privy to the sham and shame that is "due process" in Chapter 11.

The denial of due process can take place outside of bankruptcy court. If the debtor company had been wronged by another party and sued the alleged wrongdoer prior to filing, a delay of years in the matter coming to trial can in itself be instrumental in precipitating the bankruptcy. Certain judges who do not manage their calendars well can be notoriously slow in bringing cases to trial. The reader will learn of one federal judge who *three years after being given a case on which a company's life depended* ended up turning over the case to yet another judge whose own calendar was full up for nearly another year; this circumstance alone was a denial of due process.

Skilled defense lawyers can find countless ways of dragging out a case, and many judges have become accustomed to playing ball with these antics that defeat due process. Federal courts are supposed to be much faster than state courts, but that depends on which federal judge is assigned to a case. It's done by lot, which means due process becomes a game of chance. If you get an efficient judge, your case will be heard. If you get an inefficient judge with a backlog resembling Fibber McGee's closet, you can be denied due process and there is nothing you can do about it. A federal judge has the only occupation I can think of in or out of government that is not accountable to anybody. The job is for life. He can be overruled by appellate courts, but the way he runs his calendar is entirely under his control. If he is not a good manager, he may have hundreds of cases piled up and waiting. If he runs his courtroom in slow motion, or likes the publicity of high-visibility cases, two-week cases can stretch to two months or half a year while justice for other cases shrivels until it is useless, like good soup left too long on a back burner.

There's an old saw most lawyers know that's credited to William Gladstone: *Justice delayed is justice denied.* The reader of this book will encounter a case where a company ultimately was forced to file for "protection" under Chapter 11 because of a dawdling judge.

Once a company files, it's in a different kind of court than the CEO may have previously experienced or heard about. That's because a bankruptcy judge has absolute power. It was reported that Judge Howard Schwartzberg told Texaco's attorneys at the outset of their case, "You better tell your client that this is a bankruptcy case. They just can't do things without our permission." Judge Schwartzberg happens to be one of the most highly regarded bankruptcy judges in the nation, and unlike the dawdlers in the judiciary he makes his determinations from the bench or within two working days. But as he told Texaco, he's the boss. And if he wants to hear only one side of a case or not read briefs before making important decisions, as in Stein and Day's case, that's his prerogative even if it denies the debtor due process. And if, unlike Texaco, your company isn't in Westchester County, you will draw one of the 286 other bankruptcy judges in the United States, who may be a free-swinging "cowboy" or a strict adherer to the bankruptcy bible. You need to learn quickly how that judge operates because one of the things he will be operating on is the life support system of your company.

Lie Number 5. *As a corporate executive, you will not be attacked personally.*

False. As Tom Towey has warned, you will be vilified and humiliated (I was warned it was part of the game; now you are warned). Just prior to and during the ordeal of Chapter 11, Towey's position was changed, he resigned, he was retained as a consultant and then as chief executive officer, as if he were caught in a revolving door. Your instinct for self-preservation makes you want to get out and away. But if like Towey you've got thirty good years invested in the company and you've finally reached a point where you are allowed to run things without interference, you say to yourself you can't start all over again, let's give it a shot. You're not a young man of forty any more!

Crisis manager Kenneth Glass says, "The CEO is the lightning rod, but in some companies all of the high-profile executives come under personal attack. That's true of anyone who speaks for the company. They are identified as being part of the problem whether or not they are guilty."

David Ferrari, president of Argus Management in Natick, Massachusetts, a ten-man firm that specializes in helping troubled companies, speaks of instances in which executives get angry and threatening calls at home from irate creditors—or worse still, their spouses get the calls. He warns his clients that they could be subjected to lawsuits filed for harassment purposes.

What if you didn't do anything wrong? It doesn't matter. You will find yourself scrounging up retainer money for your personal defense. You will spend hundreds of hours working to defend yourself even in cases in which the judge thinks the action against you is just this side of ridiculous and invites a motion for summary judgment so he can dismiss the case. (The easiest way to get someone to settle is to show them that it will cost more to defend than to settle. If you defend an unjust attack on principle, beware. The justice system of the United States is not equipped to deal with principle.)

Do you have any idea of the thousands of dollars it costs to go for a motion to dismiss a case, even if the judge says he would welcome it? Please remember that during this period you are not likely to be paid your normal salary. Your company's lawyers, while sending bills at their usual hourly rates, may ask you to cut your pay in half, as ours did. Though I couldn't possibly afford to do it[3], I agreed to it only as part of a consensual stipulation that would permit the company to practice its business of publishing—and not otherwise. Nevertheless, the company's lawyer "volunteered" the pay cut in open court without any agreement among the parties and therefore without my permission. He knew I was determined to save my business. He used that weakness to accomplish whatever he had in mind instead of what I wanted. The moral is: *To be effective in a bankruptcy proceeding, you have to have nothing at stake—or be able to behave as if that were true.* Otherwise, you may be taken advantage of not only by the creditors and their lawyers, but by the company's lawyers as well.

According to the most experienced lawyers, family-owned or family-run businesses suffer the most pain. One of the "class acts" of the bankruptcy bar in the Midwest is that of Gerald F. Munitz, head of the bankruptcy department of Winston & Strawn in Chicago. He says that "the smaller the company, the more the personal involvement. The executives who are the worst hit are the ones where the grandfather founded the company way back when, and the present CEO is the third generation and the busi-

---

3. In my case, the interest on the money I borrowed on my home to lend to the company plus taxes on my home and life insurance premiums came to more than half of my income. Therefore half salary meant negative spendable income.

ness is failing. It's traumatic. An ordeal. But," he cautions, "the personal pain is not an excuse for not filing." Tom Towey, who is not part of the family that owned Neptune, confirms attorney Munitz's scenario. He says the members of the family were insulted and demoralized at every turn. He feared for the health of the "completely devastated" member of the family who made the decision to file for "protection."

Towey says that at the time of filing Neptune was hurting from the government's deregulation of its industry. In addition, virtually all of Neptune's facilities were unionized, making it extremely difficult to offer the discounts that nonunion carriers were offering their customers. Both factors created a cutthroat environment throughout the industry. Neptune had at one time touted itself as being "the largest privately-owned carrier not affiliated with a van line," with numerous terminals throughout the country. The family took pride in being an anomaly in the industry, but they failed to take swift and necessary steps, such as closing down the terminals that were losing money. Notwithstanding its problems, at the time of filing Neptune had not exhausted its line of credit with its major lender. However, when a family member sought to borrow approximately two million dollars more to finance a leveraged buy-out, a relationship with the bank that had endured close to one hundred years deteriorated rapidly as the bank scrutinized the feasibility of the takeover and the total financial picture of the company.

Tom Towey, though not a principal of Neptune, got a piece of the action for business he brought in. That compensation was in the form of stock in a profitable subsidiary of Neptune. Towey figured that the stock would be worth half a million dollars down the road. But as part of the Chapter 11 negotiations that subsidiary's profits were pulled into the parent company. Towey, though he was the man who guided the company to survival, lost the half a million before it ever got to him.

It took two years to bring Neptune around, with the

best of legal help. And in the process, it wasn't just money that Towey lost. He says, "They beat you psychologically. They show you disrespect. And you turn it into being beaten physically."

One turnaround specialist talked of the frequency with which executives with companies in Chapter 11 undergo so much frightening stress that they end up losing their spouses and children. One CEO whose company survived Chapter 11 admitted that his marriage did not. As a well-known bankruptcy lawyer put it, "When money goes out the door, love often goes out the window."

There's more to come. If you think torture consists of having your fingernails pulled, you've obviously never undergone the psychological torture that many brave people feel is worse than physical torture, especially if it lasts for years.

Lie Number 6. *You are the client. The lawyers are working for you.*

In the topsy-turvy world of Chapter 11, the truth is that unless you are paying your lawyers currently (instead of them having to wait to be paid out of "administrative costs"), there's a strong chance your lawyers will be in charge of the case and you will be their puppet. Ken Glass says, "You find lawyers calling the shots. The lawyer representing the Creditors' Committee, instead of providing advice, will start making business decisions. Attorneys," he says flatly, "are generally not good businessmen."

Chicago-based Gerald F. Munitz agrees that "lawyers are not business people. But when the client is paralyzed—in smaller cases the people get apoplectic—lawyers fill the gap and assume the normal prerogatives of clients."

Daniel Morris says the Chapter 11 situation is often an ego trip for the lawyers and a "dis-ego trip" for management. "Yes, lawyers assume some of the normal prerogatives of clients. The client permits it because he's in a state of shock. He wants to have trust and faith in his 'doctor.' Many bankruptcy lawyers think they can solve business problems.

That's not true in a large number of instances." He comes down with a maxim. "Good lawyers know businesses have to be run by businessmen."

Anyone who knows me knows that by temperament and experience I am not inclined to be anyone's Charlie McCarthy; I once defied a direct order from General Eisenhower when I thought he was dead wrong. But what I found in our Chapter 11 case was that *your lawyers can sign crucial agreements even when you are totally opposed to them because they are unworkable.* If you tell them in writing, in effect, "Hey, I'm the client and I do not want you to sign anything without my prior written consent," you will be harassed by your own lawyers, who will demand your appearance in distant courts on trivial matters in which there is a small possibility that something will require your consent (which you could easily give on the phone and, if needed in writing, could be telefaxed immediately).

The fact is that if you are what's called a debtor-in-possession—that is, you're still in charge of the company—it is your absolute right to instruct the attorney for the estate, for instance, to put a certain matter before the court for a hearing. But that doesn't mean he'll do it. He may prefer to "negotiate" a consent order with his "colleagues," meaning the opposing counsel, so that an agreed stipulation can be presented to the court. Some judges encourage this practice; it saves them work, however much it contributes to the destruction of due process. The court is kept from deciding key issues by listening to the arguments of all sides. Instead, the arguers argue (often interminably, while their fee clocks run) and come to an agreement behind the judge's back, as it were.

I repeatedly instructed our company's attorneys to go after monies owed and not paid. They didn't do it. They waited till the last day to apply for a new cash collateral order, putting the entire company's expenses at my sole risk unless and until a retroactive cash collateral order was approved. On more than one occasion I was only able to get the company's attorneys to put an important issue before the court by composing a letter to the judge and threatening to have it hand delivered if the lawyer didn't follow the client's instructions. Was Stein and Day's attorney typical of a part of the bankruptcy bar? Chapter 11 is a world straight out of *Alice in Wonderland.*

Lie Number 7. *Chapter 11 makes it easier to sell your business.*

In one sense, this is true. One person—the judge in the bankruptcy case—after listening to testimony from all the parties, has the absolute power to order a sale of the company's shares or its assets if he thinks it will benefit the creditors. A buyer is protected from later legal attack because he has a court order. The best title you can get to property is under Section 363 of the bankruptcy code. In addition, says lawyer Gerald Munitz, "bidding within Chapter 11 can flush out a price."

Attorney Brian Loftus of the same firm, who characterizes himself as a relative newcomer to the bankruptcy bar, says, "Chapter 11 makes it more difficult to get a good price. No matter what the company is selling, the price goes down. The only thing that can raise it is competition." Yet Loftus pointed to one example in which a court-held auction caused a 50-percent increase in the price of a unit in a large corporation (the unit went for $60 million).

Sounds good? For giant companies with divisions that can be disentangled, perhaps. Selling a smaller company or its assets in Chapter 11 might work if the case is being superintended by one of the minority of virtuous professionals. But if the company is small and gets stuck with the other kind of lawyer, all Chapter 11 provides is a better chance that the business can be sold to the vultures and piranhas who prey on Chapter 11 cases, hoping to pick up assets at enormous bargains from which they will make a tremendous profit, usually to the detriment of the creditors and original shareholders. In many cases a sale to a legitimate and prestigious buyer is made much more difficult, perhaps impossible, because the bureaucracy inherent in Chapter 11 is anathema to most businessmen.

Executives in some businesses are used to dealing with government bureaucracies. They have learned to stomach the flood of unnecessary paperwork, unnecessary meetings, and elaborate approval processes. But even they can be overwhelmed by the bureaucracy of Chapter 11. D. P. G. Cameron, vice president and general counsel of the Public Service Company of New Hampshire, knows what a utility company has to put up with in terms of government regulation. But when his company became the first investor-owned utility to file for Chapter 11 protection since the Depression, he was quoted as saying "The proceedings . . . left us breathless." If the bureaucracy and regulations imposed on a Chapter 11 company leave a public utility executive "breathless," can you imagine the effect on the companies that don't operate under the constraints of government regulation?

When on the African plains a small wildebeest loses its place in the thundering herd, it is almost certain to attract the attention first of the predators, the lions, and then of the scavengers—the hyenas, jackals, wild dogs, and vultures. A smaller company that falls victim to Chapter 11 can be said to be on an African plain on which the lions have all been fully fed and only the scavengers remain. In fact, some of these human scavengers have been given a name: vulture capitalists.[4]

Tom Towey of Neptune saw or spoke to about fifty individuals and groups that prey on Chapter 11 companies. He reported that finding the records these people wanted and photocopying them repeatedly was one of the most frustrating experiences of Chapter 11. He usually saw these offerers of uninvited buy-outs on Saturdays and Sundays.

---

4. *Turnarounds & Workouts, News for People Tracking Distressed Businesses,* January 1989. Published by Christopher Beard, this semimonthly newsletter published out of Washington, D.C., can also be useful to distressed businessmen being tracked.

"They're looking to pick up companies cheap and fast," said Towey. "Some of the deals we were offered, we would have been better off in liquidation."

Towey did have praise, however, for Robert Ehrlich, who is in the business of being the middleman in the buying and selling of troubled companies. Neptune paid Ehrlich a retainer. Ehrlich appraised the business and in so doing strengthened Neptune's resolve. "We didn't know we could survive. Ehrlich's analyses convinced us we could. He showed us there was a respectable core business in Neptune. He also helped convince the creditors. Even though he didn't find us an outside funder, his fee was worth many times what we paid."

After half a hundred experiences with the scavengers, Towey didn't find a one that had something acceptable to offer. Neptune's outside money came from inside. The family that owned the company was able to put up additional money to fund the emergence from Chapter 11.

In Stein and Day's case, it was the distinguished law firm of Weil, Gotshal & Manges that sent around the worst of the vulture capitalists that the company got to see.

Turnaround specialists have mixed feelings about finding a buyer for a business when it's "in an eleven." Adam Radzik, one of the most optimistic men in his field, feels that once a company files, it's harder to sell because "the confidence level" disappears. Still, he says, if Chapter 11 is understood by the buyer, it can be a "tool" that can make acquisition easier. David Ferrari says it depends on the buyer. "Some people will never buy out of an eleven. They are affronted by the open bidding. Others like it and are ready to listen, to be convinced. The vultures are a last resort." Ferrari will use one of the scavengers as a stalking horse to start the bidding process, but he says he'll rarely sell to them.

Daniel Morris is quite specific. "The liabilities are defined. The rush of the pre-eleven period is over. And the price is lower." Yet he sees the other side. "The buyer may not want the business badly enough to mix it up with street-smart lawyers because they want one or another asset." Kenneth Glass, who deals in mid-size to larger companies, thinks selling in an eleven is, in general, easier. Glass thinks the turnaround manager and the lawyer can be used as shields. "But," he cautions, "most buyers don't understand how it is done in an eleven. They need to be educated. They're missing a bet if they don't learn." Glass prescreens potential acquirers because he cannot waste time on the vultures.

Yet respected turnaround people like Dan Morris, who can see the vultures coming, believe "No one is difficult to deal with if you know what the likely result is going to be." Adam Radzik, who deals with smaller firms also, says his aim is "to try to save the business for the principals and to preserve income for the employees and their families." That, in most cases, rules out the scavengers.

Lie Number 8. *Filing for Chapter 11 is a voluntary act.*
The language used in reporting bankruptcy cases in the press is in part responsible for this widely held misapprehension. Businessmen are said to "take" their companies into Chapter 11, which makes it sound like a voluntary step. One thing nearly all the professionals involved agree about is that Chapter 11 is "never" or "almost never" voluntary. "In 98 percent of the cases economic pressure forces the company into the eleven." David Ferrari is absolute. "It's never voluntary," he says.

The average layman's understanding of bankruptcy is oversimplified and in most respects dead wrong. The widely held view is that bankruptcy means that three or more of a company's creditors gang up and put it into involuntary bankruptcy, as in Chapter 7, and that when a company, on its own, seeks the protection of the law from those same creditors, it files under Chapter 11 *voluntarily.*

Chicago attorney Brian Loftus says point blank, "No management would do it [go into Chapter 11] voluntarily. It is a last resort. It is very expensive, and the results are not what you hope they might be." However, he points out, "Continental Airlines used it to get rid of labor union obligations. Of course, the law has since been changed, making that more difficult."

When Frank Lorenzo took Continental Airlines into Chapter 11 on September 24, 1983, the airline canceled all domestic flights. Within three days, Continental had repudiated all union contracts,[5] cut wages, cut fares, and resumed service with a limited number of flights to selected cities, using only a third of its employees. Chapter 11 was Frank Lorenzo's way of making an airline efficient, and then rebuilding it.

It is true that a small percentage of companies do file voluntarily. Attorney Gerald Munitz is convinced that most major bankruptcy cases are in some respect voluntary. "Texaco," he says, "is the classic case to enforce an automatic stay." A Texas jury had found against Texaco and awarded Pennzoil $10.53 billion, the biggest damage award in history, for interfering with Pennzoil's acquisition of Getty. But Gary E. Hindes, who ran for lieutenant governor of Delaware in 1988 and whose career specialty was dealing with companies in distress, when asked if Texaco had lost control of their bankruptcy, said, "Absolutely. I don't think that they really realized when they went into bankruptcy what bankruptcy is all about."[6] Hindes went on to caution businessmen that going into bankruptcy because of some special circumstance is not a way to solve a business problem because in Chapter 11, "You're not the master of your own destiny." Yet Texaco management would ask what else could they do with a $10 billion judgment staring them in the face? Management would say that they didn't seek protection voluntarily—if that word still has any meaning left in it. A cynic might say going into Chapter 11 saved Texaco quite a few billion dollars, but management quickly learned how easy it was for even a strong company of Texaco's size to lose control of its affairs once it filed.

---

5. A revision of the law, sparked by Continental's action, now forbids unilateral repudiation of such contracts.

6. Quoted in *Turnarounds & Workouts*, Vol. 2, No. 12, July 1, 1988.

"Big" judgments are relative. Munitz tells about the case of "a solid, mid-size company that was in court defending itself against another party's $25,000 claim." That defendant company reaped a judgment of $10 million in punitive damages, which forced them to file for protection over what was initially a small claim. The "protection" cost them many dozens of times the original demand (though less than $10 million).

Munitz knows of a case where a class of creditors—except for a few holdouts—was willing to make a deal with the company. The lingo is "composing" their debts, which means negotiating how many cents on the dollar each creditor would be paid. Such a deal might also involve an extension of credit to the troubled firm. In the example cited by Munitz, the holdouts held out. So the company filed in order to take advantage of the "cramdown"[7] power of Section 1129B of the Bankruptcy Code, which binds an entire class of creditors, willing or not.

There are benefits, for instance, to the chain of retail stores that is stuck with a lot of leases for unprofitable stores. Once that chain is in an eleven, the law permits the leases to be voided, rejected as executory contracts, which fixes the landlord's damages and enables the chain to start up again eventually with its profitable locations unimpaired. What has to be measured is the cost of Chapter 11, always very high, against the benefit of getting rid of leasehold liabilities. Goldblatts, a chain of twenty-seven Midwest department stores, had twenty of its operations losing money. It filed under Chapter 11, got rid of its leases on the twenty unprofitable locations, and reorganized, coming out with its seven profitable stores intact.

Once upon a time, companies in the garment industry,

---

7. A "cram-down" is a way of forcing recalcitrant creditors, who refuse to go along, say, with a settlement proposal agreed to by other members of the same class of creditors, to accept the settlement by court order. Settlements are supposed to be *voluntary* agreements, but not in the topsy-turvy world of Chapter 11.

for instance, would file every few years as a means of "legally" reducing debt. Then they'd start all over again with a clean slate. That practice is frowned on in the Bankruptcy Code. It has also become uneconomical in many cases because Chapter 11 entails major outlays *in addition to* the normal expenses of a business. As people wise in that game sometimes say, "Better call Max the Torch."

Aside from these relatively few examples of special situations, the economic insanity of Chapter 11 is such that if lawyers warned businessmen what would happen, would any rational executive put his company into Chapter 11 voluntarily?

The fact is that in the vast majority of cases it isn't at all voluntary. Here are some other examples:

Zenith, a pharmaceutical company, had several recall problems after an FDA inspection. The new CEO who took over was a specialist in turnarounds in that very industry. But a tough group of banks, according to Zenith's bankruptcy counsel, Murray Drabkin of Cadwalader, Wickersham & Taft, "was intent on pulling their allegedly secured interest as fast as they could. . . . Their attempt to cause the company to be liquidated by a receiver [was] destructive to virtually everyone else's interests in the case."[8] Zenith, which had tried desperately to avoid Chapter 11, was forced into Chapter 11. Was this voluntary?

Kraus is an example of a company that, according to its president, was in good shape as far as cash was concerned. It was up to date with its payments to suppliers and had no significant problems in its business of supplying out-of-print technical journals and books to libraries. However, as a result of a lawsuit by former shareholders, the company suddenly found itself facing a seven-figure judgment it couldn't pay. Its only available course of action was to file under Chapter 11. That could hardly be termed voluntary. Nor could the appearance of a very sick person in court be termed voluntary. Once the Kraus company was

---

8. Quoted in *Turnarounds & Workouts*, Vol. 2, No. 12, July 1, 1988.

embalmed in Chapter 11, the principals became subject to the demands of lawyers without apparent regard for age or health. Patricia Day happened to be present when lawyers on one side of the controversy were demanding that the other side produce Mr. Kraus in person so that he could be interrogated on the witness stand. According to Mr. Kraus's attorney, Kraus's physician had said the aged Mr. Kraus was too sick with Alzheimer's to appear in court. Miss Day reported that the lawyer demanding Kraus's presence was insistent, but Bankruptcy Judge Howard Schwartzberg, who normally requires evidence from the witness stand, made an exception in the case of Mr. Kraus. Three days later Kraus was dead.

A successful builder of fine homes in one of the most expensive areas in the United States, a man of stature highly regarded in his community, had the prudent practice of incorporating each project separately. He had a busy life with involvements in other related businesses that he owned, and so in one project he took on a financial man as a partner. The houses in this development were superb, although they all contained one remediable flaw, which delayed the sale of some of the houses. The financial partner in the development, seeing trouble on the horizon, fled. The development was forced to seek protection in Chapter 11. When I asked this well-known builder what mistake he made that could have been avoided, he said, "Leaving the financial picture to a financial man who said, 'Leave it to me.'" When I asked him what advice he might have for any business person in a similar situation, he said, "Never go into partnership with anyone."

When the development filed under Chapter 11, several trustees were appointed, each earning fees of one hundred to two hundred dollars an hour. Naturally, the builder said, the one getting two hundred dollars an hour did most of the "work." That venture went into Chapter 11 in 1985 and at this writing *is still in it*. The chief executive, whose other projects and businesses never faltered, said the

Chapter 11 filing transformed him. The mental anguish was enormous; he couldn't sleep. "You are not in control of your life," he said. "Why did you do it?" I asked. "I had no choice," he answered. Would any equally successful person in a similar situation be said to be going into Chapter 11 voluntarily *if he knew what it was like?*

The sad fact is that the orchestrated anxiety of Chapter 11 is very good for the specialist lawyers and the trustees, and very bad, obviously, for the businessmen and -women who get caught in its web and find it takes years and years to get out. And most of them do not enter the chamber of horrors voluntarily. Many allow themselves to be pushed or talked into it because neither they nor their long-term lawyers know how bad it is.

Lie Number 9. *The key to reorganizing is to get a funder—some person or company that will put up the money needed to get the business running well again.*

It's absolutely true that this is the key to reorganizing because the secured creditors can keep you from using *any* incoming cash to run the business if what they really want is to have it liquidated as fast as possible. But if you have to line up that outside funding ahead of time, before you file, it doesn't seem to make sense. If your business is in trouble, you're obviously looking for help. And if you get a funder before going into Chapter 11, you may be able to avoid filing if the creditors will make a deal with the new funder—or if the new funder demands such a deal as a requisite for his investment. Alternatively, the funder may want your company to file before he puts up the new money because then he is likely to be able to negotiate a senior secured position.

But if a company's chief executives are spending time developing an outside funding relationship, that's time taken away from management. And what often happens is that things get worse, and suddenly Chapter 11 is standing at the door with a beckoning finger, and your funder isn't in place yet.

I asked some turnaround specialists who try to forestall Chapter 11 filings whether a company should have a funder lined up ahead of time. What I heard was a resounding "Yes!" followed immediately by, "Most of them don't."

So the company files, and the three-ring circus starts. Management is no longer in whatever business it was in; it is dealing with Chapter 11 full time. If, despite these shackles, the company comes up with an outside source of funds for running the business while trying to reorganize, as Stein and Day did, it can find itself with a new adversary. In Stein and Day's case the attorney for the company reported that the attorney for the Creditors' Committee was opposed to the outside funding. The funding proposal was never presented to the court! One could spend a year and a half, as we did, trying to find out *why* the outside funding was blocked and not get a reportable answer. If it could have saved the company, its seven hundred authors, and twenty-five years of hard work, and therefore was "good enough" for management to approve, why was it blocked in a way that never gave the court a chance to decide whether it was "good enough"?

Could it be because an outside funder who lends money to a company in Chapter 11 usually gets a preferred position in the hierarchy of creditors? The other creditors presumably provided services or products to the company *before* it had to file. The funder supplies new money and naturally wants some protection for it. But the creditors' attitude can be, "You won't get ahead of me in line even if none of us gets to see the movie as a result." Complaints should come from the shareholders, who, in Stein and Day's case, would have had to give up 50 percent of their equity to the funder. The shareholders winced, but were ready to sign the contract with the funder because half a loaf is better than none.

One could reasonably ask why it wasn't the responsibility of the attorney for the company, whose management wanted to make the deal with the funder, to oppose the attorney for the Creditors' Committee and take the matter before the court. Couldn't he at least insist that the committee meet with the funder and the company's management? Why did he let this funder slip through the company's hands when such a deal might well have saved millions of dollars worth of assets whose value depended on their use? Later, when fees were carved out—meaning when lawyers took pieces out of the proceeds from the sale of assets—the court order revealed that in the allocation of fees the lawyer for the company and the lawyer for the Creditors' Committee were both compensated, sometimes without regard to which one did meaningful work in connection with that asset sale.

Thus you can go by the rules, get an outside funder after you've filed, and still be blocked from saving your company. Consider yourself warned.

Lie Number 10. *Filing for Chapter 11 is a step toward health.*

This is one of the worst lies of all. Even if a company survives Chapter 11, the process will be devastating to the health of the company's management.

We are said to prize health above all. Normally a person will try to avoid eating tainted food or exposing himself voluntarily to carcinogenic substances. Yet, without proper warning, when we enter Chapter 11 it is as if we were stepping into a center for disease control in which all the test tubes and petri dishes have been smashed and infection is inevitable. The health of a laboratory worker, under normal conditions, is protected. The key people in a company that files are unprotected.

Sam Metzger, the forceful CEO of Chipwich who had a successful Chapter 11, considers himself lucky. He suffered only a divorce and the loss of hundreds of thousands of dollars. According to Metzger, one of his partners became so incapacitated as to be bedridden. The man couldn't breathe. He had bruises that wouldn't heal. The partner was taken to one of the best hospitals in the country, Johns Hopkins in Baltimore. Metzger thought the man was going to die because, assaulted by the problems of bankruptcy, he caved in. As any veteran of Chapter 11 will tell you, whatever the symptoms, the underlying cause is "Chapter 11 disease."

Crisis manager Daniel Morris reports that the experience "has a tremendous impact" on the physical and mental health of the executives involved. "The degree depends on their preparedness. Some few become stronger. The majority physically deteriorate, lose objectivity and their ability to focus and establish priorities. You see more drinking, smoking, drug-taking."

Kenneth Glass, whose firm has managed crises coast to coast, reports that the principal executives "seriously deteriorate, get physically sick. Stress is noticeable in all senior level executives. Personality problems come to the fore. They drink too much coffee, they drink too much alcohol."

David Ferrari, whose practice is mainly with New England companies, says, "The emotional impact is gut-wrenching, tough, terrible, especially during the first couple of months. There's the social stigma, news stories, embarrassing phone calls, and the utter frustration of not having time to run their business."

Adam Radzik reports that the key executives "lose weight, have headaches, spend sleepless nights, find their sex drive inhibited. The conflicts make them short-tempered. It's only when they see light at the end of the tunnel that they calm down." That, of course, is usually years down the road.

One of the more insightful overviews of this deplorable situation appeared in a study done from the point of view of the workout banker,[9] in which a midwestern banker

---

9. "The Human Side of Problem Loan Workouts," John Burlowski and Joan Sampson, M.S.W., A.C.S.W., in *The Journal of Commercial Bank Lending*, May 1986. Mr. Burlowski is a vice president of the Norwest Bank Saint Cloud in Minnesota. Ms. Sampson is a family counselor with the Central Minnesota Mental Health Center in Saint Cloud.

and a social worker collaborated. They warned bankers that when a loan goes bad, the reaction in the business borrower can be dramatic. The usual image of the entrepreneur is that of a self-confident, buoyant person who "often seems to succeed because of his sheer enthusiasm and belief in his own abilities." The unexpected event of a workout can be particularly stressful because the events are perceived by the individual as being beyond his or her control, which exacerbates the stress.

In their study, Burlowski and Sampson remind us that in a society where money and wealth are seen as indicators of power and status—and businessmen are more likely than other groups to believe in those indicators—"financial setbacks are often seen, both by the person himself as well as by family, friends, and the community, as major failures." They not only experience a loss of status with regard to their position in the community, but even their role within their family is tar-brushed. And their belief in their own "lack of worth can become self-fulfilling."

In another study,[10] the researchers examined certain events such as job change, death of a spouse, and divorce, and measured them as to the amount, severity, and duration of the stress associated with each event. Of the thirty-five most stressful events, at least ten "are present to some degree in most problem loan situations."

The common physical manifestations found by Burlowski and Sampson "include insomnia, loss of appetite, fatigue and lack of energy, and susceptibility to colds and other mild infections." Emotional reactions "can include depression, apathy, withdrawal, confusion or an inability to concentrate, and lack of perspective." They add, "The last can be particularly damaging since it often involves doubt about one's capacity to deal with the problem." One notices swings in mood and energy level. Also

---

10. Holmes, T. H. and R. H. Rahe, "The Social Readjustment Rating Scale," *Journal of Psychosomatic Research*, 11(2) 1967.

noted is the fact that the borrower's stress extends into his home life and that rebounds onto the stress already present in the business.

Burlowski and Sampson point out the similarities between the reaction to bankruptcy and the death of a spouse. They point to the studies of Elisabeth Kübler-Ross and others who have found that dealing with grief, such as in the death of a spouse, comes in stages: shock, denial, anger, bargaining, depression, and finally acceptance. They then show the similarity in the reactions of an executive whose economic world is suddenly in disarray and whose company may die. However, there is an essential difference. When a loved one dies, there are rituals for dealing with the loss. But for the borrower in trouble, "there is no accepted or ritualized way of dealing with the loss. The distressed borrower may have a real sense of being alone."

The biggest blow would seem to be the sudden puncturing of the business person's self-esteem. The CEO may be unable to respond or make decisions. Negotiations may break off. If pressed, the executive may respond with anger, hostility, and belligerence, sometimes directed at the wrong parties, including himself. "This can't be happening to me," he tells himself. When the anger is directed inward, guilt and shame may lead to thoughts of suicide. Burlowski and Sampson say, "It is a myth that if a person talks of suicide, he will not do it. In fact, this is often a call for help, and the person is a high-risk candidate for suicide."

The banker is counseled to "help the borrower manage his stress by focusing on the causal factors." But bankers are not psychiatric social workers, and undoubtedly very few are up to handling the extreme stress of the borrower in a constructive way. In practice, despite the well-meaning advice of people like Burlowski and Sampson, bankers who find themselves empathizing with the distress of the lender probably look to escaping from the workout area, where the stress can be catching. And those who remain can include a fair share of those who derive a measure of sadistic pleasure from the executive's pain, exacerbated by the lust for getting even with a once-powerful CEO who earned more than the banker and has now fallen from grace into the tar pit of shame.

Because how each individual is affected is not only painful but intensely personal, I will report on the Chapter 11 company I know best.

Several months after filing every key executive in our firm was sick. One awoke every night broken out in hives, another had her blood pressure soar, yet another had symptoms that took half a dozen medical specialists and two hospitals to unravel. All of these proved to be the kind of psychogenic illnesses caused by intense, unrelieved stress. Is this because people in publishing are especially sensitive? Not at all. Only one of the three I mentioned above is mainly involved in the publishing process. Moreover, Chipwich is in the food business. And Neptune is in the moving and storage business. The fact is that in every case I investigated, no matter what the industry, the same pattern was there: Chapter 11 makes you sick.

It doesn't make the judge sick. It doesn't make the lawyers sick. It makes the executives sick.

It is said that in smaller businesses the personal effects of Chapter 11 are greater. But that's based on the assumption that people who run large corporations are insensitive to humiliation and to the stigma that attaches to bankruptcy. In a country known for businessmen who strive to succeed, the role of overseeing a process that is characterized as failure is very hard to take at any size or level, especially when the formerly efficient executive watches the unnecessary prolongation of the Chapter 11 process.

What is common to almost all executives in every industry and in every size of company that finds itself in Chapter 11 is that they are no longer in control of their lives, and the result can and usually is a sudden deterioration in health.

Which may point to the need for an intermediary who

can depersonalize the situation, defuse the pain as much as possible, and prepare and guide the executive during his time of trial. In exceptional circumstances that intermediary can be a lawyer. More often it is likely to be a consultant, a crisis manager, a turnaround specialist, to whom the shocks are tactics to be dealt with, and who can protect the borrower when he is most vulnerable and the recovery process most at risk.

Now one can take the ten lies about Chapter 11 and without any difficulty convert them into ten truths. They are:

1. You can hire a lawyer of your choice only if you have a large enough, uncompromised cash reserve for a handsome retainer and if you are not blocked by a creditor on a real or specious conflict-of-interest claim. You must be able to cast a cold eye on referrals by other attorneys who may be motivated by self-interest you are not in a position to perceive. And you need to check a bankruptcy lawyer's track record with regard to success as you would a surgeon on whose skill your life depended.

2. To rebuild your business in Chapter 11 you have to have a source of money that is not claimed by secured creditors.

3. Filing under Chapter 11 will put you at the mercy of creditors who do not know how to run your business but will insist that you run it their way even if it hurts all the other creditors as well as the company.

4. Your company could be denied its constitutional right of due process under law. Mine was, twice.

5. Though it's your company and not you that is in Chapter 11, you can be sued personally, lose whatever's in your personal bank accounts, have checks bounce without your knowing it, and be otherwise harassed and humiliated financially, while having to defend

yourself at your own expense at a time when your income will probably be sharply reduced. And if you raise any of these matters with the many lawyers involved, the moral cretins among them will respond as if with one voice, "Those are your problems, not the company's."

6. You are the client in name only. Unless you can afford to pay fat fees to the attorneys for the company on a regular basis, or you are fortunate enough to hire one of the top ethical professionals, you'll find that the lawyers will be working to protect each other's interests, making key decisions as if they were the businessmen, and in some cases even signing documents as if they were empowered to do so by you.

7. Chapter 11 can make it impossible to sell your business, even to a willing buyer who would have paid off all the creditors and used the assets instead of liquidating them. You need an experienced intermediary who knows the difference between the legitimate prospect for rescue and the piranhas who swim in Chapter 11 waters looking for bones that still have meat on them.

8. Filing under Chapter 11 is almost always an involuntary act.

9. Though the key to reorganizing is to get a funder to put up the money needed to get the business running well again, your reorganization can be blocked by committee lawyers who think they're businessmen and who aren't. You have an absolute right to bypass the blocking attorneys and bring any funder's offer before the court—if you've got the kind of lawyer that will let you.

10. Filing for Chapter 11 puts the key executives' health at risk. You do not get "relief," though that is what is promised. What you get is an entrance ticket to an unrelenting, pain-filled succession of days, weeks, and

months that almost always stretches into years. Every CEO I talked to spoke of the humiliation, anguish, and pain that the process generates, and the very real illnesses they cause.

The manager of a business that files for Chapter 11 "protection" will live through a bureaucratic nightmare that will remind those familiar with twentieth-century literature of Kafka's *The Trial.* Except it won't be happening in a novel that he can put down or finish. The manager's nightmare is kept never-ending because the system permits people to benefit from the cruel and unusual punishment he will be exposed to. He can be forbidden to talk to his creditors, even if they are friends trying to help him. I found it astonishing that businessmen I spoke with who were used to frustration admitted there were times during the night (and sometimes during the day) when their anger was so great they could only think of killing either someone else or themselves.

When you file you are no longer in whatever your business is, you are in the Chapter 11 business. The chairman of Texaco learned it. Tom Towey learned it. And if you do not have deep pockets, what you learn is that the Aztecs weren't the last in this hemisphere to go in for human sacrifice or to try to cut your heart out. There is a relatively new business in the land, a haven in principle and in practice an abomination, a feast for certain lawyers who look on the rest of the world as their prospective victims.

All of this will be proven in the course of this book.

CHAPTER 2
Is This Trip Necessary?

"A goose flies by a chart which the Royal
Geographical Society could not improve."
—Oliver Wendell Holmes

PEOPLE are not geese: They often take off in the
wrong direction. "Wrong-way Corrigan," as he
came to be called, intended to fly from the east coast
to California and landed in Ireland. Businessmen
whose companies are in crisis are in the right frame of
mind to do something equally inappropriate, and sometimes an inappropriate action is motivated by decency and
a respect for life.

Consider the man perched on a rooftop ready to leap.
There'll almost always be a few miscreants in the crowd
down below yelling, "Jump! Jump!" But civil citizens who
don't know the jumper will cry out for the man not to
jump and to allow himself to be saved because they
instinctively conceive of every human life as precious.
Though corporations are, under law, "persons" too, not all
are necessarily fit to live, and liquidation may be a form of
euthanasia not to be dismissed without thought.

Heading for Chapter 11 may not be the smart course.
Not every troubled company is a candidate for rehabilitation in order to solve its ills. Some companies have passed
their moment of commercial usefulness. Some never had
any in the first place. Others lack any economic justifica-
tion for continued existence. Therefore the entrepreneur
or manager and his professional advisors, faced with the
multitudinous problems of a troubled company, must ask

themselves two essential questions: Should this company be saved? Can it be saved?

The usual reaction to such a prompt is to reexamine the balance sheet. But Joshua Angel, when first sitting down with a prospective client, is more interested in what the company can do if it obtains relief than what the company has in the way of assets and liabilities. In short, he believes the key issue to be, "Can this company make it in the competitive business world if it obtains relief from its debts—can it make a real profit?" Angel, with some thirty years of experience at the bankruptcy bar, is mindful of the fact that sometimes an attempt to reorganize can actually exacerbate rather than alleviate the problems besetting a business owner.

As an example, one which entrepreneurs are loath to consider, there is the company that has pledged its assets as collateral to a bank, and the pledge is buttressed by the owner's personal guarantee of payment. If the company has a reasonable chance of becoming profitable once it is reorganized, Chapter 11 may be an answer. But if the enterprise under no reasonable forecast can be expected to make a profit, and indeed is likely to suffer additional losses if it continues operating, then an attempt at reorganization may harm the owner more than if he had opted to discontinue operations so that the assets could be liquidated, the bank paid off, and the threat of the overhanging guarantee removed.

In other words, if losses were to continue by the operation of the business, the assets that provide the primary collateral for the secured lender would be diminished or wasted, and the likelihood of the individual guarantor having to make good becomes more probable. Under these circumstances, an attempt to reorganize the business can be a threat to the owner's personal financial well-being. Liquidation may be the best damage control.

But the ability to judge whether or not to file is most difficult for the individual who is emotionally tied to the business. He may require the dispassionate review of an experienced professional, an attorney specializing in bankruptcy, or a turnaround expert. If with the best of advice the decision is reached to cease operations and to liquidate, the advisors can still apply knowledge gained from their experience to work out a plan of liquidation that will do the least damage to their client. With one proviso. The business manager or owner has to be sure that his advisors are not the kind who prefer to milk a case rather than to get the painful operation over with expeditiously. Alas, the milkers at the bankruptcy bar not only may constitute a majority but sometimes, tragically, are the only ones available, and their advice to the client may be tainted by their primary motive: greed.

Let us assume that a decision has been reached to try to save the company. The next step is poker.

This poker game doesn't take place in a smoke-filled room in the back of some sleazy restaurant. Its likely locale is a conference room in the offices of a bank's attorneys. If it's in a city of any size, the CEO should look around at the nicely upholstered chairs, the carpet on the floor, the pictures on the wall, and the rich-looking wood of the conference table itself. If the furnishings look expensive, the CEO should keep in mind that he'll be paying for their amortization as if it were equipment he owned.

In this poker game the CEO's opponent is not Paul Newman. He's a less handsome fellow, and he's from the workout division of the CEO's bank.

They say that people playing poker should study the players. Chances are the man from the bank will hold his cards close to his chest and let the lawyer sitting beside him do the talking. In fact, in many instances the banker will have two lawyers at that meeting, the senior one whose client the bank is, the "rainmaker," and the less senior one who is one of the firm's bankruptcy specialists. The CEO should study this last fellow closely because if the meeting doesn't come to a favorable conclusion, he's going to be seeing a lot of that lawyer and he's going to be dunned for hundreds of his hours at a very high hourly rate, along with footing that lawyer's fax and Federal Express bills, indulging his penchant for chauffeured limousines, and, if the client and the debtor are not in the same city, paying his hotel bills, meal bills, and a lot of other "collection" expenses.

On the CEO's side of the table will be his bankruptcy lawyer. How that CEO will live for the next few years and whether or not his company will survive depends largely on the skill of that one man.

The CEO of a troubled company teetering on the edge of Chapter 11 depends on his bankruptcy counsel for advice as much as a newborn needs a bottle or a breast to survive. Unless the CEO has been fortunate enough to be able to hire one of the relatively small number of high-minded bankruptcy lawyers who is also a terrific negotiator, he would be well advised to bring along also a turnaround specialist, who is a businessman and can deal with the business needs of a beleaguered company, as well as draw the heat normally directed toward management. A turnaround specialist wants to be in for the short pull, not the long haul, and therefore has a kinship with the CEO who has spent his life solving business problems rather than prolonging them.

What is important before the meeting starts is that the CEO has picked a good lawyer to advise him and front for him.

Kenneth E. Glass of Canton, Ohio, one of the turnaround specialists I referred to in the foreword of this book, said it was "extremely difficult" for a CEO to find a really good bankruptcy lawyer. "You need to know who the good guys and the bad guys are," he said. "You need to find the ones that will act on behalf of clients and not themselves."

Daniel Morris, President of Morris Anderson Associates of Glenview, Illinois, and one of the foremost turnaround people, underlined that it was "extremely difficult" for any executive anywhere in the country to find a good bankruptcy lawyer on his own. David Ferrari, a New England turnaround expert, gives two of the reasons for this. "Ninety-nine percent of the corporate lawyers," Ferrari says, "don't know who's good in the bankruptcy area. If they don't have a bankruptcy department in their firm, they don't want to make referrals out of fear of losing business."

I have talked to any number of CEOs who went into Chapter 11 with a lawyer in whom they didn't have full confidence. The problem most mention is having had to hire a bankruptcy lawyer in a hurry. They didn't have the time, nor did they know how to judge the person's expertise. Neither did the lawyer they normally used. Besides, some lawyers, it's been said, may just possibly steer clients to a particular specialist in their own rather than the client's economic interest.

More than one CEO said, in effect, that when they first met the bankruptcy lawyer he didn't inspire confidence. When pressed for details, they hesitated, but the conclusion that was finally dredged out of them was that the lawyer didn't seem to understand their business or wasn't clever enough to learn the essentials quickly.

Let this serve as a warning: The CEO must find out what types of businesses this prospective lawyer has represented. It is crucial for the CEO to obtain a list of the attorney's success stories, if any, and check them out. If in the vast majority of the lawyer's cases he has represented creditors rather than debtors or has been parochially narrow in representing businesses different in kind from the CEO's, the CEO should be wary.

It is not essential that the CEO have a perfect rapport with the man or woman who is going to represent his company in Chapter 11. But it is absolutely crucial that the lawyer understand enough about the CEO's business to be able to go about saving it successfully.

When one hires a bankruptcy lawyer one needs to know not only his experience with debtor companies, but what kind of negotiator he is, how he is on his feet in a courtroom, whether he has experience in the jurisdiction where you're filing, what his attitude is toward saving companies, whether he is full of ideas for getting a company out of Chapter 11 once it's in. The key attitude one is looking for is: Does this bankruptcy lawyer think like a lawyer or a businessman?

Most lawyers are not litigators. Litigation has become a specialty of the law. Experienced litigators differ almost as much from their corporate-law colleagues as do British solicitors, who work with clients, from British barristers, who are picked by solicitors to represent a case in court.

The ability to litigate successfully requires a penchant for careful preparation prior to a court appearance, plus an ability to act on a moment's notice in the courtroom. The litigator has to challenge questions with immediate objections, he has to have a knack for picking up things on the fly. When an opponent or an opponent's attorney says something on direct examination that could open up a Pandora's box, the litigator has to be ready to jump in and release the catch. Perhaps most important, the litigator has to be an actor, able to play a part appropriate to the circumstances. Even when there is no jury, as is usual in bankruptcy court, the litigator has an audience: the judge, and the other litigators.

I have seen an experienced litigator enter a roomful of combative lawyers and win their attention and respect with just a sentence or two, or even by his mere presence and reputation. It's asking a lot for a bankruptcy specialist to also be a first-rate litigator. *But the fact is that the real battles in bankruptcy are fought in the courtroom, and the skills of a litigator are an absolute requirement.* If you pick a bankruptcy specialist whose paperwork is near perfect and who is a good negotiator in the conference room but a wimp in the courtroom, your case will have a hard time in front of a judge who wants his decisions based on what he hears in sworn testimony and not on what's in the filed position papers.

Even if the lawyer has been recommended by another

lawyer you trust, if he appears to be a waddler or a wimp, run the other way. If you see him that way, the judge might too, and the opposing lawyers certainly will. If you wouldn't hire the lawyer as a senior executive in your business, be careful, because he will in effect become that. And if you wouldn't trust him to defend a child of yours in serious trouble, don't trust him to protect a business of yours that's in trouble.

When it comes to picking an attorney, if you have a choice, he should not only be good on his feet, but—this is important—he needs to have experience in the particular court you'll be in and have litigated successfully before the judge who is going to determine your case. Otherwise, you'll both be on an unfamiliar stage—the halt leading the blind.

If the businessman is not told what the game plan is by his lawyer before the filing, he'd better not file—or get himself a different lawyer. As one key executive said, "We were caught in a dance in which we didn't know the steps, our lawyer didn't want to teach us the steps, but we had to keep dancing."

Again and again I heard from the CEOs of companies in distress that they had to hire somebody on the run because filing had become an emergency. A taxing authority or a creditor might have gotten a lien or judgment and was trying to execute and grab collateral. Banks have trigger-happy "asset recovery teams" that can show up at a company's door, post guards, seize inventory, and not even let employees remove their personal belongings from their desks.

Under that or a similar kind of pressure, or simply because their company was in hot water with its bank and they wanted the pain to stop, some pretty able CEOs abandoned their usual caution and hired a lawyer about whom they had a lot of reservations. Mistake.

I thought I was lucky because I had a friend who could smell trouble a long way away. On his advice, I consulted a partner in a major firm specializing in bankruptcy *nearly two years before my company actually filed.* This lawyer, then a partner in the distinguished bankruptcy firm of Levin, Weintraub & Crames, seemed intelligent, knowledgeable, mature. We discussed the pros and cons of filing. Months later we talked again, and again we agreed that the disadvantages outweighed the advantages. Our discussions with him and one of his colleagues, by phone and in person, stretched over a year and a half, plenty of time to prepare for D-Day, should it come. *I never asked him what kind of retainer he would require, and he never told me;* nor did he mention the need for a war chest or outside funding, or that we begin to think about the kind of plan that would be required should we have to file. So when D-Day came in the form of a paralyzing restraining order that made filing inevitable, I learned to my dismay that this seemingly excellent lawyer's firm required a large retainer we couldn't manage on such short notice. He recommended a former associate who was practicing on his own and whose retainer requirements were half that of his. That's how we ended up hiring a half-price lawyer on whom the future of our company depended.

Once a bankruptcy lawyer has got your retainer in his bank account, he has to drop almost everything else he's doing and file a massive set of papers on your company's behalf. The half-price lawyer that had been recommended to us, whom I will call Joe Doaks, left out the value of the company's two largest assets in his first filing. I pointed out the errors. It made the difference between our assets being higher than our liabilities by several million—or a lot lower. This so-called bankruptcy specialist said it didn't matter (meaning why should he take the trouble to run the papers through the word processor again). These glossed-over errors could have gotten us thrown into Chapter 7 immediately. They may have influenced the opposing lawyers into forcing us into a Chapter 7 liquidating mode while we were in Chapter 11 seeking protection. A year later the *Wall Street Journal* was still quoting the wrong numbers that lawyer put in our first papers.

The point, of course, is that hiring the right bankruptcy lawyer from the start may be one of the most important acts of a CEO's business career. The manufacturing company run by one chief executive I talked to uses a large law firm that has a bankruptcy specialist right in the firm. This executive thought the partner who oversaw the year-in, year-out corporate work for his firm was terrific. What the executive learned when his company got into trouble was that just because his regular lawyer was terrific didn't mean the bankruptcy partner was also terrific. Nor was the bankruptcy partner long on experience as counsel for a debtor, which is a different kind of ball game than being counsel for one of the creditors. Naturally, the executive's regular counsel didn't volunteer that his bankruptcy partner's courtroom style was more like ping-pong than fierce tennis volleys at the net. Nor, naturally, did the CEO's good counsel suggest that the client nose around to find someone else. As a result, the executive, who'd almost always had legal advice he considered first-rate, wound up with a klutz from the same firm. By the time the executive realized that the bankruptcy specialist in that firm wasn't up to snuff, years of hard work had run down the Chapter 11 drain.

A debtor has to find a bankruptcy lawyer who is turned on by the excitement of helping a company pull up out of the hole and back into daylight, who shares with it the spirit of entrepreneurship that drives businessmen on their way up.

The sad fact is that in the vast majority of cases, a CEO hires a bankruptcy lawyer *after* panic hits. He's been under the gun for some time. He is full of fear, anger, uncertainty, and he's fighting confusion and anxiety. He lives in a society that prizes economic success, and he is riding a bronco that is momentarily going to toss him into the dirt. And the crowd watching isn't cheering him on but waiting for him to be thrown off. That's not an optimum condition for making a wise decision that could affect the CEO's life as much as his marriage does (except getting a divorce from a bankruptcy lawyer can be harder than getting a divorce from a spouse). Torn in all directions, all the CEO can think about is being safely in the hands of a doctor who knows his trade. Of course a shocking percentage of practicing physicians don't know their trade well. Why should bankruptcy specialists have a higher percentage of competence? After all, it's only the life of the company that's at stake.

The bankruptcy lawyer on the CEO's side of the table is either one of the small minority of "class" experts, recognized as such by their colleagues and by the judiciary—let's call him a type "A" lawyer—or he is one of the other kind, a type "B," who looks to milk a case for what it's worth and who, inside his head, can't wait till he files because that's when the case becomes a real money-spinning machine for him. Of course between the smart, diligent, and honest A's and the venal B's, there wallows in the bar a surfeit of just plain lazy and incompetent lawyers who are a hazard to all they touch.

At the meeting with the bank it is the bankruptcy lawyer who is likely to do most of the talking, at least at the start.

One of the type A's, attorney Brian Loftus, a partner in Winston & Strawn, Chicago's oldest law firm and one of the country's largest, has this advice about a prepetition meeting with the bank: "In good times the manager of a business tries to keep his bankers happy. But when he gets into a troubled environment, the manager's attitude has to change. Bankers who are unsecured may threaten to pull the plug. The manager has got to be firm and get tough. Banks bluff. The CEO must realize that it is not in the bank's best interest to have a client company file for an eleven, so talking about going into an eleven is a good threat. The bank is better off keeping the company alive. What the bank wants is to get a secured position if they don't already have it because if they do, and the company has enough assets, the bank is assured of getting one hundred cents on the dollar even if the company files. However," Loftus says, "sometimes a compromise is in order. The bank threatens to cut off credit or to call a loan that can put the CEO's company out of business. But it isn't to their advantage necessarily to force a company to seek protection in an eleven. Perhaps negotiating with them, giving them some security is in order. At the same time, getting some accommodations from trade creditors will give the business a chance to turn around."

Joshua J. Angel says a bank that is secured could cut a company's credit lines and threaten to pull the plug because in an eleven, with a secured position, the bank is assured of getting paid before other creditors and has at least a chance of getting one hundred cents on the dollar. Angel believes the threat to take a company into an eleven works best with banks in an unsecured position.

Whether the chief executive gets an A or a B lawyer for this poker game with the bank may depend on whether his company is large enough or has assets enough to attract one of the A "class" players, whether he has stashed enough cash to provide for a healthy retainer, and perhaps most of all, whether he knows enough to have been able to choose a bankruptcy lawyer with care.

A CEO's chances of picking the right bankruptcy lawyer are much better if he's chosen the other person on his side of the table first, the turnaround specialist, whose motives are the same as the company's: to fix the business problems as quickly as possible and at the lowest feasible cost. He's seen this kind of situation before. The CEO hasn't. The consultant can provide detachment and experience. If it's too late for the consultant to effect a rescue outside of Chapter 11, at least he can help make the right choice of bankruptcy counsel.

One articulate turnaround consultant, himself a lawyer, sees his role as being in economic competition with bankruptcy lawyers because his job is to keep companies out of Chapter 11 by stabilizing the business. And one of the ways these crisis managers achieve this is by negotiating effectively with banks because most banks don't want a borrower company to file. They know how expensive it is. They know how long it takes. And they know that once the company's in Chapter 11, the judge, who has a great deal more leeway than other federal judges, will have a responsibility to look out for the interests not only of secured creditors like the bank, but also of the army of unsecured creditors.

That's why poker time is an ideal opportunity for a strong representative of the company to strike a deal with a bank. As one chief executive said, "Sometimes the bankruptcy lawyer's presence at the poker game with the bank is a plus even if he keeps his mouth shut. Just his being at the table advertises the hand he'll play if the bank doesn't cooperate."

The executive whose company is on the brink of Chapter 11 still has to shave every morning. When he looks in the mirror, what he normally sees is someone who heretofore knew how to solve business problems. But that's in a *normal* business environment. If he's dealing with a financially troubled company, or one suddenly under the gun because of an unforeseen event such as a huge judgment the company can't meet, he's looking in the mirror at a man whose ego is in no shape to play poker with the bank where the essential question is: Will a lender who thinks the borrower is shaky lend him more money or at least not foreclose on assets that will force the borrower to elect Chapter 11 as his only remedy?

If Chapter 11 is inevitable, as in the case of a huge judgment against the company, the poker game with the bank takes a different turn. Can the bank be persuaded to agree in advance of filing to the company's use of cash collateral, the money that comes in every day from receivables, so that the company can continue its business? For that task the CEO has to look at his bankruptcy lawyer and think, "Is this the man I'd send to negotiate a loan from the bank in the first place?" Sad to say, that would rule out a majority of lawyers simply because they are not businessmen, don't think like businessmen, and don't know how to negotiate a business deal, which is what a bank loan is and what a cash collateral agreement also is.

The CEO needs an expert whose involvement in case after case has taught him how to act in the eye of a hurricane when the CEO can't do so effectively. When it comes to making decisions about filing for protection, or negotiating pre- or postpetition deals with creditors, the CEO lacks t! ɔ essential experience of having been there before. Choosing the right expert is critical.

Executives who've been through the Chapter 11 experience agree that the right time to win the Chapter 11 war is in the weeks before it starts.

Tom Towey of Neptune World Wide Moving provides a good example of how to go to war. He had a first-class bankruptcy lawyer who then recommended that he also retain an expert financial consultant. They gave him the technical strength and moral support to be able to hold on to the reins of his business. Any lawyer who objects to a CEO's staying in charge of his company and fortifying himself with the best team—including experts with business savvy—has got a weak ego, which is not characteristic of a winner.

Picking the right turnaround specialist may be as tough a call as choosing the right lawyer, and the same cautions should be exercised. The turnaround barrel is said to have its share of inedible apples. Some lawyers will point to the fact that crisis managers may or may not be trained lawyers or accountants. What should count most to the CEO is whether the turnaround specialist is experienced in dealing *as a businessman* with a business in crisis. The CEO can't take comfort from a license because turnaround people aren't licensed. Then again, all lawyers are licensed and presumably regulated, but if that gives any businessman comfort he probably believes in Santa Claus, and that all cops and congressmen are honest.

There is one important caution about hiring a turnaround specialist. There are instances where the problems of the business have so eroded the chief executive's confidence or perceptions that he is not the right man to put Humpty Dumpty back together again. This means that the crisis manager will have to take over the reins of the business and function as a temporary CEO. Some of them require the right to do so as a condition of taking on the assignment. As one lawyer put it, "He's in and you're out!"

Even at cliff's edge, there can be a great advantage in trying to work out a deal with a bank. If the CEO doesn't do that, he will find that short as he was of cash before he filed, once he's in Chapter 11 he has zero cash that he controls without permission of the secured creditors. The price of that permission is usually a lien against newly created receivables, thus making the need for permission endless. When the "price" of permission is negotiated under the worst of circumstances, a consensual order after filing, the secured creditor, in addition to getting a lien against newly created receivables, may ask for and get concessions that will improve the secured creditor's position. He may also require management to institute certain cash-saving procedures, usually starting with a punitive cut in pay for the top people.

Prepetition negotiations are usually a waste of time unless the CEO has one of the honorable professionals at his side. Negotiations involving solely the other type of bankruptcy lawyer will be useless on both sides (except for hours billed) if the lawyers are really chafing to get the Chapter 11 underway because that's where the gold is—for them.

We will now assume that the decision to file for protection under Chapter 11 has been made. The bankruptcy court clerk will record the date and time of the filing, which will be significant throughout the case. Everything that was owed or threatened, and even any judgment that was levied, are all stayed by virtue of the filing.

What happens next depends on who the CEO has hired to advise him. For him Chapter 11 is an uncharted ocean, and he is in a leaky lifeboat suddenly attacked by sharks.

CHAPTER 3

Presumed Guilty: The Six-Ring Circus During Those Crucial First Few Days

> "Why may not that be the skull of a lawyer? Where be his quiddities now, his quillets, his cases, his tenures, and his tricks?"
>
> —Shakespeare, *Hamlet*

HARRIS S. is a CEO as well as an engineer and inventor who heads a company making precision instruments mainly for the Navy. His company is successful, and he is in this book for only one reason. Harris S. has had several good friends whose businesses ran into trouble—or had trouble run into them—and who had to file for Chapter 11 protection. And what those people went through during the days in which the decision to file was made, Harris S. says, looking at it from the outside, reminds him of the time he was lying on an operating table in one of New York's reputedly great hospitals, awaiting a major operation on which his future depended. Harris S. heard the surgeon and the anesthetist squabbling. This wasn't just a minor fracas, it was a shouting match conducted within two or three feet of the sedated patient about whether the correct pre-anesthesia preparations had been performed—or overlooked.

Afterward Harris S. was glad that the operation, though urgent, was aborted. He put himself into the hands of another hospital in another state, and at this writing is back at the helm of his business. But when he told what happened to him to a friend who had just gone through the early stages of Chapter 11, it brought both laughter and tears over the similarity of the experiences. Any executive in Chapter 11 has got to be prepared to do the equivalent of lying, perhaps somewhat sedated by tranquilizers, listening not to doctors but to squabbling lawyers waiting to operate on the company without regard for what the executive who built and ran the company thinks.

Every entrepreneur I ever talked to said he felt *the company was his,* particularly if he was a major (or sole) shareholder. Entrepreneurs whose companies are in Chapter 11 quickly learn the company belongs to the creditors—and in the words of one bankruptcy lawyer, *it is from his creditors that the entrepreneur has to buy it back!*

With what? With future earnings, but only if the creditors allow the company to function. Or he can buy it back through the sale of one or more of the assets that he needs least to run the company. Or he can find himself a new partner with money. However, he has to get the agreement of the creditors to take in the new partner if the newcomer wants the new money secured going in.

The chief executive will be hearing repeatedly a term that will change his conception of money: cash collateral. Unless his attorney has been able to work out a prefiling agreement with the secured creditors for the use of cash, the CEO will find that the first assembly of creditors in front of the judge will be about the use of cash collateral. The executive will learn, to his surprise, that any money that is in the company's till from receivables doesn't belong to the company any more; it belongs to the secured creditors who had receivables as collateral. Therefore it requires their approval to use. And for that approval, they usually want something.

What happens at the first hearing has what theater people refer to as a "text" and a "subtext." Cash collateral is usually the surface plot. Beneath that surface, the "sub-text" is about the jockeying of the creditors for position.

Position means any creditor's place in relation to the other creditors. In the lineup to collect what they can out of the company, it allegedly benefits some creditors to have their attorneys create an atmosphere of confusion.

It starts in the public hallway outside the courtroom. A dozen or two dozen cases can be down on the calendar for the same time and the same day. If it's a "minor" item like the bankruptcy of an individual, a routine hearing might involve only the individual's lawyer, but for most cases, there are at least two lawyers and sometimes several. For a new case, before the judge for the first time and involving a company of any size, there could be ten or fifteen lawyers and some of their principals milling about, indoctrinating, preaching, predisposing, proselytizing, swaying, and noisily trying, by and large, to influence other creditors. It is the Mad Hatter's Tea Party come to life. Worse, the head of the debtor company feels caught in a mob that doesn't want to wait for the courtroom doors to open—they have the rope and are looking around for a tree.

I remember vividly a scene in the hallway before Stein and Day's first hearing. Amidst the bedlam, Martin J. Bienenstock, a partner in Weil Gotshal, was pointing a finger of blame directly at my nose. "You did it!" he said. I tried to say that no, we'd been a relatively prosperous company until certain third parties ... blam! Nobody wanted to hear "excuses." The verdict was in before the trial began. I was guilty.[1]

What had greater repercussions, however, was the clatter made by Bienenstock's client, Randy Kuckuck, representing BookCrafters, a trade creditor. Kuckuck, a lawyer by training, was trying to persuade all who would listen

---

1. Ten months later Martin Bienenstock was telling my partner, Patricia Day, "I never understood how awful it's been for you." Yet his client was BookCrafters, the creditor who hurt us most.

that Stein and Day, which had finally filed in order to resume publishing, should not be allowed to print, publish, sell, or even liquidate its inventory. On the face of it what he was saying didn't make sense. You either published or perished—meaning you continued as a going concern or were liquidated. But Kuckuck was proposing contradictions: Don't let them publish, but don't let them liquidate their inventory either. Patricia Day later said that in her opinion Kuckuck seemed like the Red Queen in *Alice* that day, shouting, in effect, "Off with their heads!"

Sam Metzger, the CEO of Chipwich, the ice cream sandwich purveyor, himself a lawyer, was startled by the "ton" of lawyers present at his first hearing. "You'd think we were Texaco. You couldn't see because of the sheer number of lawyers. When the judge asked the lawyers in the Chipwich case to come forward, the first three rows in the courtroom stood up as a man and headed for the bench. There wasn't room enough for all of them. Then the judge took charge."[2]

At the first hearing, in addition to the gaggle of attorneys, a representative of each secured creditor will also be present, ready to testify to the basis of its secured position.

---

2. At the time of Chipwich's filing, its main office was located in upstate New York and the case fell into the jurisdiction of the bankruptcy court in White Plains, which meant that the judge was Howard Schwartzberg, who was also the judge in the Texaco, Neptune, and Stein and Day cases. The CEOs I talked to who came before Schwartzberg spoke of his fairness, efficiency, and control of the courtroom. Metzger, himself a lawyer, thought Schwartzberg "fabulous. Nobody can bullshit him. When he took over, you had a feeling of a protector who is a wise, understanding, experienced individual." Debtors in other jurisdictions should not assume that they will necessarily come before so expert a judge. Metzger also made the point that "outside the courtroom"—meaning when Schwartzberg was not around to supervise the conduct of the parties—"was a different world." In Stein and Day's case Judge Schwartzberg seemed to be indifferent to what was going on behind his back "outside the courtroom" even when it was reported to him in front of the participants.

(Unless their secured position in the collateral is established, they cannot oppose the use of cash.) Sometimes these representatives can serve as additional cast for beefing up the confusion. And sometimes, as in Kuckuck's case, they can play a leading role.

Why does the first hearing in court frequently resemble a circus in which every performer speaks a different language? What is the new ringmaster, the judge, trying to find out? Is there a way a judge can cut through the words of a lawyer who is less than competent? And why should the babble and activity out in the hallway before the hearing often be of greater importance than the hearing itself?

Regrettably, in many cases the turmoil of the first few days and weeks after filing is purposeful. It is part of the process of taking the management of the case and the company out of the hands of the chief executive and his staff and putting it into the hands of the creditors' lawyers.

Unless the CEO has been well prepared by an experienced attorney and they both come to the hearing with a high level of confidence in concrete plans for that first cash collateral hearing, the businessman will feel himself to be in the middle of a painful farce. If the lawyers, underneath the shouting, don't seem to care particularly what happens, it's because chances are they'll get their money even if the company goes under, as happens in the large majority of cases that come trustingly into the system.

The commotion benefits the better-versed bankruptcy lawyers and bank workout officers who have been through this scene before. What benefits them can hurt the debtor most. Therefore, before the circus starts, what the CEO needs to get from his lawyer is a clear briefing so that he will not be taken in by the deliberate confusion. As the target for the day, he needs some emotional insulation, a barbproof vest. The CEO also needs to be assured that his lawyer knows exactly what evidence or arguments he will use to enable the business to function.

Chances are the CEO will feel like a new recruit in an old army. It pays for the creditors to keep the CEO confused, angry, uncertain of what is happening or what he can do. It depletes his power. A good lawyer will protect the CEO. One of the other kind will simply help set the stage for a many-seasoned run of a bizarre play.

At cash collateral hearings involving small and medium-sized companies, the main witnesses will usually be the chief financial officer and the CEO. The attorneys for the secured creditors are likely to cross-examine both with ruthless ferocity. As for the CEO, they know that he is at his weakest, full of anxiety and pain, having just taken a step that brands him as a loser. At a time when the CEO needs all the strength of his experience and character to steer his company through the eye of a hurricane, the creditors' lawyers pounce. Their object is to tear down the debtor in the eyes of the court, to deprecate, denounce, defame, condemn, and revile him, and to besmirch whatever reputation he may have had. Their intent is to leave him demoralized, disheartened, discouraged, depressed, and shaken. Even the most expert bankruptcy judges can do little to protect the debtors from these savage attacks. The CEO is the lightning rod for all the heat in the courtroom.

The motivation behind the attacks varies. However much the chief executive of the debtor company has tried to keep his creditors informed as to the causes of the problem and his attempts at solution, time has worked against him. If he has tried different avenues for raising capital without success, each failure diminishes his credibility. If he has tried to sell the company or some of its major assets and failed, in the eyes of creditors that damages his trustworthiness, and they come to the first hearing, as one specialist put it, "loaded for bear." Very often the person in the creditor company who becomes the chief contact with the case is the credit manager or chief financial officer. That person, by extending credit, rightly or wrongly, to the company that is now in serious trouble, is now the object of fire in his home port. He is angry. And his anger is usually directed not at himself for extending credit but to the company that took it when it was offered.

And there is also the unsecured supplier whose largest account receivable by far is from the debtor company and who is terrified that his own company is now in jeopardy, that he might also be precipitated into bankruptcy. He is told that all those lawyers for the secured creditors in the courtroom are going to run up huge costs that are going to be added to their secured claims. Those claims are going to shove ahead of him on line. He may end up getting cents on the dollar or nothing. If he is a civil, understanding person like Glenn Corlett of Comp House, who saw his most important customer thrust down the drain and saw his own family firm possibly going down the tube also but managed to act reasonably and fair throughout, he deserves a medal. And then there is the exact opposite, the mean-spirited, unforgiving, relentless, vengeful, merciless, spiteful, vindictive, even sadistic creditor who is out to pull the pillars so that the whole house will come tumbling down.

Whatever the motive, the human target is the same: the most visible executive in the debtor company. And faced with so much hostility from so many sources, it is easy for the CEO to lose control of any hearing in its first few minutes.

The judge, who is trying mightily to determine the facts of the case in a whirl of contentious conduct, cannot do much about protecting the debtor from attack. That is up to the CEO's lawyer, who can object over and over again whenever the attacking lawyers cross the line, and try to put things back into an accurate perspective in redirect examination—if the company's new-found bankruptcy lawyer has those skills and is willing to use them.

There is usually a limit to the degree to which the highly outnumbered counsel for the debtor will fight back against his "colleagues." As Luz-Maria Moreno, general counsel for Neptune World Wide Moving put it, "It's a highly incestuous arena." It is important to keep in mind that the day this purposely confusing circus atmosphere is launched will also be the judge's first exposure to the case. Like most bankruptcy judges, he will know some if not most of the players, because the specialist lawyers will have been before him on another case last week or last month or last year. There will even be nods of recognition and greeting between the bench and the lawyers. At the opening of the formal proceedings, the lawyers stand and each announces his name, the name of his firm, and whom he or she represents. The one person who in all likelihood is unknown to the judge is the CEO, now known as the debtor.[3] And the judge will be forming an important first impression. Ideally, the CEO should seem self-controlled, responsible, confident, mature, reserved, and poised—a trustworthy person. In actuality, his insides feel like what the captain of the *Titanic* must have felt—and it usually shows.

The noisy first hearing is the beginning of an overlong series of courtroom events in which the CEO has to learn to play a role as if he were an actor and as if the others were actors in a play also. Even if the CEO's emotions are bubbling like a Jacuzzi, he will need to learn the fine art of observing the action *as if he were an outsider looking at a show.* Unless he steels himself to be an observer, he will end up a sure victim of a system that makes him play the contradictory roles of the perpetrator of the insolvency and the victim of the creditors at the same time.

If, however, the businessman can detach himself from the proceedings enough to witness them with a cold eye, he will begin to see what the lawyers are up to. He will watch their ploys to get star billing in this new tragedy.

---

3. In actuality, it is the company that is "the debtor," not the executive in charge of it, but the two meanings get to be used loosely and interchangeably to encompass the CEO as well as the company. Similarly, if management continues in place, the company is known as a debtor-in-possession, but in common parlance the term is also used to describe the CEO of a firm in Chapter 11.

He will be able to see their interaction and notice who is working with whom. For, as he will soon find out, one of the basic stratagems of the bankruptcy professionals is to form backstage alliances.

Most people smart enough to initiate and run a previously successful business will have learned how to study the humans in their surroundings. The problem is learning to do so when you have so much at stake. You're in a new theater that the other actors know well and you don't. They are acting for the benefit of offstage characters (the creditors), and you are there at center stage in person, beads of moisture on your forehead, hoping you know your lines. Your vocal cords are tense. You want to seem self-controlled, responsible, confident, mature, reserved, poised, and a trustworthy person.

When the creditors vie for ranking, it is for a very real objective—who gets paid back first. Secured creditors come first, with the mass of unsecured creditors following. But if there is more than one secured creditor, they vie with each other for position. True, if there's a bank involved and its loan was secured, the bank usually comes first. But a bank's papers may be faulty, it may have filed a UCC[4] (to perfect a security agreement) in the wrong jurisdiction, or it may have failed to file in a county where important collateral is kept. I've personally observed instances of all of these things, so there must be a fair amount of sloppy bank work around. And any weakness in a bank's position will be exploited by others. For instance, if no one has filed a UCC in a place where some collateral is housed, the unsecured creditors may lay claim to it at once. Better yet, if the debtor has a smart lawyer, the company may get to use that collateral to help save its business, particularly if that collateral is something that can be sold more quickly than other collateral.

---

4. The abbreviation stands for Universal Commercial Code. The UCC is a multiple-copy form that should be filed in each county and state where secured assets are located.

One bankruptcy attorney put it to me this way: When you see the creditors jockeying for position, you have to think of it as if you've just inherited George Orwell's *Animal Farm*. All the animals are equal, but the pigs are more equal than the others.

While the creditors joust for position, sometimes for months or years, what about the shareholders who owned the company? While stockholders in a company the size of Texaco may survive the Chapter 11 process with most of their equity intact, the hard fact is that in the hour before filing the shareholders owned the company, and from the moment of filing, for all practical purposes, the creditors own the company because they control the assets. In the Chapter 11 hierarchy shareholders come last, and to assess the attitude toward shareholders, listen to the president of a capital corporation that specializes in buying companies out of Chapter 11. "Stockholders? Forget them, they're dead. What do I have to do, line them up against a wall and put a bullet in their heads?"

It is only in the largest companies that the stockholders can come out of an eleven with their equity intact. And very often not even they can.

The CEO soon learns that although the ostensible object of Chapter 11 is to maximize the assets so that the largest number of creditors will benefit, and the court is there for the protection of the unsecured creditors also, each of the secured creditors will be represented by one or more lawyers, and they will outnumber and usually outgun the lawyer for the Creditors' Committee. That committee represents all the unsecured creditors. There can be hundreds or even thousands in a relatively small bankruptcy case. Who picks the lawyer representing all those people?

The process works like this. The top twenty unsecured creditors (meaning the ones owed the most money) are polled to see who is willing or insists on serving on the Creditors' Committee. Often the most aggressive of these twenty unsecured creditors will choose the lawyer who is going to represent the committee, especially if the others don't have a clue as to whom they might hire.

Some years ago lawyers were permitted for the first time to advertise their services. This provided a field day for negligence lawyers—the "ambulance chasers" of legend. In Chapter 11, this new right of attorneys to actively solicit business means that sometimes the attorney for the Creditors' Committee picks himself. He hears of a case in a field that interests him. (They like to think of themselves as industry specialists, though in my experience, corroborated by others, they frequently know precious little about the industries they get involved in.) He then solicits the largest unsecured creditors by phone and puts himself forward as the fellow who will protect their interests best. The pitch some make is to tell the top twenty how awful the management of the company is.

That technique can backfire, because in many businesses the suppliers trapped in a Chapter 11 situation have had long-term relationships with the heads of the business, are sometimes friends, and some of them look forward to a continued relationship with the debtor company, though on a cash-up-front basis until the Chapter 11 "blows over." They don't realize that the Chapter 11 company has received an indeterminate sentence that is likely to last years.

And so the CEO may receive phone calls from these creditors, saying in effect, "Hey, this lawyer called me and told me what a bastard you are and would I take his firm on as counsel for the Creditors' Committee." That's how the CEO learns of the sales pitch, which barely skirts slander. He will begin to wonder about people who make their livings this way, a handsome living to be sure.

The members of the Creditors' Committee usually "pick" the lawyer who is to represent them before they see him in action and find out whether he's any good or not. In practice, this lawyer will then ostensibly act on behalf of *all* the unsecured creditors, including the many hundreds that may not be represented on the committee.

And though he "polls"—or pretends to poll—the members of his committee (yes, it is now his committee) on important issues, he is quite capable of making monumental decisions on his own and then getting the committee to rubber-stamp his "recommendation." Of course he isn't supposed to be doing things like that, but he does, believe me.

If the committee finds the lawyer is not doing a good job and the Chapter 11 case is going nowhere, or the secured creditors are blocking any chance of the unsecureds having anything left, does the committee fire the lawyer who is controlling the fate of the vast majority of creditors? Not on your life. It can happen, but it doesn't. Corrective action is very rare.[5] Members of the committee are often in the dark, too, about what really goes on. The unsecured creditors who may be friendly to the company and want it to emerge from Chapter 11 sooner or later learn that they're stuck with the attorney who solicited them.

The strange part for the CEO is that the lawyer for the Creditors' Committee who defames him (usually before they've ever met) will be paid out of monies generated by the company! Not too much later, the lawyer who represents the Creditors' Committee may cuddle up to the CEO and try to convince him that they're on the same side. And the lawyer for the debtor company will also urge the cuddling up with the lawyer for the Creditors' Committee. This sweetheart arrangement comes about because the lawyers for the secured creditors are usually being paid for hours billed on a current basis, while the attorney for

---

5. One of the rare exceptions took place in 1988 when the Creditors' Committee of the Kaiser Steel Corporation replaced the firm of Myerson & Kuhn as its counsel. "The creditors accused the firm of 'doubling up (and more)' of lawyers attending meetings and reviewing documents, failure to submit expense receipts and including a partner's billing 28.5 hours in a single day." The fired law firm put in a request for a fee of $743,604. The Creditors' Committee sought to have the fee reduced by one-third. The story was reported on the front page of the *New York Law Journal*, April 17, 1989.

the company and the attorney for the Creditors' Committee won't see the bulk of their money until the end of the line when "administrative costs"[6] are considered. And so, in general, the attorney for the "estate" and the unsecured creditors' attorney may sometimes be tempted to play ball with each other to see what fees they can carve out of the sale of assets. In some instances there is little excuse for one or the other getting a piece of the pie, but they can have an understanding between them that incoming carve-out dollars are shared by prearrangement.

Was this what the Congress had in mind when it passed the 1978 revisions to the bankruptcy law?

The circus atmosphere of the first courtroom hearing can be carried over into the early meetings with the Creditors' Committee unless interference is run by a good lawyer or crisis manager. One knowledgeable bankruptcy attorney sketched the players this way: No matter who the people involved are, "the creditors are portrayed as representing God, America, and motherhood, while the CEO and his executives are pictured as deadbeats, failures, and crooks."

Crisis manager Kenneth Glass has a technique for dealing with groups of creditors. "There's a lot of emotional energy in the room and it's got to be directed to something positive," he says. He tries to take control of the meeting by announcing, "We screwed up. We misled you, but it wasn't intentional. We made mistakes. We apologize for those mistakes. Here's what we're going to try to do."

Glass, of course, has a marvelous advantage if it is he rather than the head of the troubled company saying those words. He is the new man on the block. The mistakes were not his: He didn't screw up or mislead anyone.

---

6. So-called "administrative costs," which have a priority over all claims other than secured claims, consist of attorneys', accountants', and other professional fees incurred after the Chapter 11 filing, as well as any unpaid obligations incurred after filing, and some other preferred items.

He has made himself the substitute lightning rod for all that belligerent energy in the room. The creditors are ready to listen.

One of Glass's objectives is to find out who the most responsible creditors are. Creditors who lose their temper at meetings look like asses just as much as the debtor does when he's out of control. Ken Glass zeros in on the ones who can become allies in the reconstructive process.

An unusually perceptive bankruptcy lawyer described the process of getting used to Chapter 11 as the conflict between the CEO's wanting to get the agony over with and his need for time to neutralize his emotions, to be able to see the game that is being played with his company and his life with objectivity devoid of emotion—a nearly impossible task.

On March 10, 1989, the morning after Eastern Airlines filed under Chapter 11, *The New York Times* reported on its front page that "under a Chapter 11 filing a company can usually keep its business going with little interference from the bankruptcy court." But a day or two later, when the judge authorized payroll and certain foreign payments, the *Times* was reporting that the court was now running Eastern!

The lawyer Stein and Day had to settle for, whom I call Joe Doaks, in my opinion appeared to be ill-prepared for the first cash collateral hearing. One important moment in that hearing turned out to be crucial. In Stein and Day's budget for the next two months there was an item of $97,000 for production, the manufacturing of books for which the company had orders and that were essential for preserving the company as a going concern in its marketplace. From out of the bedlam the judge awarded exactly $97,000 of cash collateral for overhead use! Thus the company, instead of increasing its assets by filling profitable orders, was forced to use assets merely to stay alive in a nonoperating mode. And so, at that very first hearing, a nail was pounded into Stein and Day's coffin.

The $97,000 that had been asked for the production of books to "keep its business going" and that Judge Schwartzberg awarded for overhead wasn't even enough to cover the payrolls in the period unless the company cut out all other expenses except the payment of insurance, a requirement in Chapter 11.

When I pointed out to the company's unfortunate attorney Joe Doaks that the judge's allowance for overhead didn't cover the overhead, he said, "Don't worry. We'll go back to the well later."

We worried, and not about the overhead. If the court had allowed the $97,000 for manufacturing to fill existing orders for books that the trade wanted, those orders would have brought in close to a quarter of a million dollars of revenue. And that in turn would have financed production of enough books to produce $833,000 worth of sales, and the company would have been on the rebound, ready to reorganize and stage a comeback. That would have meant that unsecured creditors, who are supposed to be protected by the court, could also have been repaid in time. It was only one error over one number, possibly the misreading of a line in a document. If it had been dealt with in time by a skilled attorney able to point out the consequences before the judge had acted, if production in that amount or any significant amount had been permitted, the company might have reorganized successfully.

Money used for overhead produces nothing if there is no way to keep product going out to customers. Overhead money becomes like a life-support system for a patient that is brain dead. Eventually that same judge, one of the most reputable on the bankruptcy bench, understood the need for production. But because the attorney could not get that point across clearly at that first hearing, a quarter of a century of publishing would go down the drain.

As I said, the bankruptcy lawyer had been recommended to Stein and Day by his mentor, the highly rated lawyer we first picked. I have often wondered what the mentor thought when he heard how his student blundered.

Of course it can happen in the best of firms. There is no law firm in the country more prestigious than Cravath, Swaine & Moore. Thomas Barr, the lead lawyer defending IBM, had a mentor named Bruce Bromely, who was Cravath's senior litigation partner. On the day a crucial, twenty-nine-day trial ended, Bromely is reported to have called Barr and said, "You stupid bastard, you haven't proved any damages."[7]

The fact that other lawyers in larger cases could make bigger mistakes did not assuage our sense of doom. Stein and Day had been put into a holding pattern with seven hundred authors as passengers aboard, and we'd been told to keep circling until we ran out of gas.

The hardest point to grasp was that we were suddenly no longer in the publishing business. The most important point for businessmen to understand about the entrance into Chapter 11 is that they are changing their vocations. When, in the Texaco case, Judge Schwartzberg was reported to have lifted the last obstacle to Texaco's emergence from Chapter 11, Texaco's chief executive James W. Kinnear said, "We can all go back into the oil business." When you file you are no longer in whatever your business is, you are in the Chapter 11 business, which is a world unto itself.

---

7. *The Partners,* James B. Stewart, Simon & Schuster, 1983, p. 53.

CHAPTER 4

The Burden of Proof Is on You

> In the People's Republic of China, "bankruptcy caused by bad management is punishable by a prison sentence."
> —*Turnarounds & Workouts,*
> November 1, 1988

THE businessman is having a nightmare. He is being brought before a tribunal, his hands behind him in linked bracelets, around him a babble of lawyers citing rule this, rule that, it's in the code, it's not in the code. All around him are these harsh-voiced advocates with common experience, and the businessman, who feels himself to be truly the victim of this whole inglorious affair, *doesn't understand why they are accusing him.*

At least the judge, the administrator of justice in a fair society, will see him right.

Wrong! For the businessman, who may never have appeared before a judge in his life, and who is now wide awake, learns that the judge can only rule on what is put before him. That is the essence of the nightmare moving into his waking life. For if this isn't one of the few major cases attracting the top talent of the bankruptcy bar, the judge will be superintending a cabal dominated by the second-raters calling their bargaining shots, setting themselves up to milk the case and the company, unprepared by disposition or talent to put the businessman's case before the court. The judge may be as helpless as the executive.

True, the judge was once a lawyer—very likely, a lawyer specializing in bankruptcy. But when he stepped up from the arena to the bench, just as he gained the power of office, he lost the knowledge of what was transpiring among the members of the legal cabal. For the lawyers acting out their parts in the scene below him manipulate what the court can see and hear. The experienced judge will attempt to listen through the din and perceive the elements he needs for his decisions. But in an early bankruptcy hearing the judge is outnumbered by his former colleagues, and, sadly, outmotivated. He is looking to put a lid on a pot that the cooks have brought to a boil and intend to keep at a boil for years. The judge has to keep his calendar moving, for there are always new bankruptcies to contend with. He can try to be fair. In the average small company bankruptcy proceeding, that can turn out to be like trying to prevent too much rape, an attitude never understood by the victims.

Nevertheless, the businessman now steps confidently forward. He is in a court of law. That is enough in itself to make most people a bit apprehensive, but all his life the executive has heard that a defendant is to be deemed innocent until proved guilty.

Soon enough the harsh truth dawns. In this courtroom, as in a soap opera, there are predetermined good guys and bad guys. The good guys belong to the "right" law firms, who have practiced before this bench many times and who nod their greetings to the judge once again. The bad guys, of course, are the newcomers, and most particularly the debtors themselves, who are almost always new because unless they are insane or in the garment business, who would voluntarily go through the Chapter 11 process more than once in a lifetime? The debtor CEO, in this environment, may come to be as full of fear as the petty criminal caught by the cops at last.

It cannot be. The CEO, the entrepreneur, the chief executive, is the same man he was the day before filing, is that not true? Is this court not governed as the rest of the legal system is? Isn't the whole society based on the premise that a person is innocent until proven guilty? Why is the burden of proof suddenly on the CEO?

Implicit in the proceedings is the overriding sense that he and his executive crew are *bad managers*—why else are they here? Even if the newly bankrupt is a farmer who can't control the weather, bankruptcy court is where he must prove his innocence in the face of the surrounding creditors howling for his punishment because it did not rain. It is not the late twentieth century in the United States but Paris in the eighteenth, and the creditors will have their revenge!

If this scene means nothing to you, congratulations, for you have never experienced Chapter 11.

When the time comes for a hearing, the secured creditors will put into evidence the "proof" of their claims by presenting witnesses and having their security agreements entered as exhibits. To the inexperienced debtor this parade of "evidence" can be a combination of fright and farce. For instance, in the case of Stein and Day, the bank had stopped sending monthly statements a couple of months before filing (and was never to send such statements during the entire course of the case, which meant that the company never knew how much the bank was really owed and what credits were given for payments made). A second allegedly secured creditor, BookCrafters, similarly presented its "case" through experienced counsel, though its very security agreements were later (too late) contested in federal court as allegedly having been obtained by fraud. Joe Doaks, the default attorney representing the debtor, seemed to us helpless in the face of the experienced presentations. The three secured creditors named Sol Stein, Patricia Day, and their Colophon Corporation did not even have the advice of counsel at that hearing, much less present their case. Can this kind of thing happen in a United States courtroom? It did.

Let us assume that the Stein and Day case was an atypical bungle and that our hypothetical debtor is competently represented and the court cares that it is.[1] After the secured creditors present their case, the debtor must prove his. That is, because he filed for protection from his creditors, the debtor must show that the company's liquid assets (such as accounts receivable, inventory, and rents) are sufficient to provide "adequate protection" for the secured creditors, even if some of their claims are highly disputable. That means the debtor must demonstrate to the satisfaction of the court that the value of the assets that collateralized a debt on the eve of the Chapter 11 filing will not be reduced materially if the debtor is permitted to continue to employ those assets in his business during Chapter 11.

"Adequate protection" is the most hypocritical phrase in the bankruptcy law. It is roughly the equivalent of providing police protection for a certain class of individuals in a society *and no one else.* As the law is practiced, there is no "adequate protection" for the unsecured creditors commensurate with their debt, there is no "adequate protection" for the shareholders and bondholders except in the largest cases, and there is no protection at all for the businessmen who become targets for the collective anger of the creditors and the disguised greed of the officers of the court representing them.[2]

If you ask a businessman what his company's assets are, he will generally refer to the items on the left-hand side of his balance sheet: cash on hand first, then near-term receivables and inventory, and then perhaps the less

---

1. I have seen judges in other courts be quick to admonish, chastise, and even poke fun at incompetent attorneys, getting the message through to the jury at least that the lawyer is screwing up. In the early and crucial stages in bankruptcy court, there was no such intervention on the part of the court. And, of course, no jury.

2. In Stein and Day's case there was no "adequate protection" even for three secured creditors who happened to be involved in the business. See Chapter 15.

immediate assets of depreciated equipment, real estate, long-term receivables, and notes.

The reader will have already guessed that once that same businessman is in Chapter 11, the whole universe of his company's assets may be turned upside down. The number one item, cash on hand, if it's part of the bank's security, or the security of another creditor, *doesn't belong to the company anymore.* None of the assets belong to the company any longer.

What's worse, valued inventory may suddenly be viewed by the company's customers as merchandise about to be available at bargain prices. On news of the Chapter 11 filing, receivables from customers who owe money may suddenly vanish, offset in the form of returned goods. Or some customers may just stop paying their bills on the pretext of not knowing where to send the money.

"Send it where you always sent it in the past," they are told.

"Thank you," they say. "The check will be in the mail today."

But the checks do not come as they did before the filing because the customers, for the most part, do not understand Chapter 11 and don't care, if you aren't going to be a continued source of goods they need. Despite any facts to the contrary, the debtor company is viewed by all as a victim deserving of its fate.[3]

In all but the largest companies, the debtor learns that when news of the filing gets around, there are few good-

---

3. When Stein and Day's filing for protection seemed inevitable, our distributor owed us money for hundreds of thousands of dollars worth of books they had shipped to customers and had not yet paid us for. I was ushered into the offices of Holt's general counsel, W. Mallory Rintoul, who told me that Chapter 11 was a death knell, that our company was over, finished, defunct, and our distributor Holt was not about to give us any money. Much later I realized that Rintoul, like some 700,000 other lawyers in the country, did not seem to be familiar with bankruptcy law.

hearted people around who will hurry their payments, and a great many scoundrels who will delay them.

And so when the time comes for the debtor company to "prove" its assets, management is in for a double shock. The very act of filing has had a deleterious effect on the assets. The second shock is that management's prefiling view of assets proves to be wrong. Crisis manager Kenneth Glass says that when a company's assets come under scrutiny, "they usually aren't what the balance sheet says they are." Values, he points out, tend to be "written up," while "obsolete inventory isn't written down" and "the receivables aren't as good as the balance sheet indicates."

To some degree the correctness of the asset valuation is dependent on who the auditors are and how tough they've been in testing—and contesting—management's assertions of value. Some assets are very difficult to "prove." Turnaround manager David Ferrari described the difficulty of proving the value of mailing lists, and in one New England case, of dealing with a font library appraised at $10 million but with a $100-million reconstruction cost. There were no buyers for it. Technological advancements had reduced its value to potential buyers.

Crisis consultant Daniel Morris lamented the fact that most companies do not have current appraisals and are not prepared to get them in a hurry. And so to "prove the assets," there is often a scramble to do quickly what usually takes time to do properly.

Everyone in business agrees that the best kind of assets are cash and good receivables—if they are usable. Turnaround consultant Adam Radzik speaks of "receivables" as "life blood," a company's chief immediate source of operating capital. But the banks, or any other creditor that has a secured position in receivables, can leave the company as frantic as a heart trying to beat with its blood supply cut off. Incoming "blood" or cash is subject to cash collateral orders.

Picture this: A retail store that sells fine merchandise in a beautiful setting. There is a lush carpet on the floor, elegant showcases line the walls. All of the decor, invaluable to an upmarket retailer, constitutes a depreciable asset that in a liquidation mode will lose most of its value instantly unless the rest of the assets can be moved and a similar enterprise is ready to move in. Even in that unlikely case, if the retailer ready to take over the store's fixtures from the distressed company knows what it's doing, it will have a lowball offer put into bankruptcy court for approval. That offer is subject to "a higher and better offer." But that kind of offer is likely to come only from another retailer looking for an elegant store in that same location. And if he's in a similar business, the retailer would have to wonder why the other business failed. And so competitive offers for certain kinds of assets are difficult to come by. The end result is that the beautiful showcases will go to the lowball bidder.

Everyone knows that the moment you drive a new car out of a showroom, its market value plunges; it is now a used car. Another way to consider assets in bankruptcy is to think of new inventory as suddenly turned into the equivalent of used cars. You are in an arena where a lot of the folks have business ethics roughly comparable to those often attributed to used car dealers. Inventory is a valuable asset to a going concern, but a distressed company may be forced to sell it at a fraction of its value.

The courts tend to overvalue "hard assets" like real estate, even if it is not liquid, because land doesn't get stale or evaporate. The transfer of land, however, when such transfers are subject to government approval, can be stymied by bureaucrats to the point where even the value of its mortgages cannot be realized under the conditions imposed by Chapter 11, at great personal risk to guarantors in management.

In the topsy-turvy world of asset appraisal, another potentially worrisome "hard asset" is machinery and equipment, usually carried on the books for its depreciated value. But that asset loses even that value when the going concern posture of the company is being kicked about. A truck or a fleet of trucks, merchandise that some-body will buy at distressed prices, even furnishings that are salable, are all considered hard assets. While tools are considered hard assets, they might be dedicated to the individual business or be too used or abused to be sold even at deep discounts.

Raw material can be a problem unless it is salable to someone who can use it right away, or the price is well below what it would cost the buyer on the open market. And if it hasn't been paid for, the supplier will want it back, though it's illegal to return it. All the experts I talked to came down hard on work-in-process, a "terrible" asset according to them because it takes money to finish and is unsalable in its present state.

If your customer list is a prized asset to you, it may be of value to someone else in the same business, but it is a soft asset. "Copyrights and patents have little or no value in a Chapter 11 case," says Kenneth Glass, "and can't with-stand a real attack from creditors." The experts also tend to knock goodwill, prepaid accounts, intangibles, and leasehold improvements. The businessman who wants to look at his balance sheet with a truly cold eye might ask himself, "What would these assets be worth if I filed for protection?" Or, with an even colder eye, he might ask himself whether the existence of these "soft" assets might prove to be an ace in the hole in the eventual task of set-tling with his creditors when he is negotiating a plan to get out of Chapter 11. The creditors might see receivables as worth "x" cents on the dollar and inventory worth "y" cents on the dollar. The question they might then ask is "What's left for me?" Since in most circumstances credi-tors are not likely to place an important monetary value on soft assets (though the debtor would know their potential worth if used), the debtor has something of value that may not be viewed the same way by the creditors. Thus he may be able to negotiate a better deal for the company in the reorganization plan. This kind of hard look at the value of assets in negotiation may be a useful exercise, but it is not recommended just before the executive is counting on a good night's sleep.

The wise CEO whose business is not in danger (the chairman of Texaco certainly didn't consider his business in danger when his company allegedly interfered with Pennzoil's acquisition of Getty) might take a look at his healthy balance sheet with the eyes of a liquidator. Are there secured creditors? To whom does the cash belong? To whom do the receivables belong? Would the value of the receivables sink if your customers thought they might not be doing business with you anymore? What is the inventory likely to bring if the whole world knows you're in bankruptcy court? Which assets would be viewed *by others* as hard or soft? Could any notes you hold be discounted in an emergency? Should they be converted now into a form that could finance a recovery?

It is part of a senior executive's normal job to let his experience and imagination work together. He usually asks himself questions such as "What if this or that product takes off? Or sales of that product suddenly dive? What if so-and-so dropped dead—who would I replace him with? What if a recession hit in three months' time and didn't go away for a long time? What if the federal government did this or that, how would it affect my business? But while asking themselves these questions, how many executives also think: What if company X got a judgment against my company that I couldn't pay? What if a creditor who has always been cooperative is replaced by a new man who wants to show how soft the old one was? What if my biggest customer suddenly stopped paying me? What if a major customer suddenly went belly up and I couldn't legally retrieve the inventory he hadn't paid for because the court was protecting him? What if my most important supplier found out that I was going to be illiquid for a time; would he play ball or would he cut back on my orders? What if my company was sued for x millions more than my insurance covers and we lost in a court of first jurisdiction?

I'm not encouraging the heads of solvent businesses to invent nightmares for the sake of playing Halloween. But in these days of so many *unexpected* bankruptcies even of "healthy" firms, it pays to examine your assets, liabilities, and resources as they would be viewed in extremis. Sometimes it takes the objective view of a business consultant with no emotional or historical attachments to a company's products, assets, or people to appraise the assets realistically, because long-term management is rarely able to do so.

If an ounce of prevention under ordinary circumstances is worth a pound of cure, in Chapter 11 it may make the difference between reorganization and liquidation.

As to "adequate protection," some bankruptcy judges do not place much weight on paper proof in lawyers' arguments. They want to hear sworn testimony by experts. Beware: The debtor may be asked to put up personal money to pay the experts. We were.

Beware also the fact that proving adequate protection does not prevent a secured creditor from savaging the company's assets in Chapter 11 to the point where *all* of the creditors get hurt. The principal method of wantonly destroying assets is to deprive a company of its "going concern" mode. It says something about human nature that the type of child who gets pleasure in destroying other children's property is not rare. There are adult criminals whose announcement is, "See how bad I can be!" There is also a certain type of creditor who appears to enjoy destroying other people's assets, or has a secret agenda: Put X out of business so that Y will prosper.

Why would secured creditors block a going concern mode? After all, they loaned the money (or provided goods) to a going concern and took as security assets that were valued as part of a going concern and not for their liquidation value.

Here on that subject is bankruptcy expert Martin J. Bienenstock of the esteemed firm of Weil, Gotshal & Manges, a firm that has seventy-seven bankruptcy lawyers on its staff—more than any other in the country.[4] "Most lenders do not lend against a debtor's liquidation value. Rather, many lenders make their decisions to grant credit based on conservative estimates of the going concern value of the debtor and its assets." Bienenstock then suggests that lenders should "maintain or enhance [the debtor's] going concern value, as long as that value is greater than its liquidation value." That would enable the repayment of "a larger portion of the lender's claims than it could by liquidating."[5]

Bienenstock is all for management "preserving the estate and maximizing the value of the business." Bienenstock says the debtor's goal should be to restructure the company's debt, and maybe its operations, "so that the reorganized debtor may emerge from Chapter 11 as a profitable going concern."[6]

Furthermore, Bienenstock says, "creditors whose collateral security is worth a lot in a going concern, but substantially less in liquidation, may very well lobby for the business to survive." He points out that unsecured creditors may not only compare what might be available to them in liquidation as against what they might get out of the cash flow of a continuing business, they may also give thought to the potential profit in "doing future business with the reorganized debtor."[7]

Bienenstock sounds positively on the side of the angels in portraying *what is supposed to happen*. But on occasion he lets his hair down and tells us that the warring parties in a Chapter 11 case sometimes seem like scorpions in a

---

4. *Turnarounds & Workouts*, March 15, 1989.
5. Bienenstock, Martin J., *Bankruptcy Reorganization*, Practising Law Institute, 1987, p. 5.
6. Ibid, p. 66.
7. Ibid, p. 575.

bottle. "Creditors," he says, "holding fully secured claims have little incentive to strive to arrive at a plan that preserves the debtor's business as a going concern. Those creditors are apt, in some circumstances, to support a liquidation under which their collateral security would be converted to cash. Thus, they have no incentive to act in accordance with the Reorganization Policy."

Note how "little incentive" becomes "no incentive" in a single paragraph. Didn't Bienenstock tell us that a creditor who used to be a supplier could benefit from being a supplier in the future if the business survived? Let's face it: There is potential profit in assisting a reorganization, *but not enough to satisfy those who would rather feast on short-term vengeance.* The distinguished psychiatrist Anthony Storr reminded us a long time ago that "with the exception of certain rodents, no other vertebrate [except man] habitually destroys members of his own species. No other animal takes positive pleasure in the exercise of cruelty upon another of his own kind."[8] Students of twentieth-century history are of course familiar with the enjoyment of some in depriving others of life, liberty, and the pursuit of happiness.

In Bienenstock's treatise on bankruptcy, the dark side of human nature is implicit, like a shadow that disappears when you turn to look at it. Thus, in saying that there is "no incentive" for the creditors to allow reorganization to take place, Bienenstock is doing what we all do from time to time, pretending that human nature is not what we know it to be.

Yet Bienenstock slips in what really happens as opposed to what is good for everybody or what the law intends. He speaks of warring parties, of scorpions in a bottle, and when he speaks of the plan-organizing stage, he finds "the intrigue and gamesmanship inherent in that situation typically . . . a fascinating process."

The businessman might well ask, "Fascinating to

---

8. *Human Aggression* by Anthony Storr, Atheneum, 1968.

whom?" To the judge who has to invoke the law? To the managers who, according to Bienenstock, are supposed to be putting their primary emphasis on maximizing the value of the business? Or is it the creditors and their lawyers who find this man-made spectacle of destruction "fascinating"? Bienenstock is now ready to admit the truth. "The creditor is aiming for the jugular. It is attempting to seize its collateral security, thereby often rendering it impossible for the debtor to reorganize."[9]

The hypocrisy of the Chapter 11 process is evident if we remind ourselves of Bienenstock's description of the automatic stay, which is what the CEO reaches for when, in anguish, he files for protection. The automatic stay "enjoins all entities from commencing or continuing actions against the debtor and property of the estate. As a result, the Equity Policy and the Reorganization Policy are served. Through the injunction, dismemberment of the debtor's estate is prevented."[10]

By this time the reader should not be surprised to learn that the author of *Bankruptcy Reorganization*, Martin Bienenstock, was the lead lawyer for BookCrafters in Stein and Day's Chapter 11 case, and that BookCrafters led the attack in preventing the reorganization of the publishing company by shutting down its only business, the publishing of books.[11]

---

9. *Bankruptcy Reorganization*, Practising Law Institute, 1987, p. 144.
10. Ibid., p. 97.
11. Up front in his tome, Bienenstock says, "To reorganize a debtor's business, the factors of production must be held in place." (p. 3) From the first day, Bienenstock and his lieutenant Deryck Palmer, following BookCrafters' orders, were instrumental in banning production. They were successful in preventing Stein and Day from ever again manufacturing any book even when such manufacturing to fill orders would have enabled the creditors to be paid back. What one has to remember is that even if their client was never paid back in full, the client was presumably paying the lawyers month by month in the belief that one day Stein and Day would be forced to pay their legal bills.

When it comes to liquidating assets instead of using them for the benefit of all creditors, a worst-case scenario would have a company immediately converted to a Chapter 7 case, an "involuntary." Or it can be left in Chapter 11, governed by a trustee. Either of these situations leaves management powerless, a particular hazard if management owns an important stake in the business. Control would seem to be crucial in a family-owned or closely held business. Therefore the ideal would appear to be for the person who ran the company to be allowed to go on running it in Chapter 11 as what is called a debtor-in-possession.

Theoretically, and under the law, the manager of a debtor-in-possession still has quite a bit of power over what happens to the assets. But this book will show how that power can be undermined from day one. Moreover, the whole debtor-in-possession routine may be a ploy to save the creditors money. A trustee is usually an expensive way of liquidating assets. Also, a trustee is not as likely to know how to get the best prices for specialized assets as is the existing management. Therefore, the management is kept on in a "liquidating eleven," manipulated cruelly in the false hope that the company will be allowed to reorganize.

For 120 days the CEO, now heading a debtor-in-possession company, has the exclusive right to file a plan for the reorganization of the business. What happens during the first few days may kill the development of such a plan. Some of the business people I talked to said, in effect, that if you're living in a daily hell, how can you focus on rational means for reviving a company that the lawyers and creditors are treating like a corpse? And after 120 days any creditor can file a plan for approval by the other creditors and the court, unless the debtor's exclusivity period is extended. Commonly, it is. If the CEO is doing a good job of liquidating the assets while he's trying to put a plan together, why not keep the status quo? It's cheaper than a trustee, isn't it? And the debtor's counsel may encourage this also, to give the debtor the illusion that it gives him important control over his destiny.

What it does, in fact, is keep the billing hours mounting up.

CHAPTER 5

Personal Assets:
Hard, Harder, Hardest

> Money is always there but the pockets change; it
> is not in the same pockets after a change, and that
> is all there is to say about money.
>
> —Gertrude Stein

IF you asked anyone except a business person, banker, or lawyer what his most important asset was, he'd probably say, as I would, "my health."

If you pushed for another asset, he would say, "My peace of mind."

If pressed for a more "tangible" asset, he might say, "My wife" or "my children" or "my friends."

Finally, if the pressure was to name something he could give up, that had an objectively ascertainable value to someone else, that's when you'd get the answer a businessman, banker, or lawyer is looking for: "My house."

Your house is a hard asset. Your health and peace of mind are of no use to anyone else. And the Fourteenth Amendment bars the marketability of your spouse and children even if they're prized by someone else.

It is on your house, however, that bankers, lawyers, and businessmen will bestow their highest rating, for it is a hard asset, valuable to the extent of the difference between your mortgages and the quick-sale price a creditor is likely to get in the marketplace.

Your most prized assets—your health, equanimity, and

family—are all in danger in Chapter 11 because of the loss of control over your life. But what about your house and other hard assets, are they in danger, too?

If you have personally guaranteed any bank or other loan, your hard assets—your home, your car—are at hazard, and not for what you believe their value to be. When a lender decides to move on your guarantee, his aim is not getting full value for your assets. He is interested only in getting his money out fast, which means he is perfectly prepared to cause your hard assets to be sold at a fraction of their value. He doesn't care about what you lose, only what he gains. And if he sells it for much less than it might be worth if it were sold under normal conditions and for less cash than he claims is owed, you will still owe the balance.

If that isn't fair, who promised you fairness? Did the Founding Fathers truly protect the debtor in their carefully drafted Constitution? They thought so, but in practice the intent of the Constitution is obliterated by the hard fact that as the law works, a secured creditor can shove constitutional intent into the same garbage can into which he thrusts the value of your assets.

Suppose you do not have an outstanding personal guarantee? As you will learn in Chapter 17, you can be sued successfully on a guarantee you didn't give. Moreover, there is nothing to keep other creditors from suing you personally even for the most flimsy reasons. You will then find your personal assets jeopardized to the extent that you will need to pay retainers and legal fees to defend yourself. These fees will have to come from savings (an asset) or from selling or mortgaging an asset. Of course if you win, perhaps after an expensive appeal, you will still have had to contend with a judgment if you lost in what's called "the court of first impression." Your assets can be seized if the bank can do so before you can post your appeal bond. This happened to me, even though I was surrounded by competent lawyers. One needs to react to a judgment with speed, and as one female vice president has testified, living in Chapter 11 is like trying to swim in molasses.

That's why we're talking about your personal assets as well as the company's, because you need to know how other people look at them, and what you can do to protect their value.

If you've ever had your home appraised by a lending institution—for instance, for the purpose of obtaining a mortgage—it is likely that the appraiser filled out a form that included a place for him to estimate the "quick-sale" price, which is not what your house is worth as a home for someone else, but what can be gotten for it quickly in a fire-sale atmosphere. The fact that a considerable percentage of its real value would be lost through haste doesn't worry the bank. A lending institution that is foreclosing has to take into consideration the interest (and legal) cost of keeping the loan outstanding long enough to derive the true market value of the house. The most likely circumstance is that the bank is owed substantially *less* than the difference between the mortgages and the true value, and as long as the bank comes out whole, it doesn't give a damn about your loss of equity.

Nor does a bank care about the values that are not "hard." For instance, if your home happens to have been the family farm for generations, or if the neighborhood is where your kids go to school or your friends live and where you'd hoped to live the rest of your life, those are all "soft" values that apply only as long as you own the property. The purpose of the foreclosure is to get the lender his money back fast.

You cannot say to the bank, "Hold on, doing it your way is going to cost me a lot of money plus things that are priceless. Have a heart." That's an internal organ unsuited to a banker in a workout division of a bank. That's the place "bad" loans go to, and if you file for protection whatever your company owes the bank will almost always move from the bank officers familiar to you, the ones who may have solicited your account and been your account executives for years, to a special unit called the "workout" section, whose role is not to woo, win, or keep customers but to get rid of them—the sooner the better. If you can quickly sell your company—or an interest in it—and pay off the bank with the proceeds, that's fine. If third-party circumstances prevent that, then the bank will seek to dump your assets by the fastest means possible. For that they need the kind of characters you don't see pictured in bank advertisements.

If you've never dealt with the workout division of a bank, you need fair warning. One of the new faces that comes to call on you will very likely belong to a man who will seem to be kind and sympathetic. Over lunch he will tell you the sad tale of the businessman in marine supplies who handed him the keys to the business and bid him good-bye. He suffers, and he sympathizes. He's the good guy. Remember, that's the part he's supposed to play. Later on you will meet his opposite, who comes on like Dirty Harry waiting to get his day made.

It is very easy for the CEO in Chapter 11 to get caught up in the good-guy routine. Anybody who seems sympathetic to his plight is a welcome guest. Then the bad guy comes around, and the good guy is powerless to stop him. If you suspect you are in danger of getting your marbles trapped in a good-guy/bad-guy routine, find out which one is the boss, and you've found the governor of your life with the bank. In my case the boss was the bad guy. I suspect you'll find the same.

CHAPTER 6

The Economic Insanity of Chapter 11

> "'Reasonable attorney's fees' is an oxymoron."
> —George C. de Kay, publisher of this
> book, in discussing a clause in its
> contract with the author

I F we examine the heart of Chapter 11, we get a frightening electrocardiogram.

Companies seek the protection of Chapter 11 because of an *economic* crisis. Yet the first thing that happens is that the company's economy is saddled with appalling new legal expenses, trustee expenses, court expenses, and the expense of the creditors' adversary actions it sought to avoid.

In a company on the verge of filing, management is under such pressure from creditors that it finds itself unable to manage without the help of the law. *Yet as soon as the company is in Chapter 11, it is given a new and inexperienced management.* Either a trustee is designated by the court to operate the business, or management is kept in place as a debtor-in-possession but the company is de facto managed—that is, the key operating decisions are made by a committee of lawyers representing the creditors. It's as if a ship in crisis at sea suddenly had half a dozen or more members of the Judge Advocate General's department fighting for control of the wheel.

The court itself is usually at sea because it takes time even for an experienced judge to understand a case. At the beginning all the court hears are the raucous cries of the gaggle of helmsmen vying to keep a hand on the wheel though they've had no previous experience with that particular ship.

Is it a wonder that the vast majority of small and medium-sized companies in Chapter 11 founder?

The economic insanity can begin before filing, and can affect big companies as well. When Frank Lorenzo started developing his Chapter 11 strategy for Eastern Airlines a full year before the March 9, 1989 filing, Eastern began hoarding cash. But to do so, it "went to Wall Street offering 17.25%—more than twice the then prime rate—on a $200 million note issue."[1]

Under normal circumstances, most businessmen devote some energy to controlling legal expenses.[2] Some succeed, some don't. The great difference in Chapter 11 is that legal expenses become uncontrollable. They are generated simultaneously by several law firms whose members seek each other's company on the phone or in meetings as often as they can arrange it. I have not met a single executive with experience in Chapter 11 who was not horrified at the way legal expenses suddenly ballooned. The bankruptcy judges try to control these costs by whittling the bills down. That procedure is adequately prepared for by lawyers shrewd enough to find ways of padding their bills by the amount they think the judge might take them down. It's a game played at the business's expense.

Gerald F. Munitz, head of the bankruptcy department of Winston & Strawn in Chicago, has been in practice for

---

1. The *Wall Street Journal*, March 10, 1989.

2. Stein and Day averaged about 500 contracts a year with authors, copyright proprietors, and licensees of subsidiary rights without the benefit of a lawyer. The average time taken for the negotiation and preparation of one of the contracts was less than one hour. Had these contracts been negotiated and prepared by an outside law firm, the annual cost, in some years, would have exceeded the company's profit.

twenty-nine years and speaks with strong, clear opinions. He said, "The court should sit on those bankruptcy lawyers who try to keep a case open." As to bill padding, Munitz, who has a knack for capturing a listener's attention, told of a lawyer who charged more hours for reading Munitz's motion than Munitz took to write it! What gets Munitz riled is "seventeen lawyers representing the same interest, or four lawyers showing up in court representing one client on one motion, three of whom never say a word." Munitz points out that today's hourly rates are three times what he was paid per week when he started out. He adds that companies doing under two million just cannot withstand the costs of Chapter 11. The quietest attorney for a debtor that I met during the research for this book said, "Chapter 11 is an arena with a lot of waste."

The law, as every businessman knows, has developed make-work that would put road repair gangs to shame. And it is in this environment that a large number of bankruptcy lawyers prey on companies in severe economic difficulty and in need of rescue. If there is meat on the bones they will hang onto the victim to carve out whatever they can for themselves before throwing the meatless carcass into the dustbin and clamping the lid on the case.

Each secured creditor and the Creditors' Committee are represented by lawyers, often multiple lawyers, and each of them expects to be paid. The lawyers for the secured creditors are being paid as they go; however, if they sink you, they get their collateral. If you make it, they get to stick you with the bill. If you succeed in working your way out of Chapter 11, you'll have the dubious privilege of paying *all* the lawyers and accountants and appraisers and investment bankers, and, and, and. Didn't anybody warn you? Does an ice-cream vendor display a big sign saying "lots of cholesterol sold here"?

You will hear the expression "carve-outs." What that means is if the company sells an asset—a division, inventory, real estate, whatever—the lawyers for the company and the lawyers for the Creditors' Committee will negoti-

ate with the secured creditors for a carve-out of fees for
themselves from the proceeds. That "negotiation" can
involve some real hardball. For instance, lawyers representing the company and the Creditors' Committee will
block sales that the secured creditors or debtor want and
that are to everyone's benefit, *unless they are given their
carve-out.* To be fair, in many instances it's the only way
they can get any current compensation while the case
drags on. To be fairer still, they are sometimes being paid,
as in my case, *at the sole risk of whoever still has guarantees outstanding,* because every dollar paid to a lawyer
instead of to the creditor who has the guarantee can potentially come out of the pocket of the guarantor. And that
guarantor is very often an owner or manager of the business in Chapter 11.

Accounting firms also swarm in to feed off the debtor.
One chief executive of a smallish firm said to me, his voice
choked with bitterness, "They had eleven junior accountants in here spinning their wheels and they were charging the estate more than a quarter of a million dollars for
unnecessary work and I couldn't do a damn thing about
it."

An additional cost of doing business is the quarterly fees
that are required to be paid to the U.S. Trustee, whose
office, according to most of my informants, is of no value
to the debtor. Of course the cost of preparing for meetings
with the U.S. Trustee comes to much more than the fees
themselves.

Another additional cost of doing business under Chapter 11 consists of what I call the "convenience practices" of
the attorneys. It is unfortunate that the American postal
system has atrophied to an unreliable pre-pony-express
state and that people who have to get letters or documents
to others reliably now quite regularly use overnight services. More recently, the proliferation of fax machines has
made rapid communication even faster. Very soon after
our company hired the law firm of Barr & Faerber to
replace our first lawyer in the Chapter 11 case, they

installed a used fax machine in our offices although we had gotten along quite well without one up to that point. Later, Harvey Barr, head of the firm, said[3] that Barr & Faerber had sent twenty to thirty telefaxes a day on Stein and Day business in the year and a half that they were involved in the case. And they were charging fifteen dollars per fax. A businessman using fax machines and overnight services knows he is spending money that if not spent would come down to the bottom line. Hence many businesses try to control these expenditures and resort to the U.S. mail for nonurgent matters and hope for the best.

The attorneys in Chapter 11, however, bill their clients for such services, and so even lawyers who aren't being paid on a current basis have the habit of communicating with each other and with their clients, sometimes daily, sometimes several times a day, by telefax and overnight delivery services. In Chapter 11 everything seems to become urgent. Even matters of minor significance require overnight delivery to "the parties." In a big case, that could be a dozen or more "parties" for each communication. And the copying machine is put to work to send back-up copies of the faxed documents by overnight delivery services. Of course in most law firms the copying machines are profit centers for the law business.[4]

Now no businessman in his right mind would assume such large additional costs voluntarily. It takes a brave lawyer to make his client, who is usually struggling with problems of cost reduction, really understand that once he's in Chapter 11, running his business will be much, much more costly. And while the legal and related bills are soaring, the managers will be asked to take deep pay

---

3. In Judge Schwartzberg's court, February 21, 1989.

4. I was tempted to provide as an appendix to this book a copy of one law firm's listing of its out-of-pocket expenses for one client for one month. Though the company involved is small, the single-spaced list is longer than most chapters in this book.

cuts, employees will be fired, and essential services will be eliminated.

While enormous telefax and Federal Express bills were being generated by the lawyers in Stein and Day's case, the line-by-line budget approved by the creditors (usually meaning their lawyers) did not include garbage collection, fixing nonworking toilets, or, in an area where village water from time to time resembles mud, bottled water for employees to drink. In other words, the priorities were irrational by any business or moral standard. (Moral not only because of the inhumaneness, but because the "morality" behind Chapter 11 should be to pay off the creditors, not enrich the lawyers who root in the spoils.) Big telefax and overnight delivery bills okay, lawyers' chauffeur-driven limousines okay; water, toilets, and garbage collection not okay. But the latter facilities are not used by the lawyers or the creditors, but by employees who are expected to double and triple up on work under increasingly deplorable conditions. The work is not the work they are used to doing; much of it is Chapter 11 "work" that didn't exist before.

Authorities on bankruptcy recognize that the process affects the morale of employees adversely. One such authority recommends compensation increases for key people to partially assuage the disaster that Chapter 11 visits on their morale. A businessman would understand that idea. During normal times, when he hears a rumbling rumor that some valuable employee is thinking of leaving, the businessman will find a way to try to keep that person. The lawyers in Chapter 11 do exactly the opposite: They do everything in their power to have people leave. Tom Towey of Neptune reported that the one thousand employees were narrowed down to the few loyal ones who decided to tough it out.

Is it any wonder that in Chapter 11 what is wilfully done by the creditors and their lawyers to demoralize employees harms the business and its chances for reorganizing?

If Chapter 11 makes neither economic nor managerial sense, does this mean that it is hopeless as a means of rescue? Is is doomed to continue in its present uneconomic, impractical form because it is a provident resource for scavengers?

Businesses that thrive on buying the assets of troubled companies cheap savor Chapter 11 because it provides them with a "clean" way of picking the bones. When the court approves their deal, they have assets minus creditors. It is they, not the company, who have gotten protection. These, the predators of capitalism, could do their bargain hunting without Chapter 11, though Chapter 11 does make it safe and convenient. Just as cops investigating automobile accidents are relied on by tow truck operators for timely tips, so do the scavengers keep in touch with the bankruptcy lawyers.

And that's where the real obstacle to reform lies. The large proportion of bankruptcy lawyers who would perpetuate the present uneconomic system do so because it has become a bonanza for some of them. In the Manville Chapter 11 case, the professional fees approved by the court came to more than $100 million.[5] One counsel for Manville got $28,390,121.15. Another Manville counsel got $12,968,011.98. Still another Manville counsel got $5,950,000. That's $47,308,134 just for Manville's lawyers. Large fees also went to seven other law firms, two accounting firms, and two investment bankers. None of these fees was less than $750,000, and five were in the multi-million-dollar category. The fees set no records. And they were approved by the court.

In the office of Neptune's CEO Tom Towey, when I raised the subject of the cost of Chapter 11, it is characteristic of Towey, a fighter who enjoyed beating the odds in Chapter 11, that he chimed in at once, his words swinging:

---

5. This and the figures that follow are from court documents reported in *Turnarounds & Workouts*, Feb. 15, 1989.

"You're right into COD. Right off the bat you're paying more because you're not getting credit." And the bank, he added, had seized all their cash accounts.

If you file for protection under pressure from your creditors because you're short of cash to meet your obligations, is it possible that after you file cash is even tighter?

"Look," Towey says, "You lose all your negotiating ability with suppliers. They name a price, you pay it. You're not in a position to argue about bills or defend yourself against them, especially from those who charge by the hour."

Towey also lashed into the newly added costs of accountants, appraisers, and real estate consultants that a company in Chapter 11 is saddled with. But the overriding problem, according to others as well as Towey, is that everything costs more because you're paying for it up front.

Neptune is proud of its main skill, which is relocating large companies over a weekend to avoid employee downtime. I asked Towey if Neptune lost any business. Towey, leaning forward, had an edge of bitterness in his voice for the first time. The more business Neptune did, the better it would be for the creditors. But, Towey said with fierce emphasis, "Not one creditor chose us for a relocation. It wasn't price. They said, 'We don't know if you'll be around.' " Towey told them Neptune would have been glad to post a performance bond. "It didn't matter," Towey points out. "They were working against themselves."

Chipwich, which also came out of Chapter 11 alive, was far luckier. According to Sam Metzger they were able to maintain a positive cash flow from money that wasn't tied up by creditors, so their credit held. However, Metzger did point out that before filing, Chipwich, in financial trouble, was paying 110 to 115 percent of the going rate for supplies. Once they filed, they still overpaid, but "it wasn't any worse than earlier."

Neptune's experience is more typical of companies in

Chapter 11. Small vendors who may not have known a company was in difficulty will learn about it as soon as the company files. There may be a press story, and word gets around even without a press story. Pretty soon, the Chapter 11 company is dealing with everybody on a COD basis—if they're lucky. Some suppliers will insist on payment before they put anything on a truck for delivery to the debtor. Others will wait till the debtor-in-possession check clears before shipping.

Does the CEO now have to take time away from running the business to worry, for instance, about how much fuel has been approved in the current cash collateral order? At Stein and Day, which owned its own headquarters, getting fuel was a major problem in the first winter of its discontent. While the lawyers debated cash collateral agreements endlessly, and billed for those debates at sums that could have filled the fuel tank dozens of times over, the already demoralized employees worked in sweaters and overcoats waiting for some local fuel supplier, usually a friend of a friend, who would, when he could, deliver a small amount of fuel for cash so that the burner could be started up again and the typewriters, if not the employees, could thaw.

For fuel oil substitute any other necessary commodity. In Chapter 11 you either cannot get it or it costs a lot more.

Another aspect of the economic insanity of Chapter 11 is the kind of thing no court or law protects the company against. If all you do is deposit money in a bank, the bank can still throw you out. In the case of Stein and Day, even when it was no longer permitted to have a sales force, it still received many phone orders daily from bookstores, wholesalers, libraries, and individuals. While the company was permitted to sell existing inventory, it was not permitted to extend credit to new customers. And suddenly, the company had a host of new customers who were simply unable to get the books anywhere else. And so they had to pay up front. Those who sent in checks had to wait for the checks to clear, or else it might be considered a credit sale. Those in a hurry, and most were, sent in cashier's checks or money orders. But most people did what most people do today: They phoned their order in and gave a credit card number.

That worked fine. Though Stein and Day had to turn away about 90 percent of the orders it received because it was running out of stock and not allowed to manufacture books that sold out (talk about economic insanity!), the 10 percent of orders that could be filled were charged to Visa or MasterCard. Until the Scarsdale National Bank, in which Stein and Day had been depositing its Visa and MasterCard charges for five years prior to filing, decided to throw out the account. The company then learned that no other bank would take deposits from its credit card sales under any conditions because the company was in Chapter 11. It doesn't make economic sense for the creditors or anyone else to put an end to a company's credit card sales, but sense is not what Chapter 11 is noted for. You are between a rock and a rock.

Another aspect of the economic insanity of Chapter 11 is apparent in as simple a thing as trying to keep new costs down. For instance, if a publisher files, authors, their agents and lawyers, the widows and widowers of authors long dead, will all write and ask, "What's happening? Why aren't you paying me the royalties you owe? Why aren't my books being kept in print?" They are innocent bystanders in the Chapter 11 wilderness. A few hired lawyers to make the same inquiries and sometimes to demand that the rights be returned to the authors or to assert that they had been returned by default. It was all a waste of money and effort. Most general practitioners know little if anything about how Chapter 11 works and that the contracts, under the law, are now part of the creditors' collateral.

It seemed to me that an easy solution to the many requests for information would be the creation of a one-page, polite form letter that would cover all the points that were being asked. One paragraph could cover the procedure for filing a claim, where to get a form, where to file, and how to get a receipt for your filing. Such a letter would appease a large constituency of writers and their representatives and not burden a rapidly shrinking staff with more work than it could handle. The first bankruptcy lawyer the company had, Joe Doaks, drafted a letter that "explained" the law in a manner that could only enrage the recipient. Well, when Joe Doaks was out of the way in two months' time, we asked the new attorneys for the estate, Barr and Faerber, to draft a form letter that would convey the relevant part of the law and outline steps to be followed.

Would you believe Stein and Day couldn't get such a letter out of Barr and Faerber for over a year? That hundreds of hours were wasted on the telephone and in writing individual replies? It cannot possibly be because lawyers really don't like the idea of drafting any form letter for you to use that would preclude your forwarding individual letters you receive to their firm to be answered by lawyers (from a form?) at an hourly rate that staggers the layman's imagination.

Once, in the course of an interview with a business newspaper, I answered some question by saying that our legal billings in Chapter 11 during the past year exceeded the company's legal fees for the preceding quarter of a century. The newspaper chose to extract that sentence and feature it in a conspicuous box on the same page as the interview. That elicited a foot-stomping blue-faced missive from the lawyer in which he used the words "I resent" eight times in one page, though the statement about the billing was absolutely true.

The ritual should be understood as one in which lawyers for the "enemies" of the debtor take actions not to improve the business but, for instance, to block the use of cash collateral or to terminate the automatic stay—at least with regard to themselves. And the "good guys" of the moment (sides switch from time to time in Chapter 11) fight back, but not too hard and certainly not efficiently, generally, for the purpose of the fray is to stretch the time so that the legal fees on both sides can balloon.

The side-switching is something to watch. In Stein and Day's case, the first motion to terminate the automatic stay was brought by the Michigan National Bank. Henry Swergold, attorney for the Creditors' Committee, joined our side. BookCrafters stayed neutral. We defeated the motion.[6] The next motion to terminate the automatic stay came from our warehouse, Consolidated Systems and Services Corporation. Then all the lawyers, for the bank, for BookCrafters, for the Creditors' Committee, hopped to our side (sometimes literally, by moving to the same table during the proceedings). The CSSC move did not succeed. The third motion to terminate the automatic stay was launched by the Scarsdale National Bank. Again, all the lawyers leaped to Stein and Day's side and we won. The fourth motion to terminate the automatic stay was brought on by BookCrafters, and this time the Michigan National Bank, which had brought on the first such motion, joined our side. These games of musical chairs are not unproductive; think of the hourly fees earned during these ritual dances.

At times the opposition to sensible acts can reach a level of such absurdity that it is hard for rational people to understand why the court does not act with reproof or

---

6. Someone who represents himself is supposed to have a fool for a client. I represented myself (it's called *pro se*) in this action. The attorney for the estate incorporated my papers "by reference" in his short brief in toto. We won. Encouraged by the result, I went out two days later and sold nearly half a million dollars' worth of rights in an afternoon. Encouragement works, but is rarely used in Chapter 11 cases. I continued to represent myself at all future proceedings for more than a year. At one point when I was examining a witness, I apologized to the judge for my lack of familiarity in introducing a particular piece of paper into evidence. Judge Schwartzberg said, "You're doing fine. You're doing better than most lawyers. But that isn't saying much." His remark brought down the house.

sanctions, out of self-preservation if not preservation of the debtor, which is supposed to be the purpose of it all.

Here is an example of the theater of the absurd as it is practiced in bankruptcy court. It is not science fiction. It happened Anni Domini 1988 and 1989.

Frank Tribbe is a quiet, scholarly man who in August of 1982 contracted with Stein and Day to publish a work he called *Portrait of Jesus?*, with the explanatory subtitle, *The Illustrated Story of the Shroud of Turin*. Sponsored by an editor of religious books, it was not the kind of book that as a rule makes the bestseller lists. Some four thousand copies were printed, mainly for libraries and persons with a special interest in whether the image visible on the shroud of Turin was in fact made by the body of Christ that had ostensibly been wrapped in it. Mr. Tribbe's book contained one somewhat startling color photograph, which was essential to his proof. It was not a book for the book clubs or the paperback reprint houses. It was simply a hardcover book that in due course sold out. After Stein and Day filed under Chapter 11, the author asked for his rights back because he was convinced, as most authors are, that there was a continuing market for his book.

The one possible outlet that the company could think of in this case was a hardcover reprint of the book, but not even that subsidiary right was wanted. So, there was no inventory on the book, no rights sublicensed, and, one could say, absolutely no reason to hold on to the rights except possibly to make the author miserable and to consume the time of the debtor in dealing with the author's pleas.

Some five years after the book was published, Frank Tribbe, who, "on information and belief" as the lawyers say, is not a well-do-to man, offered the estate $250 to buy his own book back along with the printing materials if the latter could ever be found. His request was accompanied by his check for $250 to avoid any possible objection or delay. The debtor's temporary bookkeeper did what bookkeepers usually do with small checks—she deposited it; technically it should have been held in cold storage until the court approved the transaction.

The debtor, wanting to help Mr. Tribbe, submitted the matter formally to the attorneys for the estate. This grand transaction apparently reached the attorneys just after they had prepared another slew of documents involving the sale of other exclusive publishing rights, and they did not wish to burden themselves with yet another document for a mere $250 transaction. That was in September of 1988, and thereafter the matter festered, with Mr. Tribbe phoning and writing and pleading that *Portrait of Jesus? The Illustrated Story of the Shroud of Turin*, with its significant question mark, be returned to him for revival or burial.

Finally this matter, which should have come before the court on September 20, was scheduled for a hearing (involving at least four lawyers plus travel time) on January 10, 1989. Nothing could have seemed more routine. Then out of the blue came a missive dated December 26, 1988, from the attorney for the Creditors' Committee, Henry Swergold, that deserves to be recorded for posterity:

TO THE HONORABLE HOWARD SCHWARTZBERG
   United States Bankruptcy Judge:

> The official Creditors' Committee ("Committee") of Stein and Day Incorporated, a/k/a Stein and Day/Publishers ("Debtor") by its attorneys Platzer, Fineberg & Swergold, respectfully opposes the Motion of the Debtor dated December 6, 1988 for an order seeking the release of any rights the Debtor may have in the book entitled "Portrait of Jesus" for the sum of $250.00 as follows:
>
> 1. The Debtor fails to give any information upon which the creditors can make a reasonable judgment. Copies of the contracts between the Debtor and the offeror are not attached to the Motion. There is no indication as to whether or not his is a published or unpublished title. If in fact the

book has been published, then the creditors should have the right to review the sales information and other pertinent information to determine whether or not this nominable [sic] offer is fair and reasonable. If in fact it is an unpublished title, information should be provided regarding the status of the manuscript, the Debtor's efforts to market this title and some evaluation as to the asset.

2. It appears that the legal fees alone in obtaining this assignment exceeds the value to the estate. [sic]

3. It is respectfully submitted, therefore, that the Motion be denied subject to the Debtor submitting additional information regarding the title in question.

WHEREFORE, The Committee requests that the Debtor's Motion be denied.

Of course attorney Swergold could have gotten that information with a two-minute phone call to any of the principals. Instead, a letter with enclosures that included the author's original contract was duly telecopied by the attorneys for the company to the attorneys for the Michigan Bank, BookCrafters, The Colophon Corporation, and the Creditors' Committee, as well as to the debtor, advising that the matter was adjourned from January 10 to January 25 "in the hopes [sic] that you will agree to allow this deal to go forward."

Finally Mr. Tribbe, for his $250, got his rights back.

The absurdity of this procedure that took half a year, and God only knows how much legal expense, is a metaphor for the essence of a system that permits such economic waste. The attorney who blocked the selling of a useless right back to its author was said to have run up billings of over $300,000 in this Chapter 11 case.

Mark H. McCormack, a Yale Law School graduate and successful international entrepreneur, is the founder and CEO of the International Management Group, which the

Wall Street Journal referred to as a "sports and entertainment empire." He is also the author of *What They Don't Teach You at Harvard Business School.* Here's what this lawyer-turned-entrepreneur has to say about how lawyers charge for their services:

". . . the 'time charge' method of billing, whereby lawyers charge clients up to $500 or even more per hour, *irrespective of whether their work produces any result whatsoever, or even if it was really necessary;*" (p. 18)[7]

"The bottom line is that *unless you ride shotgun on them, lawyers will charge you pretty much whatever they want for whatever level of service they feel like providing.*" (p. 70)

"*The practitioner bills virtually without accountability,* and does so in a climate where there is almost no standard for judging whether his price is fair." (p. 71)

In the context of writing about what's wrong with litigation, McCormack concludes, "It opens the gates to a flood of complications that take time and energy away from productive pursuits." That, in the simplest of words, is what the businessman's complaint about lawyers is chiefly about.

---

7. The stressed phrases are all in the original. All quotes are from *The Terrible Truth About Lawyers,* Mark H. McCormack, New York, Beech Tree Books/William Morrow, 1987.

CHAPTER 7

Suddenly You Are in the Camel-Making Business

> "Bureaucracy is a giant mechanism operated by pygmies."
>
> —Balzac

THERE'S a saying that a camel is a horse made by a committee. It was from Tom Towey, who successfully got Neptune World Wide Moving out of Chapter 11, that I first heard "cameling" used as a verb to describe the procedure by which a committee sits down to design a horse and comes up with a camel.

Committees, whatever their announced purpose, are ways for individuals to dodge decision-making responsibility by spreading the process around a conference table. There you get "input" (that could have been obtained by other means) in an environment in which the responders often modify their true opinions to conform to the way the wind is blowing in the meeting or to other forces that operate in a group setting.

Committee meetings can become mechanisms for watering down the views of the quickest-thinking participants with the views of the least-thoughtful participants. Or they are used as forums by smart alecks to show the idiots up. Groups around a table have an open invitation to perform before colleagues, to show off or kiss ass or do whatever their psyches drive them to in the presence of their peers.

Some committees are headed by an autocratic figure who uses the meetings to provide a facade of democracy. If that autocrat is also the person who governs promotions, what he often gets from the participants is not their best judgment but their best electioneering; they structure what they say to please the boss.

Committees can also allow cowards to pretend to participate in a process that frightens them. Cowards can have experience and insight to contribute. They might even have solutions to offer. But the thought of putting their ideas forward in public can be countermanded by a natural shyness. And so they shut up and let the extroverts monopolize the meetings.

If a committee normally meets for a scheduled hour and accomplishes its true business in five minutes, the participants will find ways of filling the hour. The cost of committees is formidable if measured by two criteria: the cumulative compensation of the players and what they might have achieved back at their normal work stations.

A committee is easy to create and difficult to abolish. Most efficient executives I've met deplore meetings, but they sometimes succumb to the ritual established by a predecessor. A committee becomes part of the bureaucracy of life, the imposition of routine with a high cost and little result. That is the best definition of what happens in the proliferation of meetings that are part of the Chapter 11 process.

Apart from the formal committees, in Chapter 11 there are the meetings that usually involve the same group of people. They are all lawyers the debtor is paying for.

Consider an example from my own experience. Harvey Barr attended a thirteen-hour marathon meeting that consumed a Sunday. Present, in addition to himself, were the attorneys for two secured creditors and the attorney for the Creditors' Committee, a small group in comparison with most. Assume $175 as the average hourly rate charged by those lawyers (low by New York standards). The thirteen-hour meeting that accomplished nothing was billed out at $9,100! And that was just for the meeting time itself. I know that one of those lawyers arrived from another county a good two hours' round trip from the meeting place, and another came from home in a different state. The chances are they billed for their travel time as well, and there you go: over the $10,000 mark for a single meeting that was characterized by its senior participant as useless.

In the real world one earns one's keep by having a productive day. Not so in Chapter 11 because its participants are chiefly lawyers doing time. That is, they are being measured by their firms for the billing hours served and not by what they actually accomplish for the client. The key word, from one of the better plays of our generation, Tennessee Williams's *Cat on a Hot Tin Roof,* is mendacity. Circumstances made it possible for me to see that play some several dozen times until I considered myself expert in its subject, but never did I witness as much mendacity as in the Chapter 11 process. In the words of a lawyer who, like Tennessee Williams's Big Daddy, was filled with disgust at the mendacity around him, "The players speak words like *God, country, fiduciary responsibility,* and *equity,* the collective meaning of which, absent the double talk, boils down to *my fee, my fee.*"

If a company is in money trouble, which is why it is in Chapter 11, how moral is it for lawyers to knowingly attend and stretch out useless meetings? Or for a legal system to condone such bureaucratic practices by judges inviting the lawyers to "work it out among themselves," when they know that the result will be lots of billable hours to be borne by the hapless company?

The meetings are only one form of Chapter 11's bureaucracy.

Turnaround specialists are among the most outspoken about the obstacles. Kenneth Glass says Chapter 11 is "loaded with bureaucracy. It's frustrating. You need court orders for every little thing."

Attorney Gerald Munitz, who has worked on cases with Ken Glass, says that the bureaucracy in Chapter 11 is "out of control. The disclosure statements have lost their function. Somebody pays for one that is 292 pages long and all you need to read is five pages."

One is reminded of the saw that "a lawyer is a person who writes a 10,000-word document and calls it a brief."

Munitz says, "There are lawyers who want to depose everybody about every document in the company's file cabinets." Is there a way to avoid the bureaucratic costs? "It depends on the ability of the court and counsel," says Munitz, who is in favor of cutting down litigation by "using the British system, sticking the loser with the costs, or some modification of that."

Daniel Morris, whose Illinois-based turnaround firm has had clients all over the country, says, "It's a case of procedure over substance. You have to deal with a multiplicity of interests, groups, and organizations. You are constantly saddled with delays. The decisions should be based on what makes the most economic sense, but frequently they aren't. It's just like divorce, where one of the parties says, 'I'm not going to pay for this particular item' rather than looking at the overall economic picture." His solution: "Let the court decide." That means avoid the endless meetings to arrive at "consensual" agreements that aren't consensual at all, but based, finally, on who's got the most muscle or the best lawyer, or the most to lose by procedural or man-made delays. It's a form of duress watched over by the blindfolded lady with two empty trays.

Based on my discussions with executives who have lived through the Chapter 11 experience, I can promise you this: If, as an executive, you are forthright in making decisions, you will go bananas in Chapter 11 because of the number of lawyers who feel they must consult with each other at your company's expense before a quite ordinary business decision can be made. The Chapter 11 process *invites* performance by committee, which frequently means nonperformance by people who know even less about the nature of the executive's business than the least efficient manager on his staff.

When Stein and Day had been in Chapter 11 for less than three months, I wrote to the lawyer representing the company, "Chapter 11 is Kafkaland. We are trying to climb a glass mountain." What I meant, of course, is that for every three steps we took toward solving a problem, we slid back two steps because of the committee bureaucracy we ran into. And sometimes when we thought a problem had been resolved, we suddenly found ourselves in a meeting in which the whole ball of yarn unraveled in front of our eyes.

According to an astute observer, what contributes most to the time-consuming meetings is that the lawyers are prepared to be bored out of their skulls by thirteen-hour marathon meetings that accomplish exactly nothing because their meters are running. *The pace of these meetings is set by the slowest and least efficient lawyer in the group.* Then come the follow-up phone calls, conference calls, and faxed memoranda. The longer it takes to reach an often simple decision, the more money the law firms make. And if in thirteen-hour marathons no conclusion is reached, so much the better for the lawyers and so much the worse for the company. When the interests of bankruptcy lawyers are pitted against the interests of a company in Chapter 11, guess who almost always wins.

There are exceptions. Sam Metzger, a football player and a "reformed" lawyer himself, handsome, poised on the outside, dapper in his gray flannel suit, ran meetings of his Creditors' Committee as if they were meetings of his board. He would seat himself at the head of the table, his Rolex watch showing, his lawyer, Joshua Angel, at his side. "I was better prepared than anybody else at those meetings," Metzger said. "I ran the meetings. I used them to form a good working relationship with those people. If they'd tried any of that stuff they've done to other CEOs, I'd have walked."

Tom Towey, also a strong executive, found the same kind of meetings used as a form of humiliation. The creditors and their lawyers sat around the table. He and his general counsel were given seats in the second row, like the underlings at the United Nations. When a meal was served, Towey's firm paid for it, but he was served last—a small thing, but it never failed to sting.

The best bankruptcy attorneys affirm that business people should be in control of reviving the business. One of the comments I heard most often was, "Lawyers aren't businessmen. They're trained for adversarial disputes. They benefit from inefficiency. They don't know how to be guided by the bottom line."

Of course, in large firms with deep pockets, the executives cannot be pushed around as much by the lawyers, which adds up to a defamation of the motto on the front of the building that houses the United States Supreme Court: *Equal Justice Under Law* does not obtain in Chapter 11. The big firms with deep pockets can try to keep control of the turnaround in the hands of businessmen; the CEOs of smaller companies, unless they have the toughness of a Sam Metzger and an attorney like Joshua Angel,[1] have to drink at a different fountain, where the spigot is controlled by manipulative attorneys.

In Chapter 11, the executive who likes to get things done will be frustrated by certain meetings that he cannot avoid.

The Creditors' Committee, which we've met earlier, should be a dominant force in Chapter 11 because it is supposed to represent the interests of the hundreds of unsecured creditors.

---

1. His basic strategy is this: If an issue is in dispute, he takes it to the courtroom instead of wasting time and energy on open-ended meetings with time-servers.

Part of the problem is that the members of the Creditors' Committee usually happen to be the credit officers of companies that have no direct experience with what goes on backstage, and according to people who've had a lot of experience with these committees, those credit officers are delighted with the opportunity the Creditors' Committee represents to them: They can get away from their books and out of the office. A credit officer is not a businessman. Moreover, he made the mistake of extending what obviously turned out to be too much credit to the debtor, and therefore the debtor is now his enemy. His mind-set is "Bury the enemy." Those aren't my words. They are from the head of one of the biggest New York debtor bankruptcy firms.

To understand both the waste and its cost, let's focus on a specific example. The date was September 9, 1987. The place was the law offices of Platzer, Fineberg & Swergold on East 52 Street in Manhattan. Those offices occupy the entire twenty-sixth floor of a majestic skyscraper. The only business of the firm is bankruptcy.

As you step off the elevator, you are greeted by the busy receptionist, who is sometimes surrounded by incoming and outgoing messenger parcels mostly coming from and going to lawyers representing other parties. Behind the receptionist is a large green marble plaque proclaiming the firm's name. The green marble matches the marble floor of the reception area. The debtor waiting in the reception room has got to feel *I'm here because my company had money problems and now I'm going to be asked to pay for part of this luxury.*

The meeting is scheduled for four o'clock. I am the first to arrive. Everybody who then arrives is kept waiting in the reception area. These include two other executives from my company, its vice president and its comptroller; then Harvey Barr and Joseph Haspel, two lawyers representing the company. I can feel their time clocks ticking, though their firm, most unusually, charges only for the senior lawyer's time when more than one of them is present. Waiting also is Greg Borri of the New York office of Drinker, Biddle and Reath, a Philadelphia law firm. Borri represents the Michigan National Bank, the chief secured creditor. It is getting well past four o'clock and the small crowd is finally admitted to the larger of two conference rooms. Deryck Palmer of Weil, Gotshal & Manges, the firm that represents BookCrafters, the creditor who in my opinion did most to prevent Stein and Day's reorganization, arrives forty minutes late. Palmer was late, it is intimated by the other lawyers, because of the bureaucratic procedures in his large law firm for getting documents copied.

Our comptroller, Vincent Diamonti, was deposed at Weil Gotshal. During his deposition there arose the need to copy documents that were becoming exhibits. Right outside the room where he was being deposed, Diamonti reported, there was a working photocopying machine that wasn't being used by anybody. But the material needing to be reproduced had to be sent to Weil Gotshal's main official copying set-up, where it got stacked up behind other work like late-arriving planes over an airport.

On the occasion of our scheduled four o'clock meeting, the cost of four lawyers, including our host, the attorney for the Creditors' Committee Mr. Swergold, for 40 minutes would exceed what some authors get as an advance for a full-length book. This isn't the cost of the meeting, it is the cost of waiting for the meeting to begin!

Finally, when the meeting gets under way, among the items these expensive lawyers discuss are salary cuts for the company's people and pulling some of the bones off the skeleton staff. It is quite possible that nobody in American publishing, including the chief executives of hundred-million-dollar firms, are paid what these five lawyers billed for belatedly sitting around to discuss cutting salaries.

It is important for the CEO to understand that the cutting of salaries allegedly has an economic motive, but the real motive is punitive. Otherwise, why spend more money than you save by talking about saving it?

Meetings with the U.S. Trustee are a small but pungent part of the bureaucratic nightmare.

U.S. stands for United States, of course, and if you're like me, you thought of the U.S. Trustee as a neutral participant watching over the interests of the parties. What you will find is that the meetings with the U.S. Trustee are an absolute waste of time, conducted by an inquisitor with no real power. Every word is recorded (though you probably won't ever get to see a transcript). You prepare for the meetings with the Trustee, you make a report, you answer questions, and absolutely nothing happens as a result—except you run up a bill you never had before, because the U.S. Trustee wants to be paid every quarter. Like many other things in Chapter 11, *it is a new expense with which to handicap the debtor company.* What you learn is that only the judge can make decisions that count.

The professionals I interviewed for this book were more loath to talk about the role of the U.S. Trustee than almost any other subject, and understandably they didn't want to speak for attribution. They called the subject "sensitive." One very experienced top-level professional said that the U.S. Trustee was not generally helpful except in "one or two cases." Another said the U.S. Trustee "could be beneficial" but most were "less than competent." He cited "low pay" and said other factors entered into it. One respondent thought that the reason many of the Trustees were not useful is that "they are lawyers thinking about the law instead of about the business." One professional had an experience very different from his colleagues. His client company had a plan and they couldn't get the Creditors' Committee to respond (a familiar lament). The U.S. Trustee got into the act, called the attorney for the Creditors' Committee, and forced a response to the plan. This professional favors using the Trustee as "leverage." The majority, however, seem to think it's like telling a dead man to push a wheelbarrow.

I was told that the U.S. Trustee can be of some use if there's evidence of hanky-panky. He can intervene and take steps to have the judge boot out a debtor-in-possession who's helping himself instead of the creditors. But most of the time the U.S. Trustee's role is bureaucratic and nonproductive.

Instead of running his business, the CEO has to prepare for meetings with the U.S. Trustee, provide reports for the U.S. Trustee, go to the courthouse to answer questions asked by the U.S. Trustee, and then pay the Trustee for listening as you would pay for a psychoanalyst who says next to nothing. Except that you can get a load off your chest with a psychotherapist, and if you try doing the same with the Trustee, you'll get the brush-off: "Only the judge can deal with that." In other words, this meeting is useless, buddy, stash it.

In all fairness, I have to say that in my naive days when I thought meetings with the U.S. Trustee might produce some useful result, they were superintended by a young woman, an attorney named Rosemary Matera, who deserves a medal simply because her eyes and expressions revealed that she wasn't hardened to the debtor's pain and she, too, was saddened by being essentially powerless in a situation in which so many people were being hurt. I didn't fully appreciate her humaneness till the day another representative of the U.S. Trustee showed up in her place and put me in mine; this lawyer had learned the stone-face routine and how to shut up a debtor's plea for relief from some insanity with one short sentence. It's not easy to take when the lawyer sitting in the Trustee's chair is younger than most of your own children.

A hard fact about Chapter 11 for any executive to digest is that *no one really administers the case from a business point of view.* Before the 1978 revision of the bankruptcy laws, the judge used to have that job. Now control has to come from the person least knowledgeable about the bankruptcy laws and procedures: the debtor himself. It takes a tough person with a powerful will to try to steer the business during a storm while lawyers and bureaucrats keep grabbing at the wheel.

Tom Towey of Neptune says that during the first six months that Neptune was in Chapter 11, he spent one hundred percent of his time on the bankruptcy and zero percent on the business. Then for a while it was seventy percent on the bankruptcy, then sixty, then fifty. In late 1988, long after his company's Chapter 11 case was officially discharged, Towey was still spending ten percent of his time on the bankruptcy. He thinks he spent so much time on the bankruptcy because his goal was to isolate the bankruptcy from the company. He and the company's general counsel moved their offices to another floor. There they worked on the Chapter 11 case and had minimum contact with other employees, trying to keep the scourge from burdening other members of the staff. Even with that intense effort, they couldn't stem the defections.

No executive in his right mind would spend hundreds of hours a year on an activity that was mostly boring as hell and productive perhaps one percent of the time. But litigators and bankruptcy lawyers do just that in examinations before trial, which have become a somnolent sport in our litigious society. These examinations, also called EBTs and depositions, are fishing expeditions that takes a lot of time and cost the litigants a lot of money—and, of course, make a lot of swag for clock-watching lawyers who can bear the boredom. EBTs are a caricature of legal process.

The officers of Chapter 11 companies may or may not have had previous experience being deposed. In bankruptcy, these proceedings are conducted under Rule 2004, which is designed to put the debtor in a fishbowl surrounded by lawyers with hooks in their bait. As one lawyer said, "They can ask you anything, including whether you got laid last night." The lawyers can then fight over the relevance.

Any time there is an adversary proceeding in Chapter 11, the first thing that will be demanded by subpoena is the turning over of several hundred pieces of paper from the company's files. Digging out those papers takes a lot of time away from the reorganization of the business. (Keep in mind that, as in Stein and Day's case, the creditor doing the deposing may not want a reorganization to take place.) The CEO will want to deputize someone with a brain to go over each piece of paper to see what's being turned over to the enemy. The company's lawyers will want to go over them, too, to make sure that nothing "privileged" is shown to the other side.

Warning: In the episode that eventually led to one company's filing, the company's adversary asked to see everything, including the kitchen sink. As is customary, a young associate from the company's law firm was given the job of weeding out privileged material. Would you believe that he let the other side have the most privileged kind of material of all: copies of correspondence between the company and its lawyers? Well, why not? It is said that some 26 percent of hospital cases are iatrogenic, that is, caused by actions of doctors and hospitals. Aren't lawyers also allowed to make mistakes a quarter of the time and charge you for it, just as hospitals do? One experienced lawyer maintains, "Doctors are kinder. They just kill you."

At depositions, officers of the company will be interrogated under oath about those subpoenaed papers and much else. There will be attempts to trick the person being deposed. He will be asked the same question at different times in slightly altered ways in an attempt to force a discrepancy that will be used to discredit him.

Businessmen who've been deposed in other legal matters know that depositions are one-sided meetings. The other side gets to ask the questions, and you are required to give answers. They are usually intolerably boring, even to the lawyers whose clocks are running at a high hourly rate.

Before you are deposed, your lawyer will usually give you a standard briefing beforehand. He will tell you to think before you speak, to answer in the briefest possible form, and never to volunteer any information. But what if common sense tells you that some questions should be answered not in the manner advised by your lawyer in order to get the truth on the record?

These depositions, under the best of circumstances, can be unpleasant for the person getting the third degree. They can also get pretty foolish. I know of one officer of a company, a woman with a 180 I.Q., who is said to make a very good witness in court because she answers questions succinctly in a manner that resonates with truth. She was being deposed by attorneys for the company's warehouse, one of whom came nearly halfway across the country for the event. On her side for this deposition were the attorneys for a bank as well as for the company. During her deposition, at one point the attorneys argued for nearly half an hour over the admissibility of a question. After all the protestations, the question was asked. The answer, now allowed to be given, was "I don't know."[2]

The law, in its infinite majesty, picks nits while Rome burns.

An entrepreneur, almost by definition, is a person who believes he has a money-making idea in his grasp and runs with it. If he runs too fast, if his need for capital outstrips his resources and he is forced to file, the runner will learn that in Chapter 11 nothing happens fast. If you get bored easily, if you're used to getting things done, Chapter 11 is certain to make you sick, sometimes literally, because you will be imprisoned in a world that unreels in slow motion, one static frame at a time—an image of a camel crossing a very wide desert.

---

2. ". . . in the real world, lawyerly discipline and logic are usually applied to issues of stupefying pettiness!" *Bankruptcy Reorganization,* Martin J. Bienenstock, Practising Law Institute, 1987, p. 31.

CHAPTER 8

"Unconscionable and Obscene": The Process by which Some Bankruptcy Lawyers Enrich Themselves

> "Two farmers each claimed to own a certain cow. While one pulled on its head and the other pulled on its tail, the cow was milked by a lawyer."
> —Jewish parable, quoted in *1,911 Best Things Anybody Ever Said*
> "In plain truth it is not want but rather abundance that creates avarice."
> —Montaigne

A FTER PTL, the television ministry run for years by Jim and Tammy Baker, filed for bankruptcy, some thought it appropriate for Federal Bankruptcy Judge Rufus Reynolds of Columbia, South Carolina, to quote the Bible when speaking about them. Judge Reynolds ordered Jim Bakker to repay PTL $4.9 million, Tammy Bakker to repay $667,397, and David Taggart, a former PTL vice president, to pay something over a million dollars. In doing so, the good judge said, "James Bakker either overlooked or ignored parts of the Bible, including Timothy 6:10. For the love of money is the root of all evil; which while some coveted after, they have

123

erred from the faith and pierced themselves through with many sorrows."

Judge Reynolds said the expenditures at PTL under Bakker's administration were a "waste of PTL's money." He accused the administrators of "total disregard for reality." He said, reportedly, that Messrs. Bakker and Taggart "approached the management of the corporation with reckless indifference to the financial consequences of their acts."

The judge's phrases, "total disregard for reality" and "reckless indifference to the financial consequences of their acts," describe quite accurately the legal billings in most bankruptcy cases.

We live, I suspect for worse rather than for better, in an era in which language is abused in a misguided attempt to elevate the status of an occupation. No one I know has a particular animus against the collectors of our garbage. And none of these good people think any differently now that they are called "sanitary engineers." Orwell told us pointedly how we use language to defraud ourselves.[1] When it comes to characterizing occupations, the instinct for elevation proves to be a two-way street. Witness my occupation and that of the law.

Once upon a time, in my own lifetime to be sure, book publishing was considered an occupation for gentlemen. I know of no one on this planet who is knowledgeable about publishing and who would use that description now without a wry smile.

Similarly, in my lifetime, the law was thought of as a learned profession. With more than 700,000 lawyers about (60,000 of them in San Francisco alone!), the majority of whom abuse their language daily and know little of the humanities that once characterized a person as civilized

---

1. George Orwell's essay "Politics and the English Language" is quite possibly the best short piece on the serious effects of the abuse of language. It should be required reading in law schools. Alas, it is not.

and educated, the law can hardly be called a *learned* profession, and it is now widely believed that in its vast nether regions it does not function as a profession at all. It is said that the law has become a business without making businessmen of the lawyers. If that is true, and there is much evidence to support that contention, then we can begin to see the danger of hordes of such individuals swarming into the arena of business in which troubled companies try to work their way out.

I will cite the opinions of two lawyers. One, Sam Metzger, was general counsel for a two-hundred-million-dollar company at a time when that amount of money was valued more than it is today. He had all the perks: the big expense account, the use of a Lear jet, and a helicopter. Then, in the general practice of law, with clients at least some of whom were household names for every American, Metzger came to the realization that what he was doing in his "legal profession" was selling himself. He had to be many different things to many different clients. He was successful at it, and knew how to dress, look, comport himself for each. "I didn't feel good," he says. "I didn't know who I was. I lost respect for myself."

Thereupon Metzger did what so many of us sometimes daydream of doing. He changed his life, which consisted in his case of changing among other things his clothes, manner, lifestyle, wife, and profession. I didn't know any of this when I first sat down to talk to Metzger, but I did sense that here was a man in control of his own life. He almost lost that control when his company, Chipwich, was squeezed into involuntary bankruptcy by two individuals. In order to protect the company, his attorney then caused the involuntary petition to be converted into a Chapter 11 case.

Not every entrepreneur is himself a lawyer or as resourceful as Metzger. A man who felt in charge of his life, as Metzger did, is better prepared to take charge of a bankruptcy. He'd previously found Joshua J. Angel for one of his own clients. Therefore Metzger had the advantage of being armed from the start with a lawyer who focuses on bringing his client's company back to health and out of Chapter 11.

In 1980, Metzger went into partnership with Richard LaMotta, founder of Chipwich, in what in anyone's eyes had to be a small business for a man who'd been a high-flying, well-paid lawyer. Chipwich's main and originally only product, for those who've been Rip Van Winkling, is a chocolate-chip ice-cream sandwich sold by pushcart vendors for one dollar. In the beginning, they operated out of a storefront in Ozone Park, Long Island, where they had a fifty-square-foot freezer, and some sixty pushcart vendors out in the street hawking the new product. It caught on and became the Cabbage Patch doll of the adult dessert business. Pretty soon Chipwich had 120 employees turning out chocolate-chip ice-cream sandwiches in a New Jersey plant for no fewer than twelve hundred pushcart vendors in twenty-seven locations around the country: Los Angeles, San Diego, Dallas, Oklahoma City, Miami, Washington, D.C., Philadelphia, and Boston as well as New York, where it all started. Success? Metzger and his partner were riding a flying carpet held aloft by air.

Chipwich bought its ingredients in a market that required payment in ten days. It took three to four months for the product made with those ingredients to go on sale. Their receivables were on a 30–60 day timetable. The business was very capital intensive. Interest rates, pushed by inflation, were 18–19 percent at the time. Chipwich's rapid success was a formula for disaster: a successful product produced by an undercapitalized company, booming sales, suppliers who want to be paid quickly, customers who pay slowly. It adds up to illiquidity.

Though Metzger personally lost some $800,000 in the Chapter 11 experience, he is not at all bitter about it compared to the other CEOs I've met. He says Chapter 11 saved him. I was therefore interested to hear his impression, as an attorney, of the behavior of the numerous bankruptcy attorneys he encountered during his Chapter 11 experience.

"Yes," he says, "it is the rule rather than the exception for the lawyers to try to prolong Chapter 11. They have a good thing going for them. Whatever there is [in the business] they'll eat it all up." But Metzger sees a good side: "The jackals won't waste time [if there's nothing to milk in the business]. They'll look for a different carcass."

Metzger says the practice of the bankruptcy bar is not that much different from the matrimonial bar or the negligence bar. In other words, the ambulance chasers and the lawyers who exacerbate marital differences in a spirit of fierce advocacy are kindred spirits to the bankruptcy specialists.

It is easy enough to say that Metzger, like an "ex" anything, is particularly against the profession whose daily practice he left. But that is not so. He has a high regard for men of the law who honor their profession.

Gerald Munitz, head of the bankruptcy department of Chicago's biggest law firm, rattles off the names of men he considers to be the pride of the profession who make the bankruptcy bar respectable. As for what he calls "the scum" in the trade, he "wouldn't have them clean out the dog shit at the back door."

Ron Stengel, a crisis manager who works out of Wayne, Pennsylvania, notes that, especially in smaller companies, by which he means those with under $10 million a year in revenue, some bankruptcy lawyers function as if they were the debtor. As Stengel politely puts it, the lawyer finds himself playing "a more active leadership role." But even in what Stengel calls big cases, "eighteen legal issues a day can fall on the client's desk, and he just can't handle them expediently." Then it's a judgment call for the lawyer, and frequently he's got to make decisions for the client. When Stengel was asked, "Do bankruptcy lawyers have an incentive to close a case or keep it open?" he said it was a "tough call." In his opinion, the good lawyers don't drag out a case.

Ken Glass had a very sharp reaction to the same question about bankruptcy attorneys. He said some of them try "to churn a case forever." Glass was once involved with a major U.S. company where the parties had reached "a mutually beneficial proposal," to everyone's relief. Then one attorney bounced into the situation, demanding to be dealt with. "He wanted to litigate with everyone in sight. He was a pain in the ass. He wouldn't even look at solutions."

Gilbert C. Osnos, president of Grisanti & Galef & Osnos, a long-established crisis management firm in New York, says that one reason to "go for the best" in bankruptcy lawyers is that "the true professionals try to wind up a case as quickly as possible." The problem, of course, is with the others, and also, according to Adam Radzik, to some degree with management. Radzik believes the tendency to drag things out is true of lawyers in general, not just in bankruptcy cases, and that it is the obligation "of the client to *manage* the professional. Treat him with respect, but suspect everything."

One of the things to be suspicious about, as I've said, is the padding of time billed. Knowing that the court may cut their fee applications down to size, the lawyers may inflate the size beforehand. This was confirmed by the two largest of the turnaround consulting companies whose key executives were interviewed. One said, "Sure, it's a common practice. Some gross it up by thirty percent." The other said he has suspected that the lawyers "expand the time" but it's difficult to prove. He's in favor of bonus arrangements for professionals, where they get rewarded for accomplishment rather than hours spent churning a case.

One turnaround specialist makes the point that the first-class firms don't pad their bills. Yet the majority of debtors are unable to hire the first-class firms.

There's something about the business of business, the concentration on getting things done and moving on, that makes lawyers-turned-businessmen into knowledgeable antagonists of their former occupation. Listen to the man *Sports Illustrated* called "the most powerful man in sports," Mark H. McCormack, himself a lawyer-turned-businessman, talk about the sport of law. He says, "The bottom line on professional courtesy is this: It is a system whereby lawyers make life easier for themselves and for each other, generally at the expense of their clients."[2]

In trying to ascertain why businessmen and lawyers are in frequent conflict, McCormack says, ". . . good faith and good communication. . . . are both essential for mutually advantageous business dealings. Both are often mucked up by lawyers."[3] He goes on to say, "And just in case there is anybody out there who harbors illusions about the general moral tone prevailing among the plaintiff's bar, let me report on the results of an interesting experiment conducted recently by *The American Lawyer* magazine. The publication sent one of its reporters, posing as an accident victim, to thirteen attorneys. She told each one that she had taken a fall *near* a construction site, *but that the fall was in no way caused by or connected to the construction.* Five of the thirteen lawyers advised her to change her recollection of the mishap, to bring it closer to the site so they could sue!"[4]

Especially pertinent to the Chapter 11 situation is McCormack's view that the so-called "protections" built into the legal system work toward demolishing fair play. "In effect, what the 'protections' do is to set up an elaborate game in which stalling tactics figure prominently and in which, since time is money, the side with the bigger war chest has a definite edge, irrespective of the merits of the case."[5]

Chapter 11 is a tough environment where survival is

---

2. *The Terrible Truth About Lawyers*, Mark H. McCormack, New York, Beech Tree Books/William Morrow, 1987, page 54.

3. Ibid, p. 119.

4. Ibid., p. 194.

5. Ibid., p. 206.

very expensive. The *Wall Street Journal*, the morning
after Eastern Airlines filed under Chapter 11, predicted,
"Labor's only accomplishment in the Eastern strike will be
to make bankruptcy lawyers richer." The famed Texaco-
Pennzoil case lasted only a year and was conducted in
front of a judge with a reputation for efficiency. Yet there
were 27,000 pages in that case that presumably had to be
researched and written by lawyers, and read by countless
other lawyers, not to speak of the judge and his clerk. At
350 pages to a novel, that's the length of more than 77 novels! Now comes this inevitable question: Did the lawyers
responsible for reading every word read every word, or
did they merely charge for their time?

Charging for time can be a kind of game, of course. At
Cravath, Swaine & Moore, an associate named Joseph
Sahid who worked on the IBM case scored a "triumph" by
billing twenty-four hours in a single day. Not to be out-
done, another associate on the same case, Ronald Rolfe,
flew to California, worked on the plane, and, by virtue of
the change in time zones, managed to bill twenty-seven
hours in a day.[6]

That, then, is the "professional" environment in which
a debtor is forced to try to save his business.

Consider this scenario: A company in Chapter 11 has
put forward a plan to sell over half a million dollars' worth
of its inventory on favorable terms quickly. A sales executive needed to execute this plan is waiting in the wings,
ready to be hired on a day's notice. The company has had
its assets valued under oath in court, and it seemed as if the
secured creditors were more than adequately protected.
On what was to be the third day of testimony, the secured
creditors and their lawyers surmise that the company,
Stein and Day, is about to get a cash collateral order from
the court.

And so the principals are invited to sit down in a body-

---

6. Chronicled in *The Partners*, James B. Stewart, Simon & Schuster,
1983.

crowded witness room down the hall from the courtroom. In the presence of their lawyers the principals quickly concur on a cash collateral agreement that will enable the company's Christmas sales plan to go forward because it will bring in a lot more cash for very little added expense. All that's needed is to put the terms into written form. A writer could do it in under an hour. A businessman could dictate it in even less time.

But such documents aren't written by writers or businessmen, they're written by lawyers. The lawyer for the creditor most antagonistic to the survival of the company volunteered to do the paperwork, and none of the other lawyers objected. *Mistake.* Possibly a mistake that for the company was the coup de grace, for as it turned out the creditor and/or his attorneys saw this as an opportunity to insinuate items into the agreement that were not part of the discussion but that were designed to improve that creditor's position as against that of other secured creditors.

A word of warning: Time works against the CEO and the company; therefore it behooves the CEO to insist that the company's counsel do the drafting of any agreement and do it immediately.

With the drafting in the hands of the attorney for the company's most hostile creditor, it took from November 5, the day agreement was reached, until about December 8 for the document to be endlessly redrafted and executed. "Executed" is the right word. The final cash collateral agreement was a camel without legs: It was thoroughly unworkable. The CEO of the Chapter 11 company refused to sign it as debtor-in-possession. Two lawyers told him that it didn't matter, if he refused to sign it the judge would order it anyway. The final document—an agreement that the CEO said made the rehabilitation of the company impossible—was signed not by the principals but by four lawyers! Yet anyone on the outside, including the judge, would assume that the CEO had authorized the company-killing document to be signed.

A footnote to the affair is worth noting. It was a relatively small company. The whole point of going to court to prove the value of the company's assets and to obtain a cash collateral order was to get the use of $70,000 of incoming funds for a constructive purpose: to bring in half a million dollars or more of sales in a few weeks' time, and to begin the process of rehabilitation. Instead, according to the estimate of Harvey Barr, the chief lawyer for the estate, *the lawyers' billings for the month-long "negotiation" came to at least three quarters of the amount of the cash collateral agreed to in the brief meeting!*

That unworkable cash collateral order was kept in force for more than half a year. The details of this episode are a real scorcher. The attorney for the company got so exasperated by the dangerously harmful stretch-out of what had already been agreed to by the principals that he wrote a letter to the other lawyers, calling their process "unconscionable and obscene."[7]

It takes a lot to get a bankruptcy lawyer to talk that way to his fellows. You do not rat on colleagues. In the Mafia, there are certain things you do not say on pain of death. The author of that brave letter had seen a company that he believed could come out of Chapter 11 with a new life finished off by the clever camel-makers.

One comes away from an experience of this sort with a sense that in a civil society such fiascoes should be avoided. All it takes is one knowledgeable attorney willing and able to fight for a company's life at a crucial moment by taking the issue *to the court* instead of to the other lawyers he graciously refers to as his "colleagues." For, along with the company's plans, his hope for collecting his own bills for participating in the talkathons vanished into the wind.

---

7. The letter, which deserves to be a classic on the subject of abuse of process in bankruptcy cases, is reproduced in full as Appendix A of this book.

CHAPTER 9

How Do You Tie Shoelaces?

> "Rarely do we hear about what really happens inside business. The whopping success stories are glorified, the failures are dissected or shunned. The rest is silence. Our demand for heroes and goats obscures the truth."
>
> —Paul Hawken in *Growing a Business*

YOU were probably so young when you were taught how to tie shoelaces you don't remember the process. But picture meeting an adult from some tropical country who has only worn sandals before and gets his first pair of shoes and it's your job to teach him to tie his shoelaces. Can you describe to him how shoelaces are tied without actually showing him? Doubtful.

There are a lot of things you take for granted, like tying shoelaces and running your business, but if you've ever had to explain the intricacies of running your business to someone else, remember this story about the shoelaces. It isn't easy, and giving someone a hands-on demonstration isn't always possible.

Very few businesses are easy for an outsider to grasp in a few minutes' time. Some relatively small or medium-sized companies produce dozens of new products a year, something that would baffle General Motors or General Electric. In actuality, a lot of specialized expertise is required in many businesses: how to design or manufacture a product, how to market it, or what makes customers in that business pay promptly. You can't expect a lawyer not previously connected with a business to be able to understand what makes it tick or to scrutinize its internal operating figures with intelligence gleaned from experience.

Yet the lawyers who swarm in and around Chapter 11 cases pretend not only to understand complex businesses, they often undertake to advise or dictate the conditions under which the company is managed. "They don't know what they're doing!" the executive yells (silently), watching the lawyers profess to understand the complexities behind the numbers they or their clients have to approve.

It takes self-confidence for a person to say, "Teach me" this or that about a business. Some lawyers will do that. But if the lawyer is trying to assert his primacy over the principal, he may not ask. As a result the company, its creditors, and its shareholders may be hurt irremediably.

Think of a high-tech company that manufactures an essential computer part. (Lots of companies in the rapidly changing computer business, where obsolescence is a given, have had to file for Chapter 11 protection.) An executive in good faith tries to explain how that part works—it's the company's chief product—to a lawyer who doesn't seem to have the time to listen carefully. The lawyer may not realize he needs to understand that essential until it becomes mightily relevant in a negotiation when no company executive is present to fill him in. His lack of knowledge may have dire consequences. But it is the company that loses out if he is underinformed, not the lawyer. One high-ranking officer of a Chapter 11 company said, "It is definitely true that the lawyers' arrogant ignorance can destroy a company, but do they care? They're just making money." What is important here is the executive's perception that the lawyers who are in effect making many of the business decisions don't seem to be concerned about making them knowledgeably.

Picture a large conference table in the offices of one of the lawyers representing creditors. Seated around it are all the key lawyers in the case. One of the subjects on the agenda is staff reduction, a part of the Chapter 11 ritual that affords the creditors some psychological benefit but that often trespasses on business sense.

Some of these meetings will include senior management. These people usually know who the most valuable and sometimes irreplaceable employees are. But it is a sine qua non of the process that management's word is tainted. Therefore the creditors' attorneys will play a crucial role in deciding who stays and who goes. Their "recommendations" may be capricious or based on the false assumption that employees are standard interchangeable parts. A classic example of this is BookCrafters' Randy Kuckuck, whose thrust in the Stein and Day case was to replace highly experienced people with inexperienced people working for him. The results were predictably lunatic.[1]

What an essential employee does that nobody else can do needn't be high tech. Suppose an electrical contractor has to file so that he can reorganize his business? Or a produce wholesaler? Suppose an essential person is "merely" an individual in the accounts receivable department who has a special relationship developed over long years with several major customers and who is able to influence them to pay their bills on time.

After a year or so, the lawyers, who have thought of themselves as "running the case" with a minimum of "interference" from a company's executives, may come to understand that one or another employee is especially valuable to the business—or to its successful liquidation. When that bright bulb of recognition flashes on, it doesn't necessarily shed light on the employee's motivations for staying—only that the employee is needed.

There's the rub. It is up to the CEO to defend a small core of essential employees from the very start before their

---

1. A month after Kuckuck took over the job of selling rights with an executive whose inexperience matched his, he reported to the attorney for the Michigan Bank that he had sold absolutely nothing.

departure wrecks the company's chances of recovery. But in that early period, any recommendations made by management will be viewed as suspect. Is the chief executive supposed to parade an elderly bookkeeper before the attorneys so that they won't suspect that he is sleeping with her and that that's the reason he deems her essential?

Here's how the ignorance works in practice. In Stein and Day's case, management wanted to produce books to fill bona fide orders from its distributor, Henry Holt. As a step toward consideration of this proposal, which was a step in the direction of reorganization by practicing the only business the company was in, the lawyers wanted to verify Holt's orders. First, Holt is a company that's been in the book business for over a century. Second, verifying orders from many hundreds of bookstores and wholesalers would be roughly equivalent in difficulty to verifying orders in a brokerage house with each of hundreds of customers before any action was taken. Even a customer's offer to prepay for five thousand copies of a single book, an entire printing, was blocked by the bureaucracy and ignorance of the Creditors' Committee.

Patricia Day said that Deryck Palmer, representing BookCrafters, proposed that the company raise money by selling all the contracts back to the authors! The *use* of those rights had generated between $6.4 and $7.2 million a year. The best offer received by the company for the *sale* of those rights (and not to the authors) was $400,000. So much for the wisdom of attorneys playing publisher.

The force of attorney ignorance came through to me most clearly in an episode that occurred on September 22, 1987, just three months after Stein and Day filed. The attorney for the Creditors' Committee, Henry Swergold, saw himself as having a special interest in book publishing and therefore as imbued with a knowledge of the field that he attributed to experience. The truth is that he'd been involved in the bankruptcy proceedings of Pinnacle Books, a mass-market paperback company whose "products" were mainly books by authors you've never heard of. There are few similarities between that reprint business, distributed nationwide through magazine wholesalers, and the book industry that tries to originate books that deserve the semipermanence of hard covers. Not only is every major step of the process different, but the people involved in the two industries are, with notable exceptions, a different species of humankind, marching to a different drumbeat.

Nevertheless, Swergold didn't have difficulty convincing the other lawyers involved in the case that he was the "publishing" man and that they could rely on his expertise.

Early in the Stein and Day Chapter 11 case, Barnes & Noble[2] made news with an unprecedented offer of $100,000 as an advance against royalties to Stein and Day for the hardcover reprint rights to fifty titles, most of which didn't exist in hardcover and were being sold by the company in trade paperback or not at all. Barnes & Noble had never licensed so large a number of titles from one publisher at one time. Their public statements to the press made it clear that they were trying to help Stein and Day get back on its feet and were trying to encourage it to go back into production. In addition, Barnes & Noble offered Stein and Day a chance to "run on" copies for its own sales at full price whenever Barnes & Noble manufactured books for its catalogue and store distribution. Being able to "run on" copies of a book has a significant monetary advantage if one understands that aspect of the business. Let's take a moment to elucidate.

---

2. Barnes & Noble is a chain of discount bookstores that also sells via a mail-order catalogue that reaches some four million people several times a year. It has a common ownership and management with B. Dalton, and is one of the two largest booksellers in America. Barnes & Noble's Marboro division publishes lower-priced reprints of mainly out-of-print hardcover books. An interesting sidelight on the book trade is that titles that fail miserably in the normal bookstore market can be big winners in the mail-order catalogue as hardcover reprints.

Whenever a book or anything else is being prepared for printing, there is a "make-ready" charge. That is the cost of preparing the machinery for printing a book and can run from hundreds to thousands of dollars. That's in addition to the cost of paper, printing, and binding. If you are allowed to "run on" with someone else's printing, they are paying for the make-ready, which means your cost per unit is much lower. Even if the make-ready cost is prorated, each book's cost is less. Manufacturing is the biggest cost by far in publishing and a saving by "running on" is a significant item.

Henry Swergold, attorney for the Creditors' Committee and the self-acknowledged "publishing expert" among the lawyers in the case, wanted to know what "run-on" means. In that instant we concluded that he was not as expert as he may have thought. The significance for the Chapter 11 case was that that very month "publishing expert" Swergold and his committee *had turned down the funding offer that would have put the company back into its sole business of publishing books.*[3] That wasn't just a nail, it was a real spike in Stein and Day's coffin.

The ignorance of lawyers about technical matters is just the tip of the iceberg. Though lawyers are no more busi-

---

3. At the time of the turndown (see Chapter 16), I talked to two members of the Creditors' Committee who told me they had never been consulted about the offer. Some fifteen months later, on December 28, 1988, lawyer Swergold, sitting across from me during a hurried lunch in a luncheonette next to the courthouse, told me that he had consulted every member of the Creditors' Committee and that all but one of the members of the committee voted in writing to turn down the offer that would have made a return to publishing possible. And Arcata, a book manufacturer, had given its negative vote by phone. Like capital punishment, once you have a corpse, discussions about whether the lawyer did the deed on his own or proselytized for the rejection of the offer, or whether it was done by the committee in full knowledge of the consequences, are moot. The fact is that none of the parties consulted with the publishers as to their reasons for wanting to take the deal (the shareholders were willing to give up 50 percent of their equity to bring in the production money).

nessmen than are soldiers or doctors, they can hurt the business operations of a medium-sized or smaller Chapter 11 company in ways that can equal the size of the company's total debt.

The lawyers pretend not to understand such simple matters as the payroll costs involved in taking orders, billing customers, or accounting for sales. Ask a lawyer to function without a secretary[4] for a prolonged period and see what happens to his work. Or ask him to do his own billing, record-keeping, and collecting. Any lawyer functioning this way, even for just a few weeks, might make better decisions with regard to what is and is not chopped in a Chapter 11 case.

Every manager of a Chapter 11 firm has his own horror stories about trying to teach the new people in his life some of the essentials of the business. I had a devil of a time convincing the lawyers that it is better to license something repeatedly than to sell it because if you license it, you are getting an advance against future royalty income *and you still have the property to sell later, should you wish.*

Patricia Day said that "the real point is that none of them gave a damn about learning how to tie their shoelaces. They were dancing the bill-more-hours minuet."

Sam Metzger, the CEO of Chipwich, saw at the outset that his role was to take the initiative in educating his creditors. "You *must* teach the [Creditors'] Committee

---

4. For the record, my own very good secretary, Marilyn Knowlton, who was efficient, pleasant, intelligent, and knew publishing, left in September of 1986, after, it was said, our chief financial officer had given her a frightening view of the future. Though I had the frequent and excellent stenographic help of my former secretary, Dawn Horstmann, who had been promoted to other duties in the firm, for the next two and a half years I typed some two thousand letters and documents in final form, some of them court documents of more than twenty pages that went through five or six drafts. Clearly, it was not the most efficient use of the company's chief executive, but efficiency is not a hallmark of Chapter 11.

your business," Metzger asserted. This makes much more
sense than trying to educate the lawyers.

Metzger sent his creditors a periodic "president's letter"
that was really a briefing device. He sent them reports,
background information, and ultimately a business plan.
"What I tried to do," he said, "was to make each of them
psychologically an investor in the business."

A big deterrent to this sensible practice can be an
injunction by the debtor's attorney forbidding the CEO
from talking or writing to any of the principals. (Harvey
Barr, attorney for Stein and Day, made such a ban a condition for his continuing to work. His purpose presumably
was to keep total control of the case.) An ever more common deterrent to the average CEO doing what Metzger did
is the fact that from day one he has been under attack as
the failure, the potential crook, the shameful bankrupt.
When attacked and humiliated, it is only natural for an
entrepreneur to fight back. The creditors fling the glove,
the CEO picks it up and finds himself in a confrontation
with his creditors. According to Metzger, *that's something he has to avoid at all costs.* He has to be a man of
steel, letting the barbs bounce off his armor. He has to
assert his role as teacher of the business.

What enabled Metzger to do this, he said, was not just
a matter of personality and predisposition, but having the
professional counsel of Joshua Angel, "who has a heart, a
soul, and is his own man." According to Metzger, Angel
"is a throwback to the lawyer of yesteryear. Like the general practitioner of medicine, he cares."

Just as it is the CEO's job to deal with the lack of specific
industry knowledge on the part of his creditors, the CEO
has to recognize that he is himself in a new business that
he doesn't know beans about—Chapter 11. And that
means he must take the initiative in self-education because
the majority of lawyers involved in his case are likely to
want to keep him in the dark.

Lawyer Mark McCormack emphasizes, "It is always to

the client's advantage to show sophistication by knowing the pertinent questions. Showing awareness *up front* is a great deterrent to being taken advantage of later on." What this means is that the CEO has to know his way around Chapter 11 right at the outset or he will be taken advantage of. But how does he find out if his lawyer doesn't tell him?

He needs to arm himself. There is a short form pamphlet encapsulating the 1978 Bankruptcy Code that is small enough to carry in one's pocket for easy reference.[5] I've seen a head of a bankruptcy department consult this pocket bible in the hallway of a courtroom.

There are also some reference tomes, that collectively cost less than the usual legal fee for an hour's time, that might usefully find their place on the CEO's shelf *at the time he is considering entering Chapter 11.* If he thinks an emergency is no time to look in a book, he should look before an emergency hits, because if he relies on asking a bankruptcy specialist, he will be assuming his goals and his lawyer's are the same. And this assumption could be a grave mistake. Instead, the CEO needs to realize that self-education is the ounce of prevention he's looking for.

---

5. The *Mini-Code* is obtainable from AWHFY, Inc., P.O. Box 1582, Santa Teresa, NM 88008 for $17.50. The *Mini-Rules* is available from the same source for the same price.

CHAPTER 10

The Courthouse: A Home Away from Home

"There is no cruder tyranny than that which is perpetuated under the shield of law and in the name of justice."

—Montesquieu

ENTERING a courthouse, except for people who work there, can be an awe- or fear-inspiring experience. In smaller towns that boast a courthouse, it is more likely to be a room than a building full of rooms. In cities, the courthouse is likely to be as imposing as official buildings get in that community. In the best of federal courtrooms, the walls are usually of wood or wood paneling, kept polished by civil servants. There is likely to be a barrier between where spectators sit and where the lawyers and their clients sit, usually at two tables; in criminal cases there's one for the prosecution and one for the defense, in civil cases, one for the plaintiff's team and another for the defendant and his counsel. The third part of the courtroom is usually raised. The judge's "bench" is not a bench but a massive podium that, like the black garment the judge wears, is designed to evoke authority and, in some people, fear. The judge, after all, is a man or a woman you couldn't tell apart from the rest of humanity in a crowd. But up on the bench, in his or her black cloak, the judge has powers that to the layman conjure up a primordial authority that can send a person to prison, or in

143

bankruptcy courts can devastate an individual's economic life.

Of course, the judge is to the judged what the parent was to the child: warning, disapproving, admonishing, chiding, blaming, censuring, rebuking, reproving, reprimanding, and punishing. The child, now grown and officially free of parental authority, is suddenly subject to it all over again. Moreover, the judge, unlike the parent, does not compensate for his sternness with cuddling or love; he rarely commends performance and never celebrates birthdays and Christmas with presents. Court is all of the bad and none of the good.

Those who forget *Alice's Adventures in Wonderland* are doomed to relive it. " 'I'll be judge, I'll be jury,' said cunning old Fury: 'I'll try the whole cause, and condemn you to death.' "

There is no person who does not feel a touch of the cold steel of authority on entering an unfamiliar courtroom. It is, according to H. L. Mencken, "a place where Jesus Christ and Judas Iscariot would be equals, with the betting odds in favor of Judas."

Sam Metzger, the CEO of Chipwich who took charge of his case from day one, had been a practicing attorney for many years and knew courtrooms. I was interested to know how he felt when he had to visit the unimposing building at 101 East Post Road in White Plains, where Chipwich's bankruptcy proceedings were held on the second floor.

"I never liked it," he said. "I hated having to go through the metal detector near the entrance. To me it was like taking a lie detector test." What one gets beneath the lines is *I have done nothing wrong—why are they putting me through this.* Metzger said, "When you go in as a debtor, it is synonymous with going in as a defendant. I didn't like to get off the elevator on the bankruptcy floor. The courtroom is designed to be intimidating. It made me uneasy."

If a lawyer experienced in courtrooms can feel this way, what is the layman to feel?

When I first asked Metzger how often he went to court, he replied, "Not that often. I went only to the key hearings." A bit later he said, "I went to court about three-quarters of the time." Not that often? His instinct was to minimize the experience, which is perfectly understandable.

Harvey Barr told an assemblage of a rare exception, a CEO who, in a case that had lasted over five years, had only had to be in court himself about twice. On the day he was to be in court for confirmation of a plan, he dropped dead of a heart attack. It turns out, however, that as of 1989, the case itself was still alive.

Tom Towey of Neptune had a cash collateral hearing in court nearly every week, as he recalls. He said he went to court at least fifty times. For him it was "a home away from home."

Attorney Brian Loftus of Winston & Strawn in Chicago, who until a few years ago conducted his practice in district courts, says that bankruptcy judges "are more result oriented than district judges." To the manager of a business, however, the result-oriented bankruptcy courts, even if managed by efficient judges, seem to churn slowly compared to the world of business. But then lawyers aren't businessmen, and judges, after all, start out as lawyers.

Loftus says, "I've heard that the older bankruptcy judges can be cowboys. They operate loosely. They want to achieve a result, and by God they will." He maintains, as other lawyers do, that there is a wide difference in how judges work their cases and that the quality of the bankruptcy bench has improved in recent years. When one disheartened CEO had this relayed to him, he said, "That's like telling a fellow the food in prison has improved. The Chapter 11 process is expensive, prolonged, riddled with bureaucracy, corruption, false claims, perjury, and a rabble of lawyers looking to milk a case. What good does it do to have a perfect judge up there on the bench if he doesn't or can't do a thing about the abuse of process, or doesn't know what goes on behind his back? What help is it to the owner of a troubled business if he can't get near classy and experienced lawyers like the ones at Winston & Strawn, and has to dig around the bottom of the barrel for the kind he can afford?"

Those not experienced with court calendars should know that in bankruptcy cases, where the judge is likely to see many parties on a single day, all are usually listed for 10 A.M. Your case can be first, or tenth, or fourteenth. The first cases can go quickly, say those of individuals whose cases are being dismissed. But even what may seem like a routine matter may on a moment's notice turn into a full-blown trial right on the spot if there is strong opposition to whatever motion is on deck. And so, as in other courts, the CEO who was used to running a company at full speed has to get used to waiting.

The waiting is always useful to attorneys who are clocking time. They may "work" the hallway, gossiping with their brethren or trying to enlist support for a particular aspect of a case. Sometimes the CEO is called over to participate in these hallway confabs. I noticed one thing: Executives who are used to reading or working while flying in airplanes do not read in the hallways outside bankruptcy courtrooms.

Businessmen have to get used to the idea of adjournments. You rush to get to court on time and find yourself gaping over the shoulders of four or five lawyers at the posted calendar that shows what's on and what's been adjourned. A simple matter like the donation of a defunct company's archives to a university, not opposed seriously by anybody, can go through four adjournments before finally getting its day in court.

Even if you go to court often, it is not something you easily get used to. A snowstorm or flooding rains might make you delay an ordinary business appointment, but if the judge is there you are there.

I remember one day in particular, November 25, 1987. Our chief witness, my wife Patricia Day, was sick with acute bronchitis. The night before her doctor had said she shouldn't be speaking, much less testifying. Knowing that she was our only qualified witness, I worked out a compromise with the doctor: Miss Day would limit her testimony to one hour. I felt like a bastard. How do you compromise someone's health? Miss Day had a bad night. Her coughing kept her awake. If she sat up, she said, she could breathe. If she lay down, she couldn't catch her breath. Sleeping while sitting up isn't easy.

At precisely nine the following morning word came through from Harvey Barr, attorney for the estate. When the case had been adjourned a few days earlier, the judge had written down 2/25 instead of 11/25. His secretary then noted the case for February 25 of the following year! When other lawyers on the case had phoned in the day before, the secretary had told them there was nothing on this case on the calendar for November 25. To top it off, we learned that morning that the hearing would have been adjourned in any event because the wife of the attorney for the Creditors' Committee was sick. Mr. Swergold's wife was not required to appear in court, but it made it inconvenient for her husband, who requested an adjournment. Obviously not all wives are created equal in a bankruptcy case!

More than a month later, on December 30, 1987, Patricia Day, still ill but having gone to work each day, dragged herself out of bed to get to the courtroom by 10 A.M. to meet Harvey Barr for a briefing prior to her appearance as a witness at yet another hearing. She showered and dressed. At 9 A.M. a call came through from Harvey Barr. The hearing was off till 2 P.M., displaced by Texaco, which was the most important bankruptcy case in the country and always took priority.

In time, Patricia Day got used to being the debtor's main witness. She had the financial facts in hand, answered questions succinctly, understood the issues, and couldn't be bullied in cross-examination. Moreover, she had been qualified formally as an expert in publishing, which permitted her to render opinions as well as facts from the stand. She played her role so well, when she finished I sometimes wanted to rush up to the witness box and put a bouquet in her hands, as one would honor any star's performance.

One does not applaud a witness.

One of the penalties of having to testify is that you have to hang around for the other parts of the same proceedings and listen. Patricia Day said she did not find the experience of being on the stand even for a long time as tiring "as listening to people lying in court all day." Late on November 28, 1988, she turned to me and said, "I find it exhausting to listen to people slandering you."

For a moment I was startled by her comment. I had gotten so used to hearing lies in the courtroom that I was watching it happen as if it concerned other people.

It was a game. When a witness tried to make mountains out of trivialities, or lied too much or too obviously, the judge allowed questions in cross-examination that "went to the credibility of the witness." But the lies continued, and if the judge didn't have the facts to counter them and the opposing attorneys lacked the skill or opportunity to bring them out, the distortions lay on the record like sausage meat that had gone bad that no one knew what to do with.

In the Stein and Day case, there was undoubtedly some benefit from having the case overseen by an intelligent judge. However, there were frustrations. I am a writer, and this judge couldn't always read all the papers.[1] When on December 29, 1988, the attorneys for Stein and Day moved to resign from the case because there wasn't enough money in it for them, I wrote papers in opposition saying that all I wanted was for the attorneys to do what

---

1. To be fair, Judge Schwartzberg, on information and belief, has read several of my novels on the law, and has indeed said so on occasion. It is my brief or briefs that at times apparently went unread before decisions were rendered.

they were supposed to do (which would also bring in money for them). My papers duly filed and unread, Judge Schwartzberg in court assumed that I *supported* counsel's departure rather than opposed it, and granted the attorney's motion.

My second frustration came from hearing Stein and Day's wealthy opponents make their affirmative case and then being denied an opportunity to have our response heard. Several times the strategy of our opponents was to present their case replete with misinformation and then force "settlement discussions" that always turned out badly for our side. Had we had the attorney of our choice, he would never have permitted these half-hearings to go unanswered and would have bypassed entirely the "unconscionable and obscene" negotiations outside of court. The judge would have heard both sides.

From a moral perspective, the Chapter 11 experience can restore one's faith in juries. The response of juries is sometimes quite simplistic. They know who the good guys are and who the bad guys are, and they try to follow the judge's instructions about the law. In the end, they rely on what their eyes and ears tell them and not on a particular section of a code. There are usually no juries in the bankruptcy court. And a quarter of a century of work can be wiped out because a calendar needs clearing.

CHAPTER 11

Freedom from the Press, or Please Leave the First Amendment at the Door

> "I, of course, accept responsibility for any errors or omissions."
>
> —Ellis Close, *The Press*

MOST chief executives don't spend much time thinking about the press. Large companies have public relations departments. Most small companies don't imagine themselves as newsworthy unless they are in an industry with high public visibility such as entertainment or publishing. But any company that files for Chapter 11 protection is going to make news *just by filing,* and this requires the CEO to give some thought ahead of time to the matter of handling the press; for whatever that first story says can have a decided influence on suppliers, customers, and even on the outcome of the case.

The food industry is not normally thought to have a high public profile. Chipwich is an exception. Sam Metzger keeps an album that contains hundreds of press stories about Chipwich and its industry. The marketing of a chocolate-chip ice-cream sandwich in 1981 drew a lot of attention then and in the years to come. Metzger says, "It's a mistake not to talk to them [reporters]." Yet he adds, "I'm very careful in talking to them. And I do so with some reluctance. The press tends to concentrate on negative stories. Those seem to please readers. It makes them feel good to read about other people's troubles."

Most executives have little contact with the press until something hits the fan. It's too late to learn the basics then.

A reporter, for starters, is in a hurry. Unless he's on a long-term feature assignment, he's trying to talk to a lot of people in the course of a very few hours in order to put together a story. If the facts in that story end up being 50 percent accurate, he's doing better than average.[1] It's up to the interviewee to do what he can to have his most important points register with accuracy. Even then, most of what he says is at risk.

Reporters use whatever material may be in their morgue files. Because it's in the file and they're in a hurry, they have to work on the assumption that what's in the file is accurate, especially if it's a clip from their own paper. Here's one startling example of what can happen in coverage of a Chapter 11 case.

As previously noted, when Stein and Day first filed for protection on June 25, 1987, the lawyer who prepared the papers for filing did not state the current market value of the company's real estate or include the value of its exclusive publishing rights to some twelve hundred copyrights.

I know how those mistakes were made. It is usual for

---

1. For better or worse, the author of this book has had over forty years of exposure to and involvement with the press. Back in the early 1950s, he was an officer in the U.S. State Department at the time that Senator Joe McCarthy was ripping into the Voice of America. That was front-page news almost daily for a period of time. The reporter covering the story for America's best-known newspaper, *The New York Times*, happened to be a former employee of the Voice of America, who knew the people and the background better than most reporters are likely to know their subject matter. Yet what we on the inside saw in that paper every day on this particular story was often only half accurate as to objectively verifiable facts. The reporter was doing the best he could on a fast-moving story. The standards of the *Times* are, of course, higher than many other papers, which means as one goes down the scale, one is likely to encounter even less accuracy.

public accounting firms (ours had been Price Waterhouse and Grant Thornton) to omit equity in real estate from assets listed on the balance sheet. And it is common practice in accounting in the publishing industry to carry the publisher's exclusive rights to the authors' copyrights at zero, though they may indeed be the biggest asset. The reader will remember that in reviewing the papers before filing, I pointed out these omissions to the attorney. The inclusion of these substantial items would have shown that the company's assets far exceeded its liabilities. The attorney, the reader will recall, shrugged the errors off as not important and failed to make the correction. Of course the wrong figures appeared in the press stories, including in one of America's most respected newspapers, the *Wall Street Journal.*

In a follow-up story more than a year later, those incorrect figures were still appearing in the *Wall Street Journal.* The reporter presumably got those figures out of the *Journal*'s own files. They had to be correct, right? Wrong. I'd wager that in the morgue files on every company that has ever been written about there are a lot of factual errors lying in wait for a new news story to break.

Many businessmen and lawyers view the press as hostile, partly because they misunderstand the reporter's purpose, which is not to print *your* story, but to include what you've had to say that's newsworthy in a story that will usually include comments from your opponents. If the opponent lies, and the reporter doesn't get back to you for verification or clarification, the lies will stick. That's a danger in any press interview.

In addition, businessmen and lawyers view the press as belligerent because of the way questions are sometimes posed even by less experienced reporters. (A good trial attorney should be used to combative questions.) Back in the 1950s, one well-known entertainment reporter for *The New York Times* used to call me once in a while with questions like, "Stein, I have information here that you were

seen fornicating with a giraffe in Central Park yesterday
evening. Is that true? If it isn't, what were you doing in
Central Park yesterday evening?"

That left me with several options. I could say "No comment." That could lead, in theory at least, to a story that
said, "Stein refuses comment on Central Park episode with
giraffe."

Most reporters will honor an off-the-record statement.
But you have to say it's off the record *before* you make the
statement. And if everything you say is off the record, it's
not a story.

Americans grow up believing that "the court of public
opinion" is an essential of democracy, protected by precedent and the First Amendment. A minority of lawyers
have learned how to take advantage of the press's appetite
for courtroom news and case scandal. For instance, one
lawyer involved in the Stein and Day case kept seeing to it
that the press was fed wildly inaccurate information.
Reporters, perhaps naively assuming a lawyer wouldn't
lie, didn't check the statements before they saw print.

However, most lawyers are gun-shy when it comes to
the press. "Many lawyers view journalists with a mixture
of fear and loathing, resentment and anxiety."[2] It is not
their turf, and *they can't control it*. Of course the very
strength of the press comes from the fact that it cannot be
readily controlled by those who make the news, and to get
anywhere with the press it often takes an appreciation of
the fine points of dealing with reporters. Most lawyers
won't hazard dealing with the press, and some won't even
take phone calls from reporters.

Moreover, if an executive's company is in Chapter 11,
he'll usually want to have any press releases initiated by
the company reviewed by attorneys, and there's the hitch.
The chances are that even the most experienced writer of

---

2. *The New York Times*, "At the Bar" by David Margolick, February
24, 1989, page B5.

press releases will find his work truncated, expurgated, bowdlerized, and sanitized by lawyers, and then not used by the papers. If a company in Chapter 11 has good news—we had some terrific news from time to time—a press release can help, particularly if a company is trying to work its way out of Chapter 11. But if what the lawyers leave you with sounds tame and watered-down, ask yourself, if you were a reporter, what would you do with it? If the answer is toss it into the wastebasket, don't waste any resources having it distributed. All a reporter is interested in is *news*.

Turnaround specialist Dan Morris is relaxed about the press. He says it "can be a wonderful tool or a killer. It's a vehicle of communication. If you can manage the media well, okay. Otherwise, avoid them." He adds, "A lot depends on the reputation of the reporter."

Morris's colleagues in the turnaround business are less laid back about the press. Ron Stengel takes the view that a smaller company has no reason to talk to the press while a larger company sometimes has to if only to get some good news out. Stengel believes, as do most of his colleagues, that news stories can influence a case, and sometimes he has to resort to "damage control." The "generic" newspaper reporter, he says, is usually "outrageously wrong in the interpretation of crisis situations."

Gilbert Osnos advises his clients to avoid reporters "like the plague. They're only interested in headlines. I don't talk to them." The only exception he cites is that of a consumer product company that didn't want people to stop buying the product because the press was reporting bad news about the company's finances. In that case, Osnos advised the use of a public relations firm to deal with the problem.

Ken Glass doesn't want his clients talking to the press, and he won't. Their stories, he says, can influence a case and are "rarely accurate." David Ferrari of Massachusetts is forthright. "Nothing you say will come out right. Avoid them." Though he tries not to talk to the press, he sometimes has to deal with them "to straighten out wrong facts." What he says to the press is "prewritten." He doesn't take chances.

Adam Radzik's response was a bit of a surprise because he himself was for a year and a half a part of the press. A column of advice by him appeared in a major, large-circulation New York City newspaper. Yet he advises his clients to avoid the press, and he avoids the press also. "A reporter," he says, "is interested in copy that will sell, and he will rephrase what you say to make a more interesting story."

Chicago bankruptcy attorney Gerald Munitz says that "there are some real crackerjacks in the press, but reporters have to dramatize things to sell newspapers, and they get the information wrong. I'll talk to the press only if it's unavoidable."

Joshua Angel says, "For the most part the press is useful at the beginning of the case (for a soft landing: 'We are confident, etc.') and at the end of the case ('We are pleased, etc.'). When it comes to the period in between, don't bother seeking out the press since you can't win your case in the newspapers and more likely than not will annoy someone by virtue of your having been misquoted. But if your company is a hot deal item and you're going to be in the newspapers no matter what, ducking a reporter is worse than answering his questions in an attempt to put your best foot forward. However, you should *never, never* try to beat your adversary with a press knock. It can only haunt you later."

The overwhelming majority of people trying to help companies felt they should avoid the press because the press hurts more often than it helps. If the choice is between truth and sensation, more often than not accuracy goes by the board.

According to *The New York Times*,[3] the tide is turning. Lawyers are being advised to "say something." A pamph-

---

3. "At the Bar," David Margolick, February 24, 1989, p. B5.

let issued by the American Bar Association[4] says that the most diplomatic way to duck is to be dull and say things like, "The story will come out in court." In other advisories, lawyers are told to expect tough questions, pause before answering, and speak English rather than lawyerese. One such[5] points out correctly that a colorful or memorable phrase is likely to be picked up, given the unimaginative language of most spokespersons. The author also suggests two tacks I disagree with. He says you should never ask a reporter to read back a quote. I think it's perfectly legitimate, given that error is endemic, to ask for important direct quotes to be played back. The author suggests taping conversations with reporters and letting the reporter know you're doing so. I believe most reporters would resent that more than being asked to repeat a quote, and, if they get a chance, their resentment will show in print.

When a widget manufacturer files under Chapter 11, it will probably get a mention in the local papers, and that's it. But some companies are highly visible because of their size (Texaco), because their filing disrupts the lives of many people (Eastern Airlines), because its CEO is a colorful operator in the business world (again Eastern Airlines), because of scandal (IUD or asbestos manufacturers with class-action suits against them), or because of the nature of their product. The last category would involve such diverse firms as Coleco (because of the onetime popularity of the Cabbage Patch dolls that were the company's undoing) and my own firm, Stein and Day, because literally tens of millions of people have read our books over the years and many millions more have heard our well-known authors interviewed on television. Book publishing is second only to movies and television in its public visibility.

---

4. "Lois Lane Is On Hold," by Constance Belfiore and Frank Trotta.
5. *NO COMMENT! An Executive's Essential Guide to the News Media* by Donald Blohowiak.

By the nature of his business, a publisher of well-publicized books would usually have a fair amount of contact with the press during the course of a working year. This would be especially true of a company that published many big-name authors, as Stein and Day did (see Appendix C). Such authors' new books were usually heralded with national television appearances and a press tour. In addition, Stein and Day also published books that made news. In one instance, a worldwide scoop, *The Bolivian Diaries of Ché Guevara*, made a four-column headline on the front page of *The New York Times*. The company released the first biography of Gorbachev, by *Times* editor Thom Butson, two days before Gorbachev's predecessor Chernenko died. With that kind of publishing you can't hide from the press. Next to Texaco, our case was getting more coverage than any other emanating from the White Plains courthouse.

After the press had shown itself, by and large, to be favorably disposed toward Stein and Day's predicament, the attorney for the company expressly forbade any press contact not approved by him in advance. If I refused to comply, he threatened to immediately resign from the case. This ballooned into a major source of friction. In one instance in the late summer of 1988, I wrote with sadness a press release announcing that our publishing company would never publish another book again because of restrictions imposed by two creditors to everyone else's detriment, and we were therefore ready to sell our exclusive rights in some twelve hundred copyrights. This proposed release, after being sanitized by the lawyers, sounded like an ad for our copyrights instead of like news. I was embarrassed to issue it in its bowdlerized form. But the *Wall Street Journal* and other newspapers and magazines had reporters who followed up the "nothing" story with phone calls and questions, and the truth got out: The company wasn't committing suicide. It had been murdered.

What did the lawyers expect me to say when a reporter called—"I am not allowed to talk to you"? If you avoid the press, *the story will deal with whatever's in the public record* (briefs and affidavits filed, decisions). And in most Chapter 11 cases, every time there's an important motion, papers are filed opposing that motion. What can be said in court papers is sometimes a lot worse than the laws of libel would permit a paper to print *unless it comes out of the court record.* You can't win by ducking the press. You can make headway by working with the reporters, with caution of course.

The press can be indispensable to a cornered debtor because it is one forum that it is illegal to shut up. But as I've indicated, most businessmen know even less than most lawyers about dealing with the press. When it comes to bankruptcy cases, no public relations spokesperson, inside or outside, is going to risk saying anything to the press that hasn't been approved by senior executives or by the firm's counsel.

What can CEOs in smaller firms do? The answer is quite a lot, including having a release prepared before filing that has something of an upbeat tone: The bad news is that the company is filing. The good news is that the company has a plan and is going to be okay. If the company was forced into Chapter 11, a prepared release can say why.

For the CEO a well-prepared press release at the onset of a case can serve his company as much as well-prepared court testimony. But keep in mind that every reporter, like lawyers in court, can cross-examine. Will whoever doesn't have a skeleton or two in his closet please stand up?

CHAPTER 12

The Culture of Chapter 11

> "You went to law school to find out how to avoid paying too much attention to the rules other people live by."
>
> —*The Childkeeper*, Harcourt Brace Jovanovich, 1975

D O you eat with your fingers when a knife and fork are available? If you go into Chapter 11 you will meet people who do. And that's the least of it.

When you enter that world, you are thrown together for long periods of time with people who by instinct or method rape intelligence, because they seem not to know how else to deal with it. You feel as if you have somehow been trapped in the Black Hole of Calcutta with the great unread. Or with lawyers like the one from a distinguished and well-known firm who sneezes into his palm just before shaking hands.

How you take the culture of Chapter 11 depends to some degree not only on the life you've led but on the nature of your business. Even day-to-day publishing usually involves you with authors and other reasonably intelligent people who have a command of their native language. It takes a while to get used to lawyers who persist in ending their letters, "I await your advices."

What is alarming about subliteracy among professionals is the quality of the mind it betrays.[1] William Zinsser,

---

1. "Lawyers are taught early on that a document does more than rec-

who has published more books about writing than anyone
else I can think of, says, "Anyone who thinks clearly
should be able to write clearly—about any subject at all."
Though some of the writing of lawyers is a mark of
subliteracy, much of it is purposeful obfuscation. If writing that is precise helps to clarify, jargon-loaded legal gob-
bledygook muddies not only the text but eventually the
mind of the perpetrator.

If courtesy is a mark of civility, what is discourtesy a
mark of? You are invited to a morning meeting in a conference room at Weil, Gotshal & Manges, which has more
bankruptcy lawyers than any other law firm in America.
This conference, like most of them, seems endless. Nothing is being accomplished except the running of the lawyers' time clocks. Lunchtime comes and goes. If you were
a prisoner, the institution would provide something. Here
the institution provides nothing. There even seems to be
difficulty in keeping the water pitcher replenished. The
meeting drags well into the afternoon. You are losing your
faculties to boredom. You wonder how the lawyers do it.
Can it be a pact with the devil that requires the waste of
their lives?

In the Vietnam War it was commonplace to use the
euphemism "wasting" in lieu of killing. Perhaps "waste"
is more descriptive of unnecessary death. In Chapter 11
there is much "wasting" of a kind that can gradually erode
the soul. I have spoken of the bureaucracy, the endless
make-work, the contrived humiliation, and such attractive practices as keeping everyone wondering whether
they will or won't be paid when payday comes and keeping people purposely in the dark as a means of controlling
them. You can't help but wonder how the lawyers take it.

---

ord facts; it also reflects the quality of the mind of the person who
wrote it. This goes for *any* sort of writing, and I believe it is the real reason why so many people find writing so terrifying." Mark McCormack,
lawyer and businessman, in *The Terrible Truth About Lawyers*, New
York, Beech Tree Books/William Morrow, 1987, p. 258.

If intellectual excitement or physical exercise connote life, what can boredom and lethargy connote? Can all those billing hours be worth it? One of the ethical bankruptcy lawyers I talked to said he could no longer stand the boredom of the business.

You learn how to flee to your friends. And you find out that some people you thought you knew well suddenly treat you as if you had developed cancer and that cancer was contagious. Of course Chapter 11 is an embarrassment. It should be an even greater embarrassment to some of those who live the life as professionals. If you ever have a friend or business colleague trapped in Chapter 11, my advice would be to act as if your friend had lost a child. Express your sympathy and get on with the relationship the same as it was before. Normalcy is rehabilitating.

Bullying is not normal among civil adults. It is accepted as part of an adolescent marine's training at Parris Island. It is commonplace among street gangs in Los Angeles, New York, and cities in between where turf is the issue. In the conduct of Chapter 11, bullying of the debtor is commonplace.

Also common is the lawyers' tactic of limiting information to the debtor. As one senior manager put it, "They never tell you enough to be able to act sensibly." Why? "To keep you dependent, as you would a child." The real purpose: running the clock.

The chief executive is warned of the humiliations to come. Small things. The chair you sit on every day breaks irreparably and you are not permitted to replace it. After all, you are going to have to sell your furniture in due course, and they're not going to let you buy any in the meantime. So what if there isn't a replacement chair about. You can sit in a substitute chair intended for someone much shorter. So what if your back hurts as a result. You're a debtor, aren't you?

As the insensitivity of the Chapter 11 atmosphere reaches down the hierarchy, the lawyers' game-playing has different results. A valued mailroom employee didn't understand that *everyone's* paycheck was delayed because the lawyers were pretending to squabble over a cash collateral order. In rage and dismay, he left the premises without notice. Someone went down to the mailroom and found a part of the company's one high-speed copying machine with torn wires sticking out of it. The company that had leased the copying machine sent a man to look at the damage. He examined the part and said it had to have been torn out. I have kept that piece of torn-out machinery as a reminder of the violence with which an innocent employee can react to the games lawyers play with human beings who never knowingly hurt them or their clients.

The headquarters of Stein and Day sat amidst eleven acres of trees and grass, a beautiful place in its prime. One meadow alone is five acres of grass. The caretaker's wife had learned to ride a big lawn mower. In season, when she finished mowing it was pretty near time to start again. In the Chapter 11 environment, we found out how high grass can grow when you are operating under a cash collateral order that doesn't allow for the repair of a lawn mower. That grass was never mowed again.

You find out that a debtor company can buy supplies dangerously—on your credit card, unless that gets taken away. I was lucky. I lost only the American Express card on which the company, out of necessity, charged such things as transportation. I've talked to CEOs who lost all their personal credit cards. When the rude American Express representative summons your card to be sent to him forthwith in pieces, you take the humiliation in stride because in the culture of Chapter 11, that's something you're supposed to get used to, though you have seldom been late in paying your personal bills. And after it is all over, your personal credit will carry a scarlet number, a permanent taint; as one young Citibank employee told me, "You were an officer in a company that filed for Chapter 11. How do we know it's not a trend?"

Some little things grate. You run out of paper towels in

the bathrooms. You try ordering some from your previous supplier. In the meantime, you have visitors. Someone runs out to pick up a roll of paper towels at the local supermarket—not something you do for yourself anymore, just for visitors. That doesn't help. Eventually, most of the toilets are inoperative. You lower yourself to the circumstances dictated by those who want to get the message through that all the employees of a debtor company deserve degradation. As one of the senior members of the bankruptcy bar put it to me, "Why do you suffer these humiliations? Not because suffering will make you a better person, but because you love your business and you cannot bear to see it die."

There are the little betrayals of civil life. Many companies play music when they've got you on hold. If you find the practice annoying or don't like their choice of music, you ask to be called back. But in Chapter 11, there may be several instances a day when a company executive urgently needs information from the estate's lawyers. And if they have the practice of not calling back, not today, not tomorrow, not this week sometimes, you are forced to learn to listen to their music, tying up the line until someone eventually will answer you.

I have spent hours listening to the kind of music I would never give a moment to, holding the instrument away from my one good ear, but not far enough away so that I won't hear this or that lawyer finally get on the phone. You will learn that different bankruptcy lawyers have vastly different music in the hold position. The law firm that represented the unsecured creditors is alleged to have once had good classical music; it still plays the most tolerable of the forced tunes. Stein and Day's Rockland County attorneys have a gift for keeping desperately busy CEOs on hold for long periods. Is it just to reinforce the involuntary nature of their lives? They force you to listen to a radio station that specializes in the kind of soft kitsch that most people of my acquaintance would find intolerable: bad songs badly played. Or you get to listen to long radio advertisements for local companies. You get—as I once got when I called on some urgent matter—a local talk show host's advice on the AIDS epidemic.

I once dared to comment about this enforced listening and was told that if they didn't play something, people on hold for a long time wouldn't know whether or not they'd been disconnected. Well, if you're old enough to use a phone correctly, you know that when you get disconnected you get a dial tone.

Stein and Day, the reader will learn in a later chapter, was once represented by a fair number of distinguished lawyers. None of them had music or talk shows on their phones. In fact, what they did if they were busy was to call you back as soon as they were free to do so. Then again, when you're in Chapter 11, your whole life is on hold.

Harvey Barr, as I've said, rarely called back. And if you were in desperate need of advice on an urgent matter and you finally asked to speak to one of the other lawyers in the firm, they told you, "Only Harvey can answer that." It was toward the end of the case that I learned how to get him on the phone. I would write a letter to the judge about the matter. I would inform Harvey Barr's office that I was about to send off the letter to the judge. That brought a callback.

Of course there are worthier aspects of the Chapter 11 culture to consider. For instance, you will learn to keep your lips together when you hear professional advice that is followed by "If you say I told you, I'll deny it."

Of all the lawyers in the case, the most adept on his feet in the courtroom was Martin Bienenstock of Weil Gotshal, whose appearances for BookCrafters were infrequent. I have always had a soft spot for talent, and I had to catch myself before I let my admiration for his courtroom skill let me lose sight of two facts: First, he was at his best in defending an action brought by the company's warehouse which for many months had refused to ship; Bienenstock's own client, BookCrafters, had done the same thing, held books hostage and refused to ship them to fill orders that were dying on the vine. Second was the fact that Bienenstock was said by the other lawyers to have had a particular animus toward one of the warehouse's lawyers, Helen Davis Chaitman, because she had dared to subpoena the lawyers and their records. Give a debtor a tough time, that's the name of the game, but including a creditor's attorney in the sport was beyond the pale.[2]

Some of the CEOs of Chapter 11 companies I talked to were warned by their bankruptcy lawyers before filing, as I was, that their lives were going to be studded with misery once they were in the trap. The big surprise for me was when I learned that the attorney for the estate, supposedly "your" lawyer, can make you as miserable as any of his opponents—which may be why he feels obliged to warn you.

If you are the chief executive of a debtor company, you have to be prepared for the humiliation that will be visited upon you. When the time came, the advance warning didn't help. But then one day in the courtroom, a primal instinct in me reared its head. Just as in very rare circumstances a prisoner will pick up his shovel and bash in the head of his guard, the same kind of rudimentary anger fired a reaction in me. In court we didn't have shovels, we had words. Greg Borri, a lawyer in his thirties and counsel for the Michigan National Bank,[3] our number one credi-

---

2. Even our excellent judge was said to view unkindly any seeming attack on lawyering, though he himself clearly got fed up with the conduct of the lawyers from time to time and reproved them. Once, on October 7, 1988, Judge Schwartzberg got so fed up with the behavior of the lawyers, who were arguing about their fees, that he said, "I'll give the debtor anything he wants," and awarded the company $147,500 in cash collateral for two months of operation without any of the many conditions that were normally set forth in such orders.

3. The bank, which wouldn't let us hire our lawyer of choice, itself chose the Philadelphia firm of Drinker, Biddle and Reath. The partner they thought they hired in the firm's New York office was Portis Hicks.

tor, had caused us a great deal of grief over many months. The proceedings, which were not always complex, sometimes seemed to float over Mr. Borri's head. In the early months he often put on a stern voice and an insulting manner as a substitute for what was needed. And so one day, when I found myself being addressed once again by him in a derogatory fashion, I couldn't keep myself from saying, "Mr. Borri, when you've been in *Who's Who* for thirty years you can talk to me that way and not until then." Borri seemed taken aback. He apologized. And before the event was over, he apologized a second time, and did his best to behave in a civilized manner thereafter.

It was only much later, when I interviewed the CEO of Chipwich, that I saw clearly that I had stumbled upon the way to deal with the insolence that seems normal in Chapter 11. Stop it in its tracks. Metzger said he positioned himself from the beginning as the man in charge.[4]

How you react to some of the expressions of the culture of Chapter 11 depends on how you've spent your life. As a publisher and editor, I've had associations, sometimes close, with prominent authors and figures in public life.[5]

But that man was present only at an early conference prior to filing, he never appeared in court, and once, when other attorneys tried to contact him to get a senior opinion on an urgent matter, he told them that he had had very little contact with the case and only Borri would know the answer. This practice is now endemic in American law. You hire a lawyer and what you get is the service of other lawyers, usually of lesser rank and experience.

4. Let us not overlook the differences in how people react to the same circumstances. As you may recall, Metzger's partner's reaction to Chapter 11 was to become ill enough for prolonged absence.

5. Among the writers I had worked with were James Baldwin, Bertram Wolfe, John Crosby, Budd Schulberg, Claude Browne, and John Simon (The Bad). Even before there was a Stein and Day, I had edited the prose of W. H. Auden, Jacques Barzun, and Lionel Trilling, and had consorted with intellectuals in as broad a range as can be typified by William Phillips, a founding editor of *Partisan Review*, and William F. Buckley, Jr., founding editor of *National Review*. My work kept me involved with such critics of our society and literature as Diana Trilling,

In Chapter 11, the measure of celebrity is somewhat different. When Jim Bouton, a onetime baseball player, was called on to testify by BookCrafters, we heard that the judge had gone to the public library to borrow Bouton's books. At one hearing, I heard the judge playfully tell a young attorney named Sandra Reimer that she had just sat down in a chair that was still warm from the chairman of Texaco. Maybe, I thought, they'll ask for footprints of Chapter 11 victims like those in front of Grauman's Chinese Theater in Hollywood. Too bad someone didn't have some liquid concrete around when Thomas Jefferson stepped into the dust and filed.

Leslie Fiedler, Sidney Hook, and Robert Gorham Davis. And once, with J. Robert Oppenheimer and Albert Einstein, I conspired with the former to prove the latter wrong. I published a prime minister and a foreign minister, and had a dinner given in my honor in Parliament. I published a shah, a leader of an Arab army, an influential Israeli ambassador, and David Frost when he was characterized as the king of multinational television. Associating with the cabal of lawyers in Chapter 11 was, needless to say, quite a comedown.

CHAPTER 13

Claims: The Meek Shall Inherit Nothing

"Nobody lives by the law. They live by human nature. That's why lawyers make a living, see."
—George Thomassy in *The Childkeeper*

IF justice were just, a businessman in trouble could count on the system to bring out the facts and to introduce equity into a troubled situation.

One could respond that if justice were just, we would not have had some of the great plays of Sophocles and Shakespeare. Oedipus gouges out his eyes so as not to see what the world is like. Lear's greatest torment is not that he is wronged but that he wronged himself. As we have seen, the executive, distressed by the inability of his business to meet its obligations, at first will feel himself bobbing on an ocean of trouble, hoping for a beach or a raft. What he gets in Chapter 11 is a lot of lawyers and creditors shouting recriminations from the shore. All agree it feels like hell until the CEO's mind-set changes. Nobody is going to rescue him. If he's to get any help, it will be from one of the small band of experienced and honorable bankruptcy attorneys swimming at his side, pointing the way, encouraging him with hope and instructions. Sometimes it seems as if the shore is getting farther away rather than nearer. There is a big temptation to let yourself drown. According to the CEOs I talked to, the only way to truly counter the feeling of despair is to gird yourself for the long swim back with all the wit, brains, expe-

rience, acumen, insight, lucidity, esprit, sagacity, shrewd-
ness, skill, expertise, adroitness, craftiness, prowess, street
savvy, talent, brass, guts, thick-skinned endurance, and
energy at your command, concentrating on getting to
shore despite the chorus of voices that would just as soon
see you drown.

The advice one gets from those who have lived though
the experience is that the passive ones drown. Or they get
sick, psychosomatically sick. They will get eaten by the
sharks. The survivors are sometimes encouraged for the
long haul by the sweet thoughts of revenge, of getting
even with the taunting creditors by exposing false and
inflated claims. That thought sustained some of the executives I talked to.

It takes great strength, and a clear view of what is happening. The debtor will find himself in an environment in
which he sees and hears all kinds of illegal conduct by others. He will have to stave off the temptation to do as others
do, especially if "the others" are lawyers. There is a double
standard in the bankruptcy courtroom. One is brought up
to believe that the judge's role is solely to interpret the law
and to see that fairness prevails. But it pays to keep in
mind that the judges are also lawyers. They tend to be
more tolerant of the shenanigans of their fellows at the
bar, if for no other reason than that they've got to deal
with the same characters in case after case. If you held
each lawyer up to the canons every time he stepped across
the line, a pall would settle over everyday life. That isn't
an environment judges want to live in. If you're a judge in
a court where you see the same lawyers time and again on
different cases, you can rationalize that these lawyers,
who are supposed to be officers of the court, are ordinary
human beings with all the flaws and virtues that description may entail. Everybody can't be smart. Everybody
can't be perfect. So bad conduct on the part of members of
the bar gets excused, but if you're a businessman, you start
out by being the new man on the block, the bankrupt, the
presumed villain, guilty until the facts come out. You'd be

wise to behave better than the lawyers, to keep a surface cool even if you are very angry. Take it all in. And wait your turn.

That might not come till late in the case, when the creditors have all gotten tired of staring at the debtor with hatred, and when you've got the job of going through their filed claims[1] to see who's trying to pull the leg of the law. In some cases it can become a time for sweet revenge.

Laymen tend to think that if people are owed money, what they want to collect is what is owed to them. Wrong. In many instances, the intent is to collect as much as they can get away with. It is, of course, the CEO and his staff who can best pinpoint the false and inflated claims.

When a company files, David Ferrari says, "The creditors put in for everything but the kitchen sink, claims they'd never put in with a going concern." Ken Glass agrees that creditors try to cheat on claims. He investigates "every claim. And if they're improper, I try to defeat them." When asked about claim-cheating, Dan Morris replies in one word: "Absolutely." Ron Stengel echoes, "Absolutely." Gil Osnos also finds some creditors trying to

---

1. When a case is first filed, all of the creditors are presumably notified. It is then incumbent upon each creditor to file a claim with the court. For a secured creditor with a large claim, that usually means "putting on a case" in the courtroom where, for instance, the debtor and other creditors could challenge the amount of the claim. The average unsecured creditor usually fills out a relatively simple one-page, two-sided form and sends it to the court in duplicate, asking that one copy be marked as received and returned in an accompanying self-addressed, stamped envelope. It's the only proof the creditor has that the claim has been filed on time. All claims have to be filed before a "bar date," after which no claims can be made. Creditors are supposed to be advised of the bar date. The creditor also has the choice of not filing a claim, taking the loss against his taxes, and chalking the event up to experience. In the case of small claims, the expense of having a lawyer fill out a claim form if it's not something a creditor can do himself (most can) may exceed not necessarily the amount of the claim, but the (small) percentage that he'll get, depending upon what's left in the pot after the secured creditors and the lawyers and accountants get theirs.

exaggerate claims. Some are "honest mistakes," others aren't. Radzik says, "Sure they try to inflate their claims. The debtor is down, they take advantage. Inappropriate charges are a common occurrence." Ron Stengel tells about a large case in which the total claims were something like $12.5 billion; after they were analyzed and contested, those claims were settled for approximately $800 million. Stengel says the biggest offender is sometimes the IRS, which may file duplicate and triplicate claims, or will file the same claim against all subsidiaries. He had one case where the IRS claims were "twenty-six or twenty-seven times what they should have been." To avoid both the larcenies and the bureaucratic "errors," what is needed, according to Stengel, is "active management of the claims examination process."

That struck an ironic note. At the very time that Stengel was telling me this, I was being badgered into signing a global stipulation that attested to the claims of two secured creditors. One of them was a bank that for twenty-one months had not submitted a single monthly statement of account, so that neither I nor anyone else could judge whether its claim was correct. The other was BookCrafters, a trade creditor that had been owed about $1 million prepetition, had been paid $238,000 on account, and was now claiming $1.7 million without submitting evidence to support the huge difference. "Sign it," I was told by my own attorneys, "or you will suffer a lot of pain and a lot of expense you can't afford."[2]

When I asked Chipwich's Sam Metzger if he came across any irrational claimants (I carefully avoided saying "phony"), he said he had, but he made it his business to know every claim personally. That may be true of the majority of CEOs who know their businesses well, but the

---

2. Naively, I even contested this wildly inflated claim in federal court, alleging that the security agreement was obtained by fraud. That case was blown away by the global stipulation exacted by means described in Chapter 16, "The St. Valentine's Day Massacre, 1989."

ones who get beaten down, who don't see their company's having a chance of coming out, or who are replaced by trustees, throw their special knowledge of claims to the wind.

There are also people, creditors or not, who try to buy—yes, buy—someone else's lien position. If a creditor does this, his goal is to move up in the line or to take control of the assets. As part of the deal, he can try to have his own inflated claim acknowledged before it can be investigated.

Tom Towey of Neptune is a guy it's very easy to like right away. To a stranger or a new acquaintance, he seems a gentle man. It's after a bit that you see the steel. He was determined to get the best deal he could for the creditors, but on one ineradicable condition: Neptune had to survive. It's a little like being chained to a spot a couple of miles from ground zero when everything erupts, and nevertheless, when the dust settles, you're still ready to do battle.

"Everything in Chapter 11 is a problem," Towey says. "The reward comes in catching the other guy doing the wrong thing."

According to Towey, one of the pleasures he found amidst the pain was the detective work in ferreting out duplicate claims. Towey found over one hundred. "Someone will have two five-thousand-dollar claims and one ten-thousand-dollar claim under a possibly different name and you don't immediately see that it's all one claim."

Every time he caught one, Towey had them expunged in court. He credits finding some of the duplicates to having the claims on computer—a word to the wise.

Towey didn't rest there. He loved battling with the taxing authorities and getting money back from them. He enjoyed the tough negotiations with the Teamsters Union. Some claimed that Neptune's union pension funds were inadequate. Towey's tack was to negotiate these claims down to an agreed liability. He got enough highs from winning battles that, once out of Chapter 11, he found ordinary business a "let-down."

A couple of months after he told me this, I ran into Tom Towey and his general counsel in White Plains Court. They had to hang around for hours while we were battling a creditor's motion to terminate the automatic stay. What I couldn't get out of my head was they had *finished* their Chapter 11 case in April and this was December 28, so what the hell were they doing in bankruptcy court? They were objecting to exaggerated claims by creditors. Is it ever over even when they say it's over?

CHAPTER 14

What's a Nice Fellow Like You Doing in a Place Like This?

"War, pestilence, traffic cut lives short, but should books, like people, be subject to premature death?"
—Sol Stein, in the Foreword to *Three Who Made Revolution* by Bertram D. Wolfe, Stein and Day, 1984

I F this book is, as it has sometimes been called, a cautionary tale, it is also a murder mystery, a whodunit. In this and the two chapters that follow, the reader will come to know how a living body of authors was entombed in Chapter 11 until it died, and who the perpetrators are. For people in other businesses who have no special interest in authors or publishing, the generally applicable theme can be stated simply. When you lose control over essentials in a business enterprise, the enterprise is usually luckless. In Stein and Day's case, when others took over the distribution of its books,[1] business skidded downhill fast. The ultimate loss of control was in Chapter 11.

In July of 1973, Stein and Day moved its publishing headquarters from mid-Manhattan to Scarborough House, a mansion in Westchester said to be haunted by the ghost

---

1. W. W. Norton in 1975-6, Kable News in 1984-5, and Henry Holt in 1987. Stein and Day was continuously profitable for a decade when it distributed its own books.

of Admiral James L. Worden, who was born there and went on to command the *Monitor* when it beat the *Merrimack* in the first battle of ironclads in the Civil War.

The move received a lot of publicity in both the trade and public press, with photos angled up at the three-story-high white columns in front and the seventy-foot-wide triangular window on the third floor that provided a view across the expanse of the Hudson River. On a really clear day, liars said, you could see Los Angeles three thousand miles away.

The first visitors to Scarborough House were Ian and Margery Chapman and their two teenage children. Chapman was the first man not named Collins to head William Collins & Sons, headquartered in London and the largest English-language publishing firm in the world. It was basically a business visit. Stein and Day had had more dealings with Collins than with any other British firm. Yet despite the primacy of trade, Scarborough House was the kind of place you could bring along two teenage children for a look-see.

Over the years many authors and foreign publishers came to visit. A usually shy Japanese publisher brought along his sister, father, and bride-to-be. Most authors and foreign publishers went away saying how right the high-ceilinged rooms with fireplaces seemed as a place to discuss the editing and publishing of books. A prize-winning young director even made a film of life at Scarborough House, one scene of which included the housewarming party attended by many well-known people in publishing, and another captured Elia Kazan and his editor conferring on a bench near a weeping copper beech reputed to be four hundred years old.

Irony is a stock in trade of writers, and perhaps publishers also, for in Stein and Day's last month at Scarborough House, January 1989, as the company finally died of Chapter 11 disease, a front-page story in *The New York Times* announced that Ian Chapman had lost the fight to prevent the takeover of Collins by Rupert Murdoch, whose book publishing empire now joined his other media girdling the globe. The papers said that some two hundred authors had signed a petition opposing the Murdoch takeover, and Murdoch was quoted as saying that he didn't much care; if they left, they would be replaced by other authors, who were perceived as standard interchangeable parts. The *Times* also noted that Ian Chapman was expected to leave the firm.

Between the visit of the Chapmans in 1973 and Murdoch's takeover of Collins at the beginning of 1989, publishing had finally passed from entrepreneurs whose primary interest was in books to executives for whom books were another means to an end: making money. Earlier in the century the trade could still be described as an "occupation for gentlemen," in which strong-willed individuals like Sir William Collins and Alfred Knopf put the stamp of their personalities on imprints, however large or small their firms were. As the century nears its end, there are very few such publishing entrepreneurs left, or even people for whom the title of publisher seems more appropriate than "businessman."

The fact that giant Collins and much smaller Stein and Day had once consorted together over books seemed anomalous in the new age, for now Collins was part of a book publishing empire that stretched from London to New York to Sydney, and what Collins bought would likely be published in the United States by Harper & Row, also owned by Murdoch, and vice versa. In that new world, what would happen to books like Stein and Day's very first, Elia Kazan's *America America*?

The book began with built-in liabilities. Screenplays did not sell well in book form. Someone had to take that screenplay through four full drafts to arrive at a shape that did not distort the original. In the end, the screenplay, transformed into narrative that resembled fiction, cast a net so wide it not only drew the accolades of such diverse sensibilities as those of John Steinbeck, James Baldwin, Harold Clurman, Archibald MacLeish, S. N. Behrman, and

Robert Kennedy but was also selected by *The Readers Digest* for its three million purchasers of condensed books. Would it be cost effective for any editor in the great Murdoch stable to spend time experimenting to see if a screenplay could for the first time be turned into a form that would give it a place in literature?

Now that Rupert Murdoch's sensibility of what constitutes commerce straddles both the Atlantic and the Pacific, perhaps one should pause to examine what is no longer likely to happen so that we understand the global change that has altered the nature of publishing, for in that change there may be much more at stake than the life of a single enterprise.

Perhaps one way of conveying what publishing used to be is to glimpse a few of the transactions that established a rapport between Collins and Stein and Day.

For Stein and Day's first book, Elia Kazan's *America America*, Collins paid five hundred dollars as an advance for the British rights, a modest enough sum. That gave Collins an option to make a first offer on Kazan's next book.

Late in 1966, months before publication of Kazan's second book, *The Arrangement*, a copy of the much-worked-on manuscript was airmailed by me to Robert Knittel, Collins's editorial director. Some weeks later I learned that Sir William Collins was in New York and wanted to call on me in our offices at 7 East 48 Street, a six-story building off Fifth Avenue that was our headquarters for many years.

As Sir William, called Billy by his friends, sat opposite me, he held in his hands three reports from London on *The Arrangement*. He said, glancing at his reports as if he couldn't quite believe what they said, that while Collins had paid an advance of five hundred dollars for *America America*, he was quite prepared to offer five hundred pounds for the new book, which translated into fourteen hundred dollars. I said thank you, no. He was holding on

to those editorial reports as if they were a passbook to the
Bank of England.

There were several forces at work in that room. Every
publisher I ever met reached a pitch of excitement at the
moment when a potential bestseller was within his reach.
Billy Collins's excitement was second hand; he hadn't read
the book, just the reports from London, and his minions
were expecting him to use his formidable personality plus
cash to win the day for Collins. However, Billy was, of
course, a Scot, determined on principle to pay as little as he
could get away with for any book. What kept me at the
bartering table was the sure knowledge that most publishers put in an effort on a book that is directly commensurate with what they pay as an advance.

When our chess game was over, Billy rose. We had
agreed on an advance not of five hundred pounds but of
ten thousand pounds, which came to $28,000.[2] As I walked
him out to the elevator, Collins said, "Why don't we just
round that up to $30,000 even?"

By that time, I knew what I had. The Literary Guild had
picked *The Arrangement* as a main selection, and we were
on the way toward a six-figure paperback deal with every
invented escalator one could conjure up. Moreover, I had
made *The Arrangement* my stake in a two-sided gamble.[3]
Kazan and I worked in my study in Scarborough nearly
every day for five months, where I learned to smoke

2. These sums seem small compared to the publicized advances paid
for major books in recent years.

3. Stein and Day, in its fourth year in 1966, was not yet profitable on
a regular basis. Patricia Day and I decided to gamble our time in order
to break out into the black and to put our company on the map at the
same time. She devoted three months to delivering a pediatrician's
baby, *How to Raise Children at Home in Your Spare Time* by Dr. Marvin
Gersh, which set a record by being taken by twenty-eight book clubs.
It received reviews that put Gersh ahead of Spock in acclamation if not
in sales. The book continued to sell in various editions until it, too, was
entrapped in Chapter 11. My part of the gamble was *The Arrangement*.

cigars in the morning to defend myself against Kazan's early morning cigars. Because of his background in film and on stage, at first he insisted that disputed passages be read aloud as one would in the theater. Though he had worked with writers, he at times resented the process of being worked with. Once he left me a note on my typewriter that said, "You bucher, why don't you write your own f——book." I left a return note for him that said, "When you can spell butcher and you get your ass off my typewriter, I will write my own book."

The fact is that Kazan had not taken his first book, *America America*, seriously. He had written it as a screenplay, entrusting the supervision of its revisions to his first wife, a remarkable woman named Molly Day Thatcher. *America America* was not perceived by him as important *in book form*. He inscribed my copy, "Sol, it's your book, Gadg."[4]

The Arrangement, however, swept Kazan into a lasting love affair with the solitary act of writing—a great change from the communal work of theater and film. He and I both went at the editorial work so intensely that we were halfway through the five months before we took note of the fact that we didn't have a contract for it! That contract may well be unique in the annals of publishing in that it calls for a zero advance. Kazan wanted success. I agreed to get it for him. We shook hands on it. He ended up, by some calculations, making about $1,600,000 from *The Arrangement*, including from the bad film made of the good book.[5]

---

4. "Gadg" is short for "gadget." Actors and others who pretended to know him well, but didn't, spelled it with an "e" at the end. Some years ago he started signing his name "Elia" and claimed to have hated the nickname "Gadg" all along. When friends of his speak of him, they always call him "Gadg."

5. Over time Kazan became much more receptive to the editing process. His fourth book, *The Understudy*, contains the dedication, "To Sol, who saw what I didn't think possible," which is a fair description of what an editor of the old school did. In his autobiography, *A Life*, pub-

It sold some 917,000 hardcover copies through bookstores and book clubs during its first year of publication, and was number one on the bestseller lists for thirty-seven consecutive weeks.

For a first on the bestseller list, it was quite a coup. The cynics in the trade said, "Let's see Stein and Day do it with nonfiction." We did, the very next year, with David Frost's *The English*. Thereafter, Stein and Day was represented on the bestseller lists for a total of nineteen consecutive years till the year the company was forced to file under Chapter 11 and was forbidden to publish. Though we had two near-perfect candidates for the bestseller lists ready to go, we were barred from publishing them (or any other books) by two of the secured creditors, the Michigan National Bank and BookCrafters, at a probable loss of many hundreds of thousands of dollars to the estate, not to speak of the loss to the two authors, whose copyrights were caught with some twelve hundred others in the Chapter 11 web, like flies fluttering their wings and unable to get away.

The Arrangement proved to be a success for Collins also, and an even bigger success in France.

The rapport with Collins was such that it was usually our first port of call on the morning of the first day of our regular trips to London scouting for new books.

On one occasion, Bob Knittel, Collins's long-term editorial director, had the manuscript of a first novel called *The Tenant*. I said if it was going to be published in the States, it wouldn't be under that title. I read it overnight and the next day made two offers: $2500 as an advance for the book rights, provided we could call it *The Listener*, and a second $2500 as an option on the motion picture rights. They happily accepted both (but not the title; in Britain the

---

lished by Knopf in 1988, Kazan said, "My publisher Sol Stein was my producer, and my editor Sol Stein was my director."

book was called *The Tenant*). We are about to witness the insane part of the economics of publishing.

A few days later, back home, I got a call from Jim Bryans, then editorial head of Popular Library.

"I hear you bought a book over in London called *The Tenant*," he said. "What are you planning to do with the paperback rights?"

"I bought a book called *The Listener*, and I expect to auction the paperback rights in due course," I said.

"That's what I'm going to prevent," said Bryans, or words to that effect. "I'm offering you a $170,000 advance for the paperback rights." Many American publishers had their spies, called scouts, in Britain, and vice versa, and "illegal" copies traveled by air across the Atlantic with regularity. Bryans would have had to have seen a copy of the manuscript I'd just bought in order to offer that kind of money.

That meant that Stein and Day had a profit of $85,000 and Collins had a profit of the other $85,000 to split with the author, *and nothing had happened yet*.

Then Warner Brothers, hearing of the paperback sale, sprang in to make an offer for the film rights we had just acquired. I was told Warners spent well into six figures trying to get a screenplay of *The Listener* from various hands, but not from the author of the book, John Gill. Gill happened to be the head of the BBC's drama department. One of the reasons I optioned the film rights in the first place was that the novel had visual impact, suspense, and good dialogue, and it was very nearly in screenplay form. What's pertinent here, however, is that it is unlikely the economic values in this story would ever have matured so quickly were it not for the working rapport between Collins and Stein and Day up to about the time that Billy Collins died.

On one London trip, what Collins had to offer was the then rough manuscript of a book by Mark Arnold-Forster based on a Thames Television series that was to run twenty-six full hours and to be narrated by one of the great voices of the century, Laurence Olivier. It was, of course, *The World at War*, which has now been seen by tens of millions of Americans, first on public TV, then in commercial syndication, and finally on cassette.

There were two problems. It seemed as if any number of American publishers had put in for the rights to the book, and that all there was to see of the television series was a "rough cut" of one episode, "The Fall of France."

In a rough cut, the shots do not necessarily mesh, the sound is sometimes out of sync, the color seems to be shades of green. Pat and I went to see it in midwinter in a small, unheated theater (Britain was undergoing one of its periodic strikes). Huddled in our overcoats alone among the empty seats, we had to see through the rough material on screen to what that series might become. We were impressed.

Up in Collins's offices we were given a copy of the manuscript of *The World at War*. There were errors all over the script, mainly having to do with American actions. They had the wrong regiment of the U.S. Infantry Division landing in Normandy. Naval warfare in the Atlantic was handled as if seven-eighths of the ocean was a British pond. I took off my jacket, rolled up my sleeves, and went to work.

Back home in the United States, the Literary Guild put out an offer to "whoever gets the American rights." Collins had to send a telegram to one and all telling them that Stein and Day would be the American publisher, period. The book was a success, the series was a success, and I auctioned off the paperback rights for a six-figure record sum for a military book. Again, Collins and Stein and Day had reason to be happy with each other.

One day Collins's editorial director Robert Knittel[6]

_____

6. Bob Knittel was married to Luise Rainer, who twice in a row won the Oscar for best actress in the thirties. She had been married to Clifford Odets and knew many of the theater people in New York that I also knew (I had been a founding member of the Playwrights Group of the

tipped us off that British parliamentarian and novelist
Maurice Edelman was going through a kind of change of
life about his publishing activities and was preparing to
switch from Hamish Hamilton, which had allegedly taken
him for granted too long, to Collins. In the United States,
Edelman had been published for many years by Random
House. Whenever the M.P. from North Coventry had
come to the States, he had been wined and dined by Bennett Cerf, but Random House had never managed to sell
more than 6,500 copies of a novel of his, they'd never gotten a book club for his work, and the best paperback deal
they'd ever done was for $4,500. Was I interested?

On a quick trip to Europe I had one day in Paris, and it
was spent indoors in my hotel reading the manuscript of
Edelman's next book, *Disraeli in Love*. It was a perfect
story. And Edelman, a handsome man with a winning
personality, was the first novelist since Disraeli in Parliament, which was a good angle to publicize the book from.
Knittel and I conspired over my offer, and before Random
House could get its wits together we had the book. In short
order, Stein and Day got a book club main selection for
Disraeli in Love (the club ended up selling 380,000 hardcover copies), I sold the paperback rights for $100,000, and
we increased Edelman's United States hardcover sales by

Actors Studio and had plays produced in New York and California).
When we got together over dinner in London, Knittel wanted to discuss
book properties and Luise, a strong personality, wanted to discuss theater. Theater usually won.

One incident is worth mentioning. I accompanied Bob and Luise to
the London opening of *That's Entertainment II*. It was a Hollywood-
style launching, huge searchlights out in the street and crowds blocking the limousines. As we were leaving the theater, narrowed into a
single file between velvet ropes, Liza Minelli was just ahead of us and
Beatle Paul McCartney just behind. With that splatter of then current
stardom, no one seemed to be recognizing Luise Rainer so she quickly
took off her hat and put it in front of her face to hide it, at which point
the crowd's attention turned to her and as if in one breath excitedly
wondered out loud who that was! It was a magnificent piece of stage
business.

a significant percentage. Edelman ended up giving a dinner in my honor in Parliament, inviting "British authors
with the wrong American publisher." It was the beginning of a relationship that would last until Edelman's
untimely death.[7]

The observant reader will now see why the largest of
the large firms and the newest of the small firms had as
many good times together as people did watching Laurel
and Hardy. The fact is that the size of a firm mattered
much less in Britain than it did in the United States. British
publishers reacted to the person across the table from
them rather than to the size or power of the institution
they represented.

It wasn't just Collins. I remember on our first frantic
buying trip to London, cramming eleven appointments
into a day, we met Tess Sacco, a director of Macmillan,
who gave us a welcome I'll never forget. She'd done a
real FBI check on us and said we seemed to have done
as well with subsidiary rights as the big boys did and
she didn't see why Macmillan shouldn't be offering us
American rights. That friendly attitude continued
through the years. Even when Stein and Day was
forced to file, with some monies for the books bought
from Tess Sacco unpaid, she wrote warm and humane
letters of support.

The upshot of the web of British relationships was that
for many years Stein and Day was said to publish a higher
percentage of books of British origin than any other
American-owned firm (St. Martin's, which publishes

---

7. On the next trip that Pat and I took to Round Hill, a place in
Jamaica that was the vacation habit of a number of publishers, I spotted
Donald Klopfer, Bennett Cerf's partner at Random House, who had just
arrived. I found my way across the dance floor to say hello, but Donald
was immediately on his feet, spluttering, "You stole Maurice Edelman
from us!" His wife Pat had to pull his jacket to make him sit down and
be civil. Klopfer was a gentleman, embarrassed by his outburst, and
bought us predinner cocktails several times during that trip to make
amends.

more British books, is British-owned). When a party was given at the Dorchester for three British prime ministers, Macmillan, Heath, and Wilson, we saw Lady Churchill and some five hundred other distinguished Britons. The only Americans present were the ambassador and Stein and Day. (We subsequently became the publishers of Heath's best-known book, *Sailing,* and sponsored a memorable day of book promotion in New York, during which the State Department took great precautions to see that Heath didn't get assassinated by an Irish militant while he was doing the"Today Show," or giving a press conference, or signing books at Abercrombie's.)

There was a strong economic basis for all this Anglo-American fraternization. We worked like hell on the books that originated on our side of the Atlantic, and hoped for a product mix that would bring us a fair portion of books on which British editors had worked. In time, however, we began to originate or edit works by British authors like Anthony Sampson, Gordon Thomas and Max Morgan Witts, and Jack Higgins, all of them bestselling authors in the States.

This brief smattering of the Stein and Day story is designed to give a sense of the fun and success of the enterprise during the early years, particularly from 1966 on. Its success in publicizing books may have reached its zenith at LaGuardia Airport one day in the 1970s. I had gone there to meet my mother-in-law, Brenice Day, who traveled by wheelchair. I was not permitted to go past the security barrier without a green card. Finally, working my way through channels, I got to see the local security chief, who asked, "What's the name of the party you're meeting?"

I said, "Day."

He said rather gruffly, "What's your name?"

"Stein," I said.

"Hey, that's funny," he said, handing me my green card, "There's a publishing company named Stein and Day!"

I handed him my calling card and ran off to meet the plane.

What that incident proves is not that the chief security guard is a book reader, but that he probably watches television, because we designed our author promotions whenever possible to expose the news of a book to as many as forty million people via television, radio, and the press.

By 1984, *The Writers Yearbook* ranked Stein and Day number four of the top fifty American publishers, their criteria all being from the point of view of authors, who are, of course, the source of everything in the industry, and who want their books edited and publicized well. Even in 1985, after calamity hit, we moved up in the rankings to number three, ahead of giants like Doubleday, Simon & Schuster, Putnam, and Harper's. Three of our employees became presidents of other publishing firms; there is a presumption, true or false, that Stein and Day trained people well. The company had built a valuable backlist, which an independent expert later testified in court had to be worth between $5 and $6 million. Each year the company came out with a list of one hundred new books, one or more of which found their way onto the bestseller lists. And it was reported that Stein and Day's subsidiary rights sales were unparalleled for a firm of its size.[8]

Because it is usually the smaller firms in every industry that are destroyed in Chapter 11, it is important to note that these firms have some attributes that are not matched by the larger firms. In the case of widgets it may matter less than in the case of book publishing simply because many millions of readers and hundreds of authors are

---

8. In 1978 Lehman Brothers/Kuhn Loeb prepared a report that showed that, according to industry statistics, companies of our then size had subsidiary rights sales averaging 11 percent of book sales. Stein and Day's subsidiary rights sales (the most profitable part of publishing) had a low of 33 percent and a high of 100 percent of book sales.

affected. Therefore another fact in Stein and Day's history may be worth noting. Authors who did well under its banner fared less well if they moved to another firm. For example, Barbara Howar, whose *Laughing All the Way* was rejected by Putnam because it didn't turn out to be a Washington peephole book, climbed to the number two spot on the bestseller list when Stein and Day published it. At our launching party for Barbara Howar at The Sign of the Dove, an "in" New York restaurant, I could see Bob Bernstein, head of Random House, sniffing around our author. Her next book, *Making Ends Meet*, didn't. It was published by Random House and sank, the only trace a bitter quarrel between Howar and her new publisher.

Anthony Sampson, author of *An Anatomy of Britain*, was turned down by Harper's for the new edition, called plausibly *A New Anatomy of Britain*. The new edition, published by Stein and Day, made the front page of *The New York Times Book Review* and was a success. Stein and Day then commissioned *The Sovereign State of ITT*, which Patricia Day edited, and it became a national bestseller. Harry Lorayne, who has published many books in his lifetime, never had anything like the financial success he had with *The Memory Book*, which held on to the bestseller lists for thirty-eight weeks. David Frost's successful books were published by Stein and Day, his not-as-successful ones later, elsewhere. When the money crunch came, Jack Higgins, whom Stein and Day published successfully for a decade, fled to America's biggest trade publisher, Simon & Schuster, for a whopping big advance and quite possibly the worst reviews of his career. Was the missing ingredient Stein and Day's editing? Even in the literary field, as distinguished a critic as Leslie Fiedler, after fourteen books under Stein and Day's banner, accepted an advance from Simon & Schuster that we could match but not pay as quickly. After that experience, Fiedler came back to Stein and Day for a three-book contract, which was thwarted only by the Chapter 11 no-publishing edict.

Perhaps the most striking example of the one-way

street was Stein and Day's most successful author of all, Elia Kazan. *America America, The Arrangement, The Assassins,* and *The Understudy,* all under Stein and Day's banner, were all successful. According to Kazan, what then happened was that Irving "Swifty" Lazar, one of the kingpins of the agent world, was hobnobbing with Howard Kaminsky, then head of Warner Books, over Richard Nixon's memoirs. Kazan reported that Swifty had said to Kaminsky something like, "You paid Stein a lot of money for the paperback rights to Kazan's last book. Would you pay a million dollars for world rights?" According to Kazan, Swifty telephoned him and said, "If I can get you a million-dollar advance for your next book, can I be your agent?" Kazan told me he said, "Sure," thinking he'd never hear from Swifty again. The upshot, after the million-dollar deal was made, was that Warner, then exclusively a paperback house, had to find a hardcover editor and publisher for Kazan's new novel. Two large firms turned the book down. Finally it was taken on by possibly the best publisher in America, Knopf, with the editing to be done by its president, Robert Gottlieb (now editor of *The New Yorker*). Gottlieb was nice enough to send me a note saying how well I had taught Kazan. But to edit Kazan you have to be willing to fight like a tiger with a tiger of a man, who is intelligent, willful, manipulative, clever, and resistant to change. Kazan's new novel, *Acts of Love,* had a single week on the bestseller list, not a way to go for a million-dollar book. His next under the same auspices was *The Anatolians,* which never made the list.

If you look at what happened to Howar, Sampson, Kazan, and others, you might come to the conclusion that perhaps the publisher makes a difference. But if Stein and Day was good at editing and publishing, how the hell did it end up in the Chapter 11 soup?

Only a small percentage of United States publishers could match Stein and Day's list of well-known authors (see Appendix C), not to mention the dozens of unsung authors of successful do-it-yourself books, scholarly works, books in the fields of biography, history, the physical and behavioral sciences, reference books, and medical books for the general reader. Stein and Day became the premier publisher of military history. What happened to bring a house with such a list tumbling down? When did the fun stop and the trouble start?

Patricia Day and I both pin it to 1975. For a decade we had been continuously profitable. Some years were higher, some lower, but that was in the nature of a business that depended on large numbers of new "product" each year. Our shareholders were happy, and we even paid dividends for a while till the directors agreed that it was foolish not to reinvest the profits in what was clearly a generally upward movement in sales and market share.

Malcolm Magruder, our star sales manager during the profitable decade, was eventually succeeded by a man he had recommended named John Maclaurin. There was nothing similar about them except their Scots ancestry. In fact, Maclaurin had a burr to go along with his ancestry. He had started professional life as a salesman for Collins, had moved to the States, and at the age of thirty-two was in his second job as sales manager of a publishing company. He was also a member of Stein and Day's four-person management committee, consisting of its chief financial officer Ed Sands, Patricia Day and myself, and now Maclaurin.

To backtrack for a moment, when Stein and Day started out, it was distributed by a two-hundred-year-old Philadelphia company, J. B. Lippincott. It was financially an excellent deal for a start-up company because Lippincott was effectively financing Stein and Day's receivables. Moreover, Lippincott had comparatively few star-quality books, and the fledgling firm soon had quite a few, so Lippincott salesmen used Stein and Day books as their door openers. Within a year and a half Lippincott had more money in Stein and Day than its shareholders did. We parted company amicably with Lippincott and proceeded to set up our own distribution. During the entire period of profitability, as I've said, Stein and Day distributed its own books. That is the key to understanding the two main events that led to the company's downfall.

Maclaurin had style. He did a good job of bringing in orders. And his assistant sales manager, Vicki Brooks, was a gem (who ended up running her own marketing company). Maclaurin, as a member of the management committee, had a proposal. Our sales force was a mix of "house men" (full-time Stein and Day employees) and commission reps. It is generally acknowledged in the industry that commission reps, sometimes representing as many as eighteen lines, don't have time to present all of a publisher's books and do their own preliminary screening, which can be the kiss of death to those books before they even have a chance to be presented to bookstore buyers. And commission reps usually don't have time to sell backlist, which is accomplished by taking inventory in a store and telling the buyer what he's sold and needs to restock.

Maclaurin's proposal was that we combine sales forces with W. W. Norton, a distinguished independent firm. Stein and Day would dismiss its commission reps, Norton would dismiss theirs, and we would combine our house men with theirs for a first-class sales force. Maclaurin had had a similar arrangement with Norton when he'd been sales manager of the New York Graphic Society, a publisher of high-quality art books.

Pat and I had few qualms. The sales manager of Norton, Walter Oakley, was a man we'd met years before when we were running a book club and he was sales manager of Oxford University Press. He was a senior in both experience and manner and would be a good Dutch uncle for young Maclaurin. We were swayed mainly because we felt that, with Oakley sharing the responsibility for sales, we'd be stronger. Wrong. We were giving up control of an essential element in any business, the sales force.

What we didn't know was that Oakley was not a power within W. W. Norton and that the sales force was in effect run by its president. Nor did we know that when we merged our sales forces, presumably with the best men of each remaining, the former Stein and Day men would be under pressure. Norton's president, George Brockway, apparently wanted to see more Norton men in place and fewer Stein and Day veterans.

On the plus side, however, was the mix; there seemed to be so little conflict between the lists. Norton's trade list, characteristically, had fairly sober books that advanced a small number of copies but sold for many years, requiring a strong capital structure. Stein and Day's books were of high visibility in comparison to Norton's, had much bigger advances, and some sold huge numbers of copies in their first year, a fine position for an undercapitalized younger firm.

Norton insisted that all the men be paid by Norton check, with a suitable memo on it that it was on behalf of both companies. It made sense for the men because the longer-established company, Norton, had better benefits. However, it was a mistake for Stein and Day to agree to that because, psychologically, a person feels employed by the company that has its name imprinted on the check.

It was agreed that the salesmen would show Stein and Day books first in one store and Norton's first in the next. What really happened in the field was that the stores got the impression that Norton was "carrying" Stein and Day's line. We had 50 percent of the fiscal responsibility but it was as if we were back in the days when we were distributed by Lippincott—without the financial advantages.

Two months into the two-year contract the news was turning grim. For many years Stein and Day had advanced large numbers of its books with bestseller potential, which is indispensable for getting books on the bestseller list. At the heart of our business, though, were books that advanced between, say, 10,000 and 32,500 copies. We had a lot of those. A few "broke out" and took off, but those that didn't brought in a lot more revenue than the bestsellers put together. What happened in the Norton arrangement was that suddenly we were advancing pretty much across the board the same small numbers that Norton was traditionally used to.[9] For Stein and Day it was an instant catastrophe. Two months into the marriage, we knew it had to end.

It was a bitter parting, fraught with recrimination, and with Norton in the driver's seat throughout. The decade of unbroken profitability ended. 1976 was Stein and Day's first loss year in all that time. It took into the early 1980s for Stein and Day to pull itself back up to profitability with its own sales force. Maclaurin departed. Despite much effort put into recruitment, we weren't able to find someone as good as Magruder or Maclaurin. With no financial reserves to build back what we'd had, I decided to sell the company.

The first offer came from BPC, the British Printing Company, which owned a number of British firms and was tempted to get into the United States market. I was impressed by BPC's ability to arrange for its two key executives to arrive at Kennedy at approximately the same time that the third would be arriving from Australia—an interesting exercise in logistics, designed to get all three to a meeting with us at the same time. I was less moved by the British Printing Company's CFO's assertions that what they wanted from their publishing companies was a 40 percent pretax profit, something that no publishing firm, to my knowledge, had ever achieved on a consistent basis. I was even less impressed by the offer they made at the conclusion of their visit.

In 1978 the hunt for a buyer was formalized. Lehman Brothers/Kuhn Loeb became our investment bankers. Michael Jackson was the managing director who came to visit at Scarborough House and take charge of our situation. The deal was the typical Lehman Brothers formula.

---

9. Ironically—this business is full of ironies—the year we got together, Norton had several whopping bestsellers, something that hadn't happened in many years.

I couldn't imagine that a company as small as ours could be of interest to them. But Jackson was enthusiastic, and his analyst, Mary Tanner, was an impressive worker.

Stein and Day found a buyer on July 6, 1979. It was Kluwer, the second or third largest Dutch publishing conglomerate. They and we signed a binding purchase agreement.

We were told that Kluwer had also bought two other United States publishing companies in unrelated specialties. Kluwer was to put a million dollars of new capital into Stein and Day and, for starters, paid in a quarter of a million on closing. The newspapers made quite a thing of the acquisition with stories like "The Dutch Have Landed—Again." Our headquarters were located very near the place where the Dutch did in fact first land, when they bypassed insignificant Manhattan Island and sailed up the Hudson. This Dutch invasion of American trade book publishing was hailed by the press not as a takeover but as a welcome event. The post-Norton agony was over.

Or so we thought. At the end of August, Kluwer decided to back out of what had been a firm deal, not a letter of intent. The directors of Stein and Day met with Burton Monasch, head lawyer and strategist of our law firm, and Arnold Stream,[10] the chief litigating partner. The decision was to sue for performance. The case was settled fairly quickly, with the shareholders receiving a six-figure cash settlement, and the $250,000 already in the till being turned into a subordinate mortgage on our Scarborough House real estate that was eventually paid off.

Then the shareholders did something most unusual. Without exception, all forty-three Stein and Day shareholders turned over the proceeds from the settlement to

---

10. Stream, who handled several legal adventures for Stein and Day both in and out of the courtroom, usually with a successful outcome, eventually became the author of a novel called *The Third Bullet*. It was published by Stein and Day shortly before filing; Stream was one of the unsecured creditors left in the lurch by the case.

the company to help bind its wounds from the Kluwer experience, which to this day remains something of a mystery. What is not a mystery is the exceptional nature of the shareholders.

Despite the shock of the Kluwer ordeal, Stein and Day gradually rebuilt its sales force and slowly restored its profitability in the early 1980s. Fiscal year 1983 was the second best year in Stein and Day's history. And fiscal year 1984 was even better.

The company's comeback in the early 1980s is attributable at least in part to a line of credit extended by the largest printer in the United States, R. R. Donnelley. That line was to prove Stein and Day's undoing.

When Charles Haffner, Donnelley's CFO, first visited the premises of Stein and Day, the company's line of credit was something like $180,000. Haffner got to know the company and its principals. He understood that the biggest problem for an undercapitalized publishing company was success, meaning orders for books that had to be paid for months before the publisher was paid by the bookstores and wholesalers. The more books you sold, the more tide-over capital you needed, or, without the capital, at least credit from a major supplier such as a book manufacturer. Donnelley's credit line went by stages from $180,000 to a peak of about a million and a half dollars. It takes two to make a fault that size. Donnelley extended the line and we took it. When Haffner moved upstairs to become vice chairman of the corporation, his place was taken by a man named James Fletcher, who seemed to the directors of Stein and Day out to prove that he was Mr. Tough. He made demands that any knowledgeable person would realize we could not possibly meet.

Again, we must step back a bit.

Stein and Day's forte was hardcover books and subsidiary rights. It started out building an upside-down pyramid, the smallest number of books that could produce the largest amount of rights. It worked. Several years down the road, in the late 1960s, the company started to publish trade paperbacks.[11] This next step was designed to make the company completely vertical, that is, to become a publisher of every major form of book—hardback, trade paperback, and rack-sized paperbacks, commonly called "mass-market" paperbacks.

Back in 1978, before the affair Kluwer matured, Stein and Day launched a small line of rack-sized paperbacks called Day Books. In this experiment, Stein and Day sold these books only to its regular accounts, that is, to bookstores and wholesalers. The company stayed away from the world of magazine distribution, which accounts for the vast majority of mass-market paperbacks sold—and returned.

Day Books[12] did surprisingly well. Returned books were only a few percentage points off from returns on Stein and Day's other books. At the beginning of 1983 the inevitable push toward expansion caused Stein and Day to move in the direction of a national distributor for Stein and Day's rack-sized books. Over the years, the company had sold about $30 million worth of rights, mainly to paperback publishers; now was Stein and Day's chance to cash in on that market directly. We hired Marvin Hoffman, a CPA who had been executive vice president of a mass-market company, to find a distributor for Stein and Day.

In fairness to Hoffman, it should be pointed out that there were reportedly about fifteen distributors of maga-

---

11. Misnamed, trade paperbacks are simply normal-sized books, printed on decent paper like hardcovers, but bound in paper. They used to be called "quality paperbacks" when they first came out in the early 1950s. For the record, the author of this book published the earliest line of perfect (glued) bound, book-sized paperbacks at the Beacon Press in Boston. The line was an instant success, despite the reservations of the sales force, and led to the director of the Beacon Press, Melvin Arnold, being invited to start similar series at the company now known as Harper & Row. Eventually he became Harper & Row's president.

12. Kable, soon to become Stein and Day's national distributor of mass-market books, required that Day Books cease publishing, they said "to avoid confusion in the marketplace," or words to that effect.

zines in the United States at that time and fewer than half distributed paperback books also. We were interested in Hearst's distribution, but Hearst owned Avon Books, one of Stein and Day's big rights customers (they published *The Arrangement* in paperback), and we heard Avon's head man didn't want competition in Hearst's distribution channels. Other distributors had other commitments. Warner's was briefly a possibility, but they already distributed a great many lines; that's a tall totem pole to be on the bottom of. That left Kable News. They apparently convinced Hoffman, and through Hoffman me, that they were capable of doing the job, that their new computer system was the most up-to-date in the industry, and— flattery will get you everywhere—that we would be their "Bantam." For many years Bantam had been perceived as the premier publisher of mass-market books not only of popular interest but also of quality.[13] Moreover, the other publishers carried by Kable did not have big-name authors whose books had graced the bestseller lists in hardcover year after year. The rumor was that Zebra, Kable's biggest line, would move elsewhere when its contract expired in August of 1984. That would make Stein and Day's paperbacks Kable's number one imprint.

Somewhere along the line I'd heard that the chairman of Kable, Daniel Friedman, was a convicted felon and had served time for mail and wire fraud. And Kable was owned by AMREP, a company traded on the New York Stock Exchange, whose chairman was Howard Friedman, Daniel Friedman's brother. Howard Friedman was also a convicted felon.

I felt backed into going with Kable because, in the end, Hoffman said they were the only mass-market distributor available. The pressure to expand the mass-market line was great. Though we were quite profitable for a trade

---

13. The New American Library, publisher of Mentor Books among others, probably had a longer list of books of quality than Bantam, but Bantam had the reputation.

book company at the time, one of Stein and Day's most profitable activities, the sale of printing materials to a company that formed leasing partnerships for tax purposes, was going to end with tax law reform. Mass-market distribution was to take its place.

Kable had a sales force of thirty-two people, almost three times the number we'd had at Stein and Day's peak. The first month, December 1983, Kable said they shipped some 400,000 books to their customers, more than Day Books had done in its five-year history.

In that briefly happy and prosperous spring of 1984, Stein and Day paid off an R. R. Donnelley note of $565,000 and started making monthly payments on a non-interest-bearing second note. Donnelley sent Stein and Day congratulatory letters on paying off that first note. Our comeback seemed secure.

That June I was invited to address a convention of the Independent Periodical Distributors Association, known in the trade as IPDA. After delivering a short speech—one of several—early in the morning in a large, sparsely filled auditorium of sales reps and buyers, I stayed on to join alternately Kable's eastern and western district managers as they held serial fifteen-minute meetings with independent distributors, called IDs in the jargon of the trade.

Then something odd happened. A distributor asked me, "Mr. Stein, how come you're sending me books I didn't order?"

"We don't send you *any* books," I replied. "They all come from Kable. We don't even know which ID orders."

At this point the Kable regional manager said something I remember quite precisely. "If we don't hear from you by the cut-off date, we send you one-third of suggested."

What startled me was that I knew that the "suggested" quota for each book title for each ID was three times the amount Kable thought they should order! In other words, it seemed that whether or not you placed the order, you got the books anyway!

The same question was asked by other IDs. And then came the same almost singsong answer: "If we don't hear from you by the cut-off date, we send you one-third of suggested."

A pang of concern raced through me. What did the IDs do with the books they didn't order, have the covers ripped off and returned for credit?[14] Those books cost good money to manufacture. What was happening?

If Kable sent twenty-five copies of a book to a particular ID, who then sold fourteen copies, that would be a 56-percent sale, which is quite profitable. But if Kable sent fifty copies of the same book to that dealer, and the dealer sold fourteen copies, that would be a catastrophic 28-percent sale, occasioning a big loss to the publisher.[15] Kable would maintain that if they'd only shipped the twenty-five, maybe fourteen wouldn't have sold, maybe only twelve would have sold because fewer were on display. (Of course many of the overshipments never got on display. The covers were ripped off and returned for credit.) Even if Kable were correct, it meant that Stein and Day had to manufacture twenty-five additional books to supply the nonordered amount, and if two of those sold, Kable made a profit because it got a commission on every

14. Not everyone is familiar with this barbaric practice. In the hardcover and trade paperback field, if a book isn't sold, it is returned for credit, usually three to twelve months after receipt. In the mass market field, if a book isn't sold, the cover is ripped off and returned for credit, destroying the book. This happens to roughly 50 percent of the books that are shipped out. Many of the books are not "distributed" at all. That is, they are not put out on the racks for customers to buy or reject, they are stripped of their covers in the warehouse. The coverless book is supposed to be pulped. If you've ever seen a coverless paperback book being sold at a bargain price, know that you are buying something that it is illegal to sell. The practice, unfortunately, has been widespread from time to time.

15. These are the actual numbers of a title shipped to a Pennsylvania ID of a March 1984 title. They had ordered twenty-five copies and gotten fifty.

book sold, but at that rate of sale Stein and Day would be losing serious amounts of money.

On arriving back home I sent a long letter to the chairman of Kable News. I was told that he and a couple of his senior executives spent the better part of two weeks replying to my letter. They were apparently taking my complaint seriously.

In the meantime, something else was happening. A national distributor like Kable usually pays for the books piecemeal over an extended period of time. The biggest payment from distributor to publisher comes first, and it usually represents enough to pay for the manufacturing of the books and sometimes some of the sales materials. But it does not cover the royalty payment to the author, or most of the color covers printed long in advance and used by the distributor's salesmen to sell the books, or the myriad other expenses, including overhead, that the publisher has. So the publisher looks to the second and third and fourth payments down the line because it is from them that he covers his costs, other than printing the books, and derives whatever profit there may be.

The short version is that Stein and Day got two second payments and none thereafter. It received no third payments and no final payments. Kable's stated reason was that the books weren't selling, that the *projected* return rate was very high. What seemed strange about the report was that at the same time that each month's books were being sent to Kable's customers, the exact same titles were going out to Stein and Day's own customers, the bookshops and wholesalers called "direct accounts," meaning the people who bought Stein and Day's hardcovers and trade paperbacks and were now buying the rack-size books also. And these books were selling very well.

We huddled with Kable's management and said, in effect, "Look, if the books aren't selling well in your market, let's stop right now." After all, Stein and Day could go back to selling the mass-market rights to other publishers, which it had done profitably for so many years.

At which point Kable's chairman, Daniel Friedman, changed his tune. He had been saying that perhaps the books weren't really "mass-market" books, though, as I've said, that was the market that had paid Stein and Day approximately $30 million over the years for the mass-market rights to its books. It wasn't the books, Friedman now seemed to be saying: The books were fine, it was the covers. That seemed strange, because Kable's senior vice president in charge of book sales, David Abramowitz, got to see the cover designs at an early stage and we reflected his input in the final covers. Friedman also said the type size in Stein and Day's books was too small and the books needed to be fatter.

Kable had the experience in their market. We fattened up the books at considerable (wasted, as it proved to be) cost, enlarging the type size in some books till they resembled juveniles, while all of the major firms continued to print many of their mass-market books with the same size type that we'd been using all along.

Kable's chairman said, in effect, "Don't go away. Let's see how these changes affect your sales." He even went so far as to point to a particular forthcoming title, a novel by Derek Lambert called *The Red Dove*. Friedman said the proposed cover was terrific and that his chief financial officer, Al Holpp, had actually read the book and liked it, "Didn't you, Al?"

What the hell was going on? Was a distributor's accountant now the editorial judge? And there seemed to be no significant correlation between "terrific covers" and sales that we could see.

At least once a month Abramowitz, the head of book sales, visited us in Scarborough to go over proposed titles, covers, and plans. He didn't mind coming up from New York City because he lived upstate and we were, in effect, en route to his home. One very significant day, he had lunch with several senior Stein and Day staffers on the second level of Dudley's restaurant in Ossining. We talked about Friedman's reports of projected poor sales. Abramowitz said that Stein and Day's real sell-through rate[16] at the end of the calendar year would be "in the high thirties or low forties."

I said, "Does that include the supposedly disastrous first few months?"

"Yes," he replied. "I swear on the lives of my children that I'm telling you the truth."

That statement hit me, for I knew that Abramowitz had actually lost a child and therefore that kind of oath had the ring of truth. But if Abramowitz was telling the truth, why was Kable not paying us? Stein and Day was falling behind in its payments to its hardcover suppliers and others because it wasn't getting those second and third payments from Kable.

In the spring of 1985, the Stein and Day board of directors had before it the first full-year report of the sales of mass-market books in both directions, through Kable and to direct accounts. The "spread," or difference, between Kable's alleged sell-through rate and Stein and Day's sell-through rate to its own customers was about fifty points![17] We checked with knowledgeable people in the industry who said a spread of twenty points was normal (bookstores keep the paperbacks on display for much longer periods of time), and twenty-five points was possible. But fifty points? Never!

We consulted lawyers and in July 1985, filed a lawsuit

---

16. This is a term that means the percentage of books shipped that actually sell to the final customer and don't get returned. In the mass market field a sell-through rate of 50 percent is considered good. Stein and Day was in a position to be profitable with a sell-through rate of only 41 percent.

17. To simplify understanding of this point, if Kable was reporting a sell-through of 30 percent (meaning three out of every ten books had been sold) and our own customers were reporting a sell-through of 80 percent (meaning eight out of every ten books had been sold), the "spread" would be fifty points.

in the Southern District of New York alleging fraud against Kable and charges against Kable's three principal officers under the Federal Racketeering Act (RICO). I had always been told that the federal judiciary moved faster than the state courts, and we desperately needed an adjudication as early as possible. The case, however, was assigned to Judge Pierre N. Leval. Three years passed before Judge Leval got around to hearing pretrial motions (Kable had moved to have the case dismissed) and deciding that there were triable issues involved. To top it off, Judge Leval turned the case over to a new judge, who set a trial date for May 30, 1989, four years after the filing!

Meanwhile, the impact on Stein and Day was ruinous. The company had funded the mass-market program with monies normally used for its successful hardcover and trade paperback operations. Because Kable did not make the second and third contract payments,[18] Stein and Day went from enjoying the best year in the company's history, fiscal 1984, to being suddenly pauperized in a matter of months. Among other delinquencies, Stein and Day was unable to keep up its monthly payments on R. R. Donnelley's second note. Eleven months after Stein and Day sued Kable, R. R. Donnelley, the biggest printers in the United States, sued the publisher in state court, where things moved swiftly on a very different timetable than Judge Leval's calendar.

In the meantime, two things were happening. Stein and Day was suffering from the domino effect of the monies not received from Kable. That meant that, say, $300,000 withheld one month in the spring of 1984 could have produced hardcover billings of about $1,050,000, of which perhaps $50,000 would have gone to pay authors, and $1,000,000 would have gone into further production. A million dollars of production money would have enabled

---

18. During pretrial discovery, Kable's auditors, Arthur Andersen, admitted under oath that, according to Kable's books, there was a credit due Stein and Day from Kable.

the company to fill about $3,500,000 of orders. When those were paid for, perhaps $500,000 would have gone to authors, and the rest would have been available for production, overhead profit, and the payment of notes.

Very early in the filing of the case against Kable, there was a partial settlement from Kable involving over half a million dollars, to cover merely three of the twenty months of Kable's distribution of Stein and Day books. Stein and Day's purpose in taking that settlement was to keep the company's mass-market books in the racks until a new distributor could start selling them beginning with the January 1986 releases. Periodically, Kable would make additional small settlement offers that would have left Stein and Day's authors out in the cold and would not have compensated Stein and Day one penny for the damages caused by the withheld funds. As of February 28, 1987, the claim for the receivable and the itemized damages amounted to $11.4 million.

So we have two parallel cases. Kable owed Stein and Day money. Stein and Day owed Donnelley money. Donnelley knew all about the Kable case. But Fletcher, the new man at Donnelley, didn't care about *why* we didn't pay; he kept making demands along the lines of "a million dollars by this Friday." At the same time, Stein and Day had counterclaim allegations against Donnelley for $3.5 million, for damage caused by Donnelley's interference in Stein and Day's publishing business. These claims were never tried because the way the justice system works, a note for money owed, if the amount is not in dispute, is a simple matter to adjudicate quickly. And so Donnelley obtained a decision from the state court that Stein and Day had to pay on the outstanding note. The parties were ordered to agree on the amount owing or to participate in a hearing to determine the amount.

On April Fool's Day, 1987, discovery was officially and finally completed in the Kable case. The two sides could stop poring over each other's files and examining each other's officers.

On April 7, 1987, McGraw-Hill told Stein and Day's investment bankers that they proposed to buy the company (and hence assume the company's debt) for a sum of not less than five million dollars. They said they wanted Stein and Day's backlist of some twelve hundred previously published books that would complement McGraw-Hill's own trade backlist.[19] They also wanted the two seasons' worth of yet unpublished books assembled by Stein and Day, most of which had already been edited and set in type and were ready to go. Third, the investment bankers reported that McGraw-Hill liked Stein's publishing outlook into the next century and wanted Stein and Day on their team.[20]

On April 9, 1987, Donnelley's lawyer, Barbara Kelly of Skadden Arps, said that Donnelley didn't want to damage or destroy Stein and Day. She simply wanted us, as the court had ordered, to stipulate to the amount owed on the note. Stein and Day did so, taking Donnelley's lawyer at her word.

On May 13, 1987, Donnelley obtained a judgment on the note in the amount of $1,011,733, which included interest, legal fees, and so on. (The amount actually owed on the non-interest-bearing note was a bit over $800,000.)

While McGraw-Hill was completing the "due diligence" investigation antecedent to a closing, Black Friday intervened. On May 15, 1987, Donnelley got a restraining order, paralyzing Stein and Day and preventing all publishing and related activities. The sheriff said the only reason he didn't padlock the door was that the caretaker and his

---

19. One McGraw-Hill official later told me that while his company's backlist was larger than Stein and Day's, the latter's was better.

20. It would have brought a happy ending to a prospective recruitment that began in 1964, when Stein and Day was a fledgling company and the publishing giant's present chairman, Harold McGraw, was delegated to persuade Sol Stein and Patricia Day to join their company and bring Stein and Day's imprint under their corporate umbrella. When Donnelley imposed its restraining order, it was reported to us that McGraw-Hill was not up to dealing with noisy creditors.

wife lived in the building. Donnelley's counsel told Stein and Day's counsel that she would have the judge throw Sol Stein in jail if he tried to publish or pay the employees. It was another spike in the coffin.

On June 1, Stein and Day filed a motion for summary judgment on the amount of money that Kable's auditors said that Kable owed.

Stein and Day was forbidden to pay its staff or to publish the books in the already distributed catalogue. To make matters worse, Stein and Day's warehouse and shipper, Consolidated Systems and Services, had stopped all shipments of orders to Stein and Day's customers on April 30, 1987.[21] It was yet another nail in the coffin. Then Stein and Day's new distributor for its hardcover books, Henry Holt, stopped selling the books in May, because they didn't want to take orders for books that wouldn't ship. That was one more nail.

Ever since the Kable calamity started, Stein and Day's management had sought advice from bankruptcy specialists such as Levin, Weintraub & Crames, and from two bankruptcy specialists at Stroock and Stroock and Lavan. The advice was unanimous: *Don't file under Chapter 11.* Unlike a widget maker, a publisher like Stein and Day was dependent on getting a hundred new books a year. It is unlikely that agents and authors would sell exclusive publishing rights to a company that had filed for protection.

But, paralyzed by Donnelley's restraining order, unable to sell a book, pay our bills, or publish, what choice did we have?

---

21. It started shipping again, feebly, about half a year later, and less feebly after being cited for contempt by Judge Schwartzberg.

CHAPTER 15
Biting the Bullet

"Most people become bankrupt through having invested too heavily in the prose of life. To have ruined oneself over poetry is an honor."
—Oscar Wilde

THE expression "bite the bullet" has evolved to a different definition than it once had. It originally meant "to suffer in silence," and came from the days before anesthesia, when wounded soldiers ready to go under the surgeon's knife would bite on a bullet put between their teeth.[1] The expression has now been extended in meaning to encompass not only taking pain, but doing something both definitive and unpleasant in order to get a matter over with once and for all.

If you bite the bullet, you might expect your leg to be cut off. You wouldn't expect to be completely dismembered. But that's what happens in the preponderance of Chapter 11 cases.

Stein and Day/Publishers, known worldwide for a quar-

---

1. *The Dictionary of Contemporary Slang* by Jonathon Green, Stein and Day, New York, 1985, p. 21. This useful reference book addressed the meaning of English-language slang expressions as used in the United States, Canada, Britain, Australia, and elsewhere in the English-speaking world, and also slang expressions used by blacks and in the demimondes of crime and sex. The American rights were acquired from Pan Books, London, for an advance of eleven thousand dollars, of which only the first half was paid. Pan became an unsecured creditor in the Chapter 11 case. The book, which would have easily earned out the advance, was one of the victims of the Michigan National Bank's and BookCrafters' ban on reprinting books that sold out.

ter of a century, was run by two publishing executives whose biographies appeared in *Who's Who in America* and *Who's Who in World Commerce and Industry* for many years, because of their work in that field. Their business was at its zenith of profitability when disaster hit with repeated punches: Kable, Donnelley, Michigan National, BookCrafters, and certain death.

In the course of this book the reader will have learned that a company can be forced to seek the protection of Chapter 11 for unpredictable reasons.

Though the purpose of Stein and Day's filing, as I've said, was to resume publishing, the only business the company ever had, two secured creditors, the Michigan National Bank and BookCrafters, a manufacturer of books, refused to allow the company to publish a single book. As a condition of permitting Stein and Day to use cash collateral, these two creditors also forbade the publishing house from reprinting any book that sold out. That meant that a company that had generated $6.4 million in revenue net of returns in fiscal year 1984, and even after the Kable trouble started, $7.2 million in fiscal year 1985, was forced to liquidate its assets, which brought in all told only a fraction of one year's revenue. This destructive action decimated the chance of other creditors to be repaid and of hundreds of authors to get the royalties due them, and blew up a quarter of a century of work and the equity created in that work. That the Chapter 11 process and the court permitted this wanton destruction of value without benefit to the majority of even the secured creditors is a condemnation of a system that has failed.[2]

---

2. There were five secured creditors. The Michigan Bank got back the money it was owed, including interest, though if a creditor is undersecured, it is not entitled to interest. The bank did not get all of the nearly $300,000 in legal fees and expenses it claimed. BookCrafters, a trade creditor that played a central role in preventing the reorganization of the company, got all the remaining assets. The Colophon Corporation, and the two principals of Stein and Day, borrowed money,

By prohibiting publishing, the two Michigan-based firms shot themselves in the foot. And that foot was on the head of all the other creditors, authors, and shareholders. The chief perpetrator of the ban on publishing was an attorney named Randy Kuckuck.

The specific damage caused by the ban can be measured. By not allowing the reprinting of Stein and Day's fastest-selling backlist books, Michigan and BookCrafters caused the company's largest asset to shrink from a value of $5 to $6 million[3] to no more than 8 percent of that amount a year later.

If you don't use your legs, they will atrophy. If you don't keep books in print, they will atrophy even more quickly than legs. If schools use your book and can't get it, they'll substitute another title. If a bookstore customer can't get your book, he'll buy another. Werner Linz, the expert who testified to the value of the backlist, said to me after his day in court, "Publish or perish." This slogan of university life, Linz said, was even more important for a publisher.

Donnelley, which pulled the trigger, didn't benefit from its action. It became just another unsecured creditor.[4] Why did Donnelley do it?

Why did the bank and BookCrafters prevent the com-

---

loaned it to the company, and though they filed UCCs before BookCrafters, they got nothing back.

3. That value was testified to in bankruptcy court by an expert, Werner Linz, the chairman of three publishing firms unrelated to Stein and Day, who had had occasion to examine Stein and Day's backlist on behalf of a European publisher just a few months earlier. His testimony could not be shaken in cross-examination.

4. The *bona fides* of Sol Stein and Patricia Day in relation to Donnelley can be established from objectively verifiable evidence. When, long before filing, they loaned money to the company to tide it over until the Kable case would come to trial, the directors voted them a security interest in all of the company's assets. When the Steins filed their UCC, they allowed a secured claim from Donnelley to precede them. Donnelley never filed a UCC and therefore became a judgment creditor, unsecured.

pany from functioning in the only business it knew when that activity would have resulted in repayment not only to them but to all the creditors? Why did Donnelley take an action that benefited no one and caused McGraw-Hill to back away from "noisy creditors"?[5]

In the century in which psychiatry blossomed, no one has explained satisfactorily the part of human nature that takes pleasure in sadism and that commits torture, wanton murder of strangers, and genocide by civilized nations. Therefore, how can one reasonably expect explanations for harmful actions in business that benefit no one?

Sidney Hook, probably the leading American philosopher of his time who dealt with public issues, once published a short piece called "The Ethics of Controversy," the thrust of which is that one should not impugn the motives of one's opponents. That code imposes a rugged discipline, and compels us whenever possible to describe actions rather than ascribe motivations as we relate the outcome of Stein and Day's passage into the "protection" of the law.

As the reader already knows, for a year and a half we were in touch with Myron Trepper, then one of the partners of Levin, Weintraub & Crames, a top-rated bankruptcy firm. Trepper, who seemed intelligent, sympathetic, and knowledgeable, repeatedly advised, "Don't file." Then, when Donnelley imposed its restraining order and filing seemed the only way to lift the ban on publishing the list of books that had already been catalogued and publicized to the trade at its annual convention, Trepper mentioned for the first time that his firm would require a fifty-thousand-dollar retainer.

---

5. John Martin of McGraw-Hill told me in July 1987, after the filing, that McGraw-Hill was just "too structured" a corporation to get involved, much as it wanted the backlist, forelist, and the management. That has been borne out in interviews with turnaround experts, who say that some staid companies just can't let themselves get involved in the way Chapter 11s are run, which leaves a wide-open field for the "vulture capitalists," the companies that specialize in buying assets from firms in Chapter 11 at fire-sale prices.

Independent publishing companies are not usually cash rich, and I can't remember a time in the company's glorious twenty-five years when it had that much spare cash for more than a day. If I had known the catastrophic consequences of not having that retainer or been warned in advance of that need, I would have tried coming up with the money somehow. In Chapter 11 you have to travel first class because coach is a cattle car headed for the slaughterhouse. I didn't know that then. And so when Trepper recommended a former associate who would accept half that much as a retainer, I did what most people do in emergencies; your doctor gives you the name of a surgeon, and you sign on for the operation. Signing up with Joe Doaks was another nail in the coffin. His was a one-man office, a sublet inside another law firm's premises. His experience turned out to be in shopping center bankruptcies.

After Joe Doaks filed inaccurate papers and was outthought, outfought, and outpaced by the creditors' attorneys, a prospective funder, Terence Herzog, a cheerful man who always wore red suspenders, put us in touch with one of the truly able bankruptcy lawyers, Joshua Angel, a cheerful man who always wore a bright red tie. Angel, as the reader knows, was so confident he could get Stein and Day out of Chapter 11 that he was willing to take the case at no cost to the estate. What could be better?

After the Michigan Bank blocked the retention of Angel on "conflict of interest" grounds, Stein and Day had to settle for Barr & Faerber, who accepted the case without a retainer, a noble act under the circumstances. They ran up over $300,000 worth of bills in just over a year, or more than six times the amount Levin, Weintraub & Crames had wanted as a retainer. This was also $300,000 more of "administrative claims" against the estate than would have been the case if Joshua Angel had not been blocked by the bank.

A key to reorganizing was finding a funder, an outsider willing to put new capital into the company for production. Barr thought we would find one, otherwise he wouldn't have taken on the case.

I had lunch with Matthew (called Joe) Culligan, a friend of the famous, a onetime marketing whiz, whose face was familiar to the public because he wore a black eyepatch to cover a World War II wound that took his eye. Culligan and I had some fun finding a way to sit at a table and talk since he couldn't see out of his left eye and I couldn't hear out of my left ear.

Culligan and I hit it off immediately. He was, in addition to everything else he did, a writer of business books, and he wanted Stein and Day to be his publisher. Before lunch was over Culligan had put in a phone call and soon we were joined by a young, handsome, and bright former Israeli paratrooper named Isaac Levi. Levi was a scout for a Houston-based, formerly Italian venture capitalist with the very un-Italian name of Dibo Attar. Attar, who was rich enough to keep a New York apartment at the Pierre for his occasional visits, had a New York lawyer named Michael Beckman, a name partner in a firm called Bell, Kalnick. Beckman and I, it turned out, had played tennis together years ago, had had some business discussions, and had liked each other. Great! Beckman's firm, however, had no bankruptcy lawyer, but they knew one they had great confidence in. His name? Joshua Angel. Great again! Angel already knew all about Stein and Day's case. Terrific! We were caught in the upswing of a soap opera that could have a happy ending.

By September 1, we had seen the second draft of a contract for Dibo Attar to become Stein and Day's outside funder. The price was tough for our shareholders, 50 percent of the equity, and Attar was to get, as is customary for an investor in a Chapter 11 company, a priority security position, and a hefty fee if the deal collapsed. But it was a way out of the ban on publishing and we took it—or wanted to.

The offer was passed along to Harvey Barr, the debtor's new counsel, who in turn passed news of it along to Henry

Swergold, attorney for the Creditors' Committee. What Barr should have done was to take the deal to court and have any opponents argue their case in front of the judge. Instead, he succumbed to the backroom "negotiation" that so many bankruptcy attorneys practice and that, in our case, led absolutely nowhere.

Barr came back with the news that Swergold had rejected Dibo Attar's offer of funding. I called several members of the Creditors' Committee. They said they hadn't heard about the funding offer. I still keep as a souvenir the torn remnant of the poster that served as a visual aid for our meeting with Attar. It showed the titles of the most urgently needed books, how much it would cost to manufacture them (they were all ready to go), and how much revenue they would produce.

On September 10, 1987, our spirits were lifted off the floor again by an unprecedented offer from Barnes & Noble that made news nationally and was received as a good sign by many in the publishing community. Barnes & Noble offered to license the hardcover reprint rights for their mail-order catalogue of fifty titles that no longer existed in hardcover. Their advance would be $100,000. John Kelly, vice president of their Marboro Division, who negotiated that and subsequent deals and was for a long time a hero of this Chapter 11 case, testified later in court that those long-dormant rights would earn between $300,000 and $400,000 over the five-year life of the contract. Moreover, they put in an order for a lot of Stein and Day trade paperbacks. They told the press they were hoping the money would enable Stein and Day to make a comeback. What the press didn't report was that the Michigan Bank grabbed $70,000 of the $100,000, which added up to 100 percent of Stein and Day's share 40 percent of the authors' share, and left the publishing house still unable to produce books and get back on its feet, Barnes & Noble's best efforts notwithstanding.

Well, if Stein and Day couldn't be in the business of publishing, at least Harvey Barr, unlike Joe Doaks, knew how to present evidence of the value of the company's assets. On October 27, 1987, and then again on November 2 and 5, Stein and Day brought on its witnesses. A certified appraiser named Eugene Albert testified that the company's real estate was worth $2 million, and if he could, he'd buy it at that price. Werner Linz, as previously mentioned, testified that Stein and Day's exclusive publishing rights to twelve hundred backlist titles was worth between $5 and $6 million. John Kelly, expert in old books, new books, and good books, testified to the worth of the Barnes & Noble deal, and said that his company wanted to do more (and they did). Claude Tusk, a Harvard Law graduate, the partner of Solin & Breindel litigating the case against Kable News on behalf of Stein and Day, found himself on a witness stand for the first time in his life; he did a remarkable job of summarizing the case, which if finally heard by a jury might provide the restitution that would enable the publishing company to return to its pre-Kable profitability.

Other witnesses testified to the accounts receivable due from various sources, and to the value of the large inventory. (Within months, over 90 percent of incoming orders had to be turned back because the company ran out of stock on its most wanted books and was not allowed to reprint them by the business-destroying order of Book-Crafters and the Michigan National Bank. In my opinion, the company and its unsecured creditors might well have had a large claim against these two secured creditors under the lender liability laws.[6])

The testimony as to Stein and Day's assets was strong and favorable. And, as the reader knows, the company had developed a new ongoing business plan that would have enabled it to do over half a million dollars' worth of Christmas business *with existing inventory,* enough to get the company rolling again.

---

6. See Chapter 18, "What Your Lawyer May (or May Not) Tell You About Lender Liability."

That's when Deryck Palmer, a sixth-year associate at Weil Gotshal, managed to turn an agreement of all the parties into the "unconscionable and obscene" talkathon described in Chapter 8. Harvey Barr should never have permitted that initiative to get out of his hands. Palmer was the attorney for the estate's arch enemy, BookCrafters. Barr would have saved himself a paper mountain of later work, and possibly put himself in a position to be compensated adequately, if he had insisted on drafting the document. Sadly, it was the last chance, really, to save the company, and Deryck Palmer took on the job of dribbling the ball for five weeks until the game was over.

One has to credit Harvey Barr. Once he saw he'd been tricked, his anger was real. That's when he sent his letter to the other attorneys—Palmer for BookCrafters, Borri for the bank, and Swergold for the Creditors' Committee—calling their tactics "unconscionable and obscene." That brave act earned him absolutely nothing except a place in this book.

One of the big bullets Stein and Day had to bite was the sale of its real estate for $1.1 million less than its appraised value. How it happened is part of this cautionary tale.

On November 6, 1987, Stein and Day signed a contract for the sale of its real estate at the appraised price of $2.6 million, to CarSem, an engineering and building firm. That was enough to pay down the bank completely (the bank claimed $1.8 million at the time of filing). The court approved the sale.

The next step was a meeting of buyer and seller before the Briarcliff Village Planning Board. In our home court we needed friends. When I spoke before the planning board, they were well aware of the company's plight, which had had plenty of local press attention. I thanked the members of the board and left the room. I then watched through the glass in the courtroom door as Ed Seminara, a principal of CarSem, made his request to build twenty units on the property. I couldn't hear what was going on. From Seminara's expression, however, I could see he wasn't getting a favorable reaction. When he came out he looked like someone who'd just taken a kidney punch. Within days, CarSem had backed out of the contract.

In the next year, we sold the property *three more times*. All three went to court-approved contract and none had any contingencies requiring planning board approval. Buyer number two and buyer number three each failed to close. Though each forfeited a fifty-thousand-dollar deposit, that didn't cover the intervening interest and legal expense. The Michigan Bank ran up a bill for half a million dollars for additional interest[7] and legal fees while we tried to find a buyer who would either have no contingencies or could pass muster with the planning board. More than seventy parties, one from as far away as San Diego, came to view the property. All who went for an informal discussion with village officials came away discouraged. Others were discouraged by the fact that an old, unused aqueduct cut a twenty-foot-wide swath diagonally through the property. The aqueduct used to carry water to New York City, and narrow strip of land over it was now a kind of state "park," a rarely used walkway that crossed streets and roads and on the Scarborough House property was a band of grass indistinguishable from the rest of the meadow. You had to lay out your plans so as not to build houses on top of the parkland and you could cross it only on the existing road. Hence it took a bit of brainwork to lay out a plan, and this discouraged some builders.

Finally, almost by accident, a developer named Norman Judelson dropped by. He had built beautiful homes in Westchester and the Hamptons and had a lot of loose cash.

---

7. Under the bankruptcy law, if a secured creditor is *under*secured, it is not entitled to postpetition interest. Though both the bank and BookCrafters claimed at various times in motion papers that there was insufficient equity in the estate (meaning they were undersecured), both continued to rack up interest charges without objection from either the estate's attorneys, the attorney for the Creditors' Committee, or the court, though I kept calling attention to that anomaly.

He offered $1.5 million for the property that had been appraised at $2.6 million, and had outstanding mortgages of over $1.9 million. I was able to negotiate an increase of $129,000 for each building lot above ten that the planning board would approve. With the approval of just a few more, the bank at least would be paid off and the Steins' home would no longer be at risk.

Judelson applied to build sixteen houses on the eleven-plus-acre property (really thirteen-plus acres if you include the unused parkland of the aqueduct). The property owners present at the planning board meeting were unanimous in support of the petition, which was most unusual since normally only dissidents show up to oppose a developer's plans.

In spite of the support of neighboring homeowners, the planning board turned us down flat. At this meeting we learned for the first time that when we sold the property to Judelson some months earlier it had been rezoned "automatically" to one-acre residential, though nobody had advised us of this automatic rezoning. In fact, we learned that evening that we were no longer legally entitled to operate a business in Scarborough House where Stein and Day had its headquarters for fifteen years, although the planning board had magnanimously decided that we could stay on for six months (which we were also not told), some part of which had already been used up.

The planning board's turndown was only a "recommendation" to the board of trustees, but local politics dictates that its recommendations are not opposed. Naively hoping that reason might prevail, I wrote to the board of trustees.

First, I suggested that any "automatic" rezoning of property might be unconstitutional.[8] I learned some weeks later that the village's attorney, who was not pres-

---

8. Briarcliff's then recent Master Plan Update said that if any business property was sold it would be "automatically" rezoned to the lowest density residential zoning in the area.

ent at the meeting, agreed with me. Second, I pointed out
that the Master Plan Update stated that "the Plan must be
responsive to the needs and desires of those it represents,
particularly as it reflects their physical, social, and economic investments."

This, I said, raised two issues. As to "economic investment," appraisals were made in good faith by professional
appraisers over a period of a decade on which the property
owners and lending institutions relied. I pointed out that
the Michigan National Bank, the principal mortgage
holder on the property, and Stein and Day as the owners
of the property, had relied on the appraisals. Even the
bankruptcy court had relied on a recent appraisal given
under oath to determine whether the secured creditors of
Stein and Day were adequately protected. If the court,
banks, and property owners cannot rely on appraisals by
experts, "particularly as it reflects their physical, social,
and economic investments" as stated on page eight of the
planning board's own Master Plan Update, then we had
precipitated all mortgagors, mortgagees, and the courts
themselves into economic chaos. I said, " Surely that is not
the intention of this Board."

I made the point that if property owners find themselves unable to pay off their mortgages when they sell
their land because of newly rendered views of a planning
board, this could be interpreted as an unconstitutional
deprivation of property.

I then raised the delicate issue of democracy. The Master
Plan Update states that "The Plan must be responsive to
the needs and desires of those it represents." At the
meeting of the Briarcliff Planning Board on Tuesday, October 11, 1988, every Scarborough homeowner present
spoke in favor of our petition. Among those present as
individuals were the president and recent past president
of the association of area homeowners.

It didn't do any good. My opinion, shared by other property owners, was that Mr. James Carey, a banker prominent enough to be listed in *Who's Who in America* and as

Chairman of the Planning Board an influential public official, had made up his mind perhaps prior to the meeting. Mr. Carey was against rezoning the Scarborough House property to the same density as most of the land in the area, including the estate across the way. He fixed on the zoning of one street inland from the property that suited his purpose: to deny the petition. Other than that street, the property was surrounded by the same zoning we were asking for, plus a church and a golf course. At the subsequent meeting the of board of trustees, the pastor of Scarborough Presbyterian Church spoke in favor of our petition, but to no avail. Without rezoning to R-30 (three-quarter-of-an-acre plots), the property had been effectively sold for little more than half of its appraised value, the mortgages could not be paid off, and we were stuck. The Village Planning Board had hammered another nail into the coffin.

The board's decision destroyed the last chance for Stein and Day to pay off the bank and for my family to be rid of the guarantee, which could still be used—and was used—as a club to get us to agree to anything anybody else in the Chapter 11 case wanted.

A local law firm experienced in zoning matters thought there was merit in a case against the planning board's unfortunate decision. It would have taken a $10,000 retainer to go after $774,000 of payments that would be due the estate on rezoning to R-30. However, most of the creditors and their attorneys were busy fighting with each other over small amounts and could not focus on this three-quarter-of-a-million-dollar issue. Barr & Faerber, the attorneys for Stein and Day, had carved out a substantial fee for themselves and for the attorney for the Creditors' Committee out of the sale to Judelson. Both attorney carve-outs were at my sole risk.[9] Despite their compensation from the sale of the real estate, neither law firm sent any-

---

9. Every dollar that went to the attorneys was at my risk as the bank's guarantor.

one to represent Stein and Day at any of the three meetings we had with the village authorities.

The thrust of this cautionary tale, if you're a debtor company in Chapter 11, is that biting the bullet means recognizing that the attorneys will run the case and that you will be helpless to oppose those who take unreasonable positions against you or your company's interests, whether they be creditors, their lawyers, or even local officials whose return for their time is an exercise of power over the powerless.

Perhaps what hurt most during this period was the fact that I had begun writing this book, and everyone I talked to in its preparation who knew Joshua Angel said that had he been allowed to be Stein and Day's attorney, as he had elected to be, the publishing company would today be forging into its second quarter century, a better-run ship because its founders had lived through the Hellsgate[10] of Chapter 11 and learned a thing or two.

When it comes to biting the bullet, Sam Metzger of Chipwich tells this story: "During Christmas week of 1983, I was summoned to Chicago to meet with a successful businessman, one of the richest men in America, who was a major creditor of my company and knew Chipwich well. He offered to take over financial responsibility for the company."

Clearly, it was an invitation Metzger could hardly refuse. "It turned out to be a two-day meeting. But this fellow's proposal came quickly. He wanted to wipe out my stockholder base. He wanted the people who'd invested in Chipwich, who'd believed in what we were doing, to be

---

10. Hellsgate is the place off the northeast shore of Manhattan where the waters of Long Island Sound swirl into the waters of the East River with a rush that causes a perpetual turbulence that all who would be safe had best avoid.

dropped by me down a deep hole through an unofficial reorganization. The administration of Chipwich would of course be transferred to this man's home base, Chicago.

"I spotted a bullet on the man's desk. I got the obvious message: It was time for me to bite the bullet. What I did was take the bullet when he wasn't looking.

"It would have been a relief to be rid of Chipwich's mounting financial problems. But I couldn't live with myself if I ditched my stockholders. The next week I returned and respectfully declined the man's proposal. He said he respected my decision, but he would never receive me again or provide me with any assistance in the business community.

"When I got back home I found a gunsmith near my upstate farm and had him empty the powder out of the bullet and put it on a dogtag chain. I wore that bullet as a reminder throughout the company's years of agony. For four years I never took that chain off, night or day. When I wore an open-throated shirt, people who didn't know me must have wondered what kind of biker I was, wearing a bullet. People who did know me probably wondered, too. Once when I was in Chicago and ran into this fellow, I couldn't resist it. I unbuttoned my shirt and showed him the bullet.

"Finally, long after the Chapter 11 was over, the chain broke. I had it fixed. When it broke a second time, I knew the occasion had arrived for me to put the bullet away in my jewelry box."

Despite Metzger's stand, in the end only the shareholders of Chipwich got hurt. The creditors got paid back. The shareholders had two million dollars in equity wiped out.

I asked Metzger for his overview of the Chapter 11 experience. He said it made him smarter, stronger, more compassionate, five times the man he'd been for having lived through the bankruptcy. He says he learned humility, to face his emotions, and how to deal with adversaries. Was he recommending the experience?

"No," he answered. "Not many people survive. Ninety-nine percent will be permanently damaged."

Every year out in the Hamptons, when the weather turns toward summer, an "autographing" for charity is staged at the Elaine Benson Gallery. Books are cadged from the publishers of all the many writers who live on the South Fork of Long Island, and although I have never owned property there, Pat and I and even some of the kids stayed so often at the Kazans', once at the Budd Schulbergs', and several times in houses rented for a fortnight or a month, that I seemed to be considered a "local" writer. In 1986 there was a stand with Budd Schulberg's books and Budd Schulberg behind it, pen in hand. There was also a Sol Stein stand piled high with books, but I was not there. The same thing happened in 1987, a few weeks before filing, and though it would have given me a chance for a reunion with several of my authors and lots of our friends, I just couldn't bring myself to go. In 1988, as far as I know, there was no Sol Stein stand. I had disappeared from where I belonged and wanted to be.

Pat and I have been "book people" all of our lives, giving in to temptation whenever we passed a bookstore in any city anywhere. On Saturday, June 4, 1988, not quite a full year into Chapter 11, Pat and I were in Mount Kisco, looking for a suit for me to appear in court in. (For the first time in my adult life, my clothes no longer fit me.) In the mall, we passed Lauriat's, a bookstore we'd dropped into dozens of times to browse, and to see how many—and which—Stein and Day books were on display. This time Pat pulled me away. "It makes me sick to go in there," she said.

Item: It is Sunday, November 7, 1987, almost half a year into Chapter 11, and by prearrangement, our good friends the Brieants bring new neighbors, Mr. and Mrs. Joseph Flom, to see Scarborough House. Brieant is, of course, Chief

Judge of the Southern District, and the fact that Stein and
Day is in a bankruptcy court in that district, in a courtroom just below his in the same building, has left an awk-
wardness in our long-standing relationship that we both
work at trying to keep at bay until this is over. Flom, as
probably all 700,000 lawyers in America know, is the head
"rainmaker" of Skadden, Arps, Slate, Meagher, & Flom.[11]

The Floms took us all to a splendid dinner. Did he know
that his firm represented R. R. Donnelley? Did he know
that Donnelley got a restraining order that effectively put
us out of business at no benefit to itself? Did he know that
one of his partners threatened to have me put in jail if I
dared to publish? Or with nine hundred lawyers in his
firm, does that kind of small stuff not drift upstairs? Flom,
to his credit, came to speak on our behalf when the local
property owners turned out in force to support our ill-
fated petition before the Briarcliff Village Board of Trustees. His wife, Claire, is a book person. At this writing more
than a year has passed since their visit to Scarborough
House. I promised to take them to *"riverrun,"* one of the
great second-hand bookshops in the United States, run by
Harper & Row's ex-sales manager, Frank Sciocia. I sent the
Floms a photocopy of an article about the place, but I
didn't take them. I will, when the pain stops.

Valentine's Day, 1988, is on the horizon, which counts
for less than the fact that it will be the fiftieth birthday of
Stein and Day's most loyal and valued employee, Dawn
Horstmann, known and liked by dozens of people in publishing and by scores of authors. We can't throw a party,
can we, we who had thrown parties that were covered
nationally by CBS and NBC television crews when we
launched an important new book? We settle for lunch at
Dudley's restaurant, where we had consorted with world-
famous authors undisturbed by the locals, and where,

---

11. At which firm, according to *The New York Times* of March 24,
1989, the partners' *average* income is $1.1 million per year.

once, on two successive days we had as lunch guests Jimmy Hoffa (a month before he disappeared off the face of the earth) and Nguyen Cao Ky, the dashing ex-prime minister of South Vietnam, and the locals wondered, some of them out loud, about the kind of people who were writing books these days.

And so five survivors plus Dawn Horstmann ended up at Dudley's. We toasted her half century. Her husband is taking her away to celebrate where it is warm. We wish her well. There is a little bit of present-giving. And then the bill comes, and I read it three times, for it says $195, less than most lawyers in the case bill for an hour's work, but to us at that stage an impossibly depressing sum.

In the spring of 1988, Patricia Day, who did her graduate work at the universities of Paris, Iowa, and Columbia, was now, by default, an order processor. And what she was telling us was that more than 90 percent of the orders that passed through her hands had to be turned away because we were out of stock and not allowed by the Michigan Bank and BookCrafters to reprint the books that people wanted most. Some quick calculations would indicate that we were turning back close to four million dollars' worth of orders a year. Everybody could have been paid back in time if it hadn't been for the irrationality of two creditors and our not being allowed to hire the attorney who knew how to deal with them.

It is said that in the United States there is a course for every possible subject of study, including the most inane. But there is not a single program in any university in the country that teaches you the skill of surviving as a manager in Chapter 11. If there were such a course, no one would take it because you take courses when you are young or optimistic about life.

It is debilitating beyond belief to do hard work totally unrelated to any field in which you have expertise. If you have had pleasure from work, as Pat and I have almost all

of our lives, it is stultifying to be in a world without pleasure, a prisoner serving time.

I note in my diary, "I'm chafing all day to get going on
something that resembles real work."

On May 12, 1988, in the eleventh month of Chapter 11,
I said to my wife over the newspaper at breakfast, "I
checked the obituary page. It's okay. I'm still alive."

When our seven children were young, I would always
read the Declaration of Independence to them on the
Fourth of July. In 1988 Pat and I didn't venture out even to
watch the fireworks at the Sleepy Hollow Country Club, as
we had for some twenty years. As for reading the Declaration of Independence, even to myself, it seemed inappropriate.

A few days later, in Stein and Day's now desolate
offices, the air conditioner in the room that housed our
company's one personal computer, formerly used by our
now departed comptroller and now by me, wasn't working properly. We tried a do-it-yourself fix that didn't work
well. We gave up, which is what Chapter 11 gets you used
to.

On Thursday, December 22, 1988, Deryck Palmer, one
of Weil Gotshal's seventy-seven bankruptcy lawyers, representing BookCrafters, the estate's mortal enemy, served
Stein and Day with a motion to terminate the automatic
stay. It later turned out they'd been working on this since
sometime in October, but waited till a day before the
Christmas weekend to spring it. And they got Judge
Schwartzberg to foreshorten the notice time and agree to
a hearing on Wednesday morning, December 28. Weil
Gotshal required answers by 6 P.M. Tuesday. That meant
it had to get to Federal Express (Stein and Day is not in the
same city as Weil Gotshal or the others to whom answering papers had to be sent) by Monday. But Monday was a
national holiday. I wondered if Judge Schwartzberg knew
or cared how boxed in we were. We had a single working
day, Friday, to prepare a reply to a complex petition that

could stop everything dead in its tracks. The only time to get comments and corrections from the attorneys on our side was the Christmas weekend.

At about eight o'clock on Christmas Eve, Laurence Solarsh of Golenbock & Barell, attorneys for The Colophon Corporation, showed up to get a copy of my papers, which I'd been laboring on all day. At 9 A.M. on Christmas Day, Solarsh telephoned for an hour, going over points in the papers so that they could be revised on Christmas Day. At 1 P.M., five of our now-grown children had assembled restlessly beneath the tree, ready for the present-opening ritual, conducted since they were very young, making the rounds, one present at a time, with always the youngest opening a package first. At exactly that moment, the telephone rang. It was Harvey Barr, attorney for the estate, with his comments. I took them down, and then, at long last, we got to the present-opening and then the holiday meal. Then, of course, it was back to work to incorporate the comments from Solarsh and Barr into the answering papers.

Thank you Weil Gotshal, thank you BookCrafters.

The words that haunted my mind throughout the latter part of the Chapter 11 experience were those I had once heard from Elia Kazan during the long months we had spent working together. "If you've got a body, bury it." That's what enabled me in the summer of 1988 to issue a release to the press that said, in effect, Stein and Day will never publish another book. I did it for practical reasons, too. I had the sense that other publishers were not vying for the rights to books in our backlist because it was unseemly as long as there was some possibility of Stein and Day making a comeback. It was up to me to bite the bullet, open the door, and invite them in to finish off the involuntary liquidation.

This cautionary tale would be incomplete without acknowledgment of the good people whose quality was never fully appreciated until we were forced to live in the moral wasteland of Chapter 11. Israel Berman, the intelligent and witty head of Viking Films, had years earlier brought world rights to a work by Dylan Thomas[12] to Stein and Day; while painfully sick with inoperable cancer, he kept calling with concern about what would happen to us. And Daniel Miller, director of the world-famous Strang Clinic, a brilliant oncologist, came to my office to inquire about the fate of his novel in the Chapter 11 process and to say that he had read the chronology of events and understood *it was not our fault.* Or the attorney-turned-novelist, Arnold Stream, who would pick up the phone every few weeks to find out how we were faring and to ask were there any legal services he could perform without fee? And literary agents, who in legend are enemies of publishers in trouble, but who in the persons of Claire Smith and Jane Gelfman, each protective of their clients, also would call to express their concern for that living thing, the publishing venture, that was, like Gulliver, tied down by small men.

Chapter 11 brought out the best in a few loyal employees, a tiny army, who stuck it out. I mean people whose talent and presence would grace any company, and who stayed with the debtor as if the company were a part of their family under attack.

Throughout the Chapter 11 experience I thought of myself as an indentured servant. If someone in that position has a chance to flee, he probably should, which is why I strike a medal here for those who didn't: Lou Ditizio, the able production manager who waited for half a year for a chance to produce the books to fill the waiting orders before taking a much-better-paying job that he

---

12. *The Beach at Falesà,* originally written as a screenplay for J. Arthur Rank and transformed into a book in a screenplay series that began with Elia Kazan's *America America.* At one point, the co-owner with Viking of the film rights was Richard Burton, who fortunately changed his mind about having Elizabeth Taylor play an eighteen-year-old Polynesian girl.

liked less; or Daphne Hougham, the administrative editor, who had dozens of new books ready to go to press and finally understood the ununderstandable, that BookCrafters and the bank would really abort all those thousands of hours of work; or Vincent Diamonte, our comptroller, who had to be restrained time and again from borrowing money on his house to put into profitable production because we knew that the system would prevent his ever getting his money back, as it had ours.

Two employees stayed to the bitter end out of loyalty. Dawn Horstmann, my good right hand whose value to the estate was realized even by the hostile lawyers, who each day had to put aside urgent work to do fruitless Chapter 11 labor or, as a newly expert paralegal, help me prepare for yet another court hearing, kept her extraordinary presence even when she was not paid and when she had to moonlight occasionally to make ends meet. Our receptionist, Idoline Rankine, also became our order-taker, typist, computer operator, purchasing agent, and God knows what else as jobs doubled and quadrupled for those who remained.

My employment (but not my work) was officially terminated by the creditors on January 27, 1989. David Stein, the youngest of our six sons, now twenty-five, who had left a good job in San Francisco to help the family firm (he took the place of four people) and Patricia Day Stein stayed on at the behest of BookCrafters, the creditor who succeeded in taking over the assets. On February 13, 1989, BookCrafters paid Horstmann and Rankine and reneged on their promise to the others. Horstmann and Rankine, both moral people who had wanted to leave a long time ago, picked up their things and left, for there was no longer anyone or anything to be loyal to. After twenty-six years, nine months, and twenty-one days, Stein and Day became a shell without publishing people. In charge was Randy Kuckuck, a lawyer.

The shareholders of Stein and Day were not financiers but people who were interested in publishing and had faith in the enterprise. The majority of shares were owned by employees and former employees of the company. One editor put her entire inheritance into Stein and Day stock. All of them lost everything. I was even blocked from keeping them informed of what was happening. When I drafted a letter, one or another lawyer would always find a tactical objection to something I was saying. Hence my real communication with them is this book.

As for me, I could look back on the largely wasted years in Chapter 11 and sum up:

I lost my life savings.

I lost all the money I had earned as a writer over a quarter of a century.

I lost the approximately $300,000 borrowed by mortgaging my home to lend to the company during the time of troubles.

I lost the money invested in defending myself from harassment lawsuits against me personally, which were really tactical maneuvers to cause me cost and pain and, in one instance, to successfully help coerce a signature out of me on an entirely different matter.

Finally, I hoped to gain my freedom from the orchestrated madness that is Chapter 11. I wanted to get out with my principles intact. That was not to be.

CHAPTER 16

The St. Valentine's Day Massacre, 1989

"Take note, take note, O world,
To be direct and honest is not safe."
—Shakespeare

*O*EDIPUS, *Lear, Alice in Wonderland,* Orwell's *1984*—the literature of manipulation and deception is art; the manipulation and deception that is allowed in courtrooms are artful dodgings of due process. The prize goes to the lawyer who outfoxes his peers.

On December 28, 1989, BookCrafters presented its case for the termination of Stein and Day's automatic stay. Had they succeeded, that might have left them mired in a long squabble with the other creditors. *They didn't really want the stay terminated.* In my opinion the real purpose of their motion was to force a settlement that would enable them to walk off with the assets of the company whose ability to continue publishing they had destroyed.

Such hypocritical motions are part of the game, just as BookCrafters' harassment lawsuits against me personally were part of the game. We will remove these threats against you if you agree to what we want you to agree to, if you sign what we want you to sign.

One begins to see the law as a playing field.

BookCrafters' motion papers were full of wrong figures that could only mislead the court. Our answering papers, duly filed, uselessly gave the correct figures and facts.

Judge Schwartzberg has said that he doesn't credit papers and pays attention only to testimony and documentary evidence. Fine, we thought. We were prepared to back up our papers with detailed testimony and hard evidence.

BookCrafters' main witness was, of course, Randy Kuckuck. He raised his right hand to affirm that he would tell the truth, the whole truth, and nothing but the truth, and then told the court that BookCrafters had about five thousand customers of whom about four thousand were United States trade book publishers, and that therefore BookCrafters was a suitable custodian of the assets, particularly the publishing rights.

Had Stein and Day been given an opportunity to respond, it would have introduced a truly heavyweight piece of evidence, the six-pound, 1,395-page 1989 edition of *The Literary Market Place*, which lists all the publishers of any consequence. Miss Day would have testified that she had counted the publishers and there were a total of 1,748, not 4,000 (even if they were all BookCrafters' customers!). Moreover, the 1,748 included many duplicate imprints within the same organization, as well as over 100 university presses that don't publish trade books. That would clearly impeach Kuckuck's testimony that they had 4,000 American trade book publishers as clients. Were there that many in the entire English-speaking world?

Before Chapter 11, I had viewed perjury as a serious crime. In 1957 I had been commissioned by the Theater Guild to write a courtroom play about the Hiss-Chambers case. I had studied the many volumes of testimony. Important scenes of the play centered on the lie for which Hiss eventually went to jail. Before its opening on Broadway, the play, *A Shadow of My Enemy*, had a run at the National Theater in Washington. On opening night there, November 25, 1957, four justices of the United States Supreme Court were in the audience, a fact that did not go unnoticed in the newspapers the next day. In our society, the punishment for telling lies under oath is like the punishment for income tax evasion and conspiracy. These are "covers" for which wrongdoers are punished when their underlying and perhaps more important offenses are less susceptible to proof. That is the way I felt about Kuckuck's lying on the witness stand. His real offense had been his eagerness to destroy Stein and Day and all its works, rather than to give it a chance to rebuild from devastation caused by the actions of others. His "cover" offense was his parade of fiction under sworn testimony on the witness stand.

In his testimony, Kuckuck, a lawyer, had not only vented an immense falsification of the number of book publishers that BookCrafters did business with, he told the court that BookCrafters' twelve printing salesmen would and could sell rights to the Stein and Day books because of BookCrafters' good reputation in the publishing community. Kuckuck's purpose, of course, was to persuade the court that BookCrafters would be a better custodian of Stein and Day's assets than anybody else.

In addition to the objectivity verifiable evidence that Kuckuck had lied contained in a copy of *The Literary Market Place*, Ms. Day was prepared to testify that she and another Stein and Day staff member had conducted a survey of the top fifty publishing companies and learned that BookCrafters *regularly did business with only one.* Several others had used them occasionally in the past for reprints of backlist. A number of the production managers had never even heard of BookCrafters and asked how the name was spelled. One, when asked if they ever used BookCrafters, said, "Not if I can help it." One major book club had an absolute ban on doing any work at BookCrafters. So much for Randy Kuckuck's sworn assertions of BookCrafters' standing in the trade and their four thousand book publisher customers!

Ms. Day was also prepared to testify that BookCrafters' printing salesmen had no experience in selling publishing rights, and, moreover, didn't even deal with the people who bought rights! She was also prepared to testify that, in anticipation of Judge Schwartzberg's decision of the matter before the court, the woman BookCrafters had already hired to sell Stein and Day's publishing rights had no experience in a field that requires a lot of expertise.[1] We were also ready to prove that Mr. Kuckuck, who had elected himself to supervise the dismantling and sale of a publishing list assembled over a quarter of a century, could not identify its leading authors. How do you sell something if you don't even know what it is?

We never got our day in court. It is a game in which one side has exclusive use of the ball and then calls time and the game is over.

The parties, meaning the lawyers, wrapped themselves in the cloak of negotiation over a global settlement that would put the case to rest. Negotiating on behalf of The Colophon Corporation (and de facto on behalf of Sol Stein and Patricia Day) was a lawyer who'd been picked, essentially, not by me but by the lawyer I'd hired. This nice enough young man proved to be adept at surrender in this case. I provided him and the lawyer for the company with my deal-breaking points and the other items I wanted considered by the parties if I was to consent to a stipulation that enabled the company that had effectively blocked reorganization of Stein and Day to walk off with the assets at about zero cost (according to our calculations, they would be getting most of what they offered to satisfy the bank from money already on its way, as it were).

BookCrafters had proposed moving all of the company records from Scarborough House to its plant in Michigan before the stipulation was approved by the court. I was opposed to the premature move for two reasons. They'd said they planned to move more than fifty filing cabinets full of paper, some of it historically but not monetarily valuable. There was a more appropriate place for the editorial

---

1. When Ms. Rhonda Wonderman was hired by BookCrafters, she went running to an executive in publishing who had bought many rights from the company and asked him if he would teach her all about rights. He immediately called us to report this nonsense.

files than in the office of a cultural ignoramus such as Randy Kuckuck (see Chapter 20). Columbia University had asked to set up a Stein and Day archive alongside those of Random House and Harper & Row, which would preserve a quarter of a century of correspondence involving some well-known authors and three heads of state, as well as marked-up copies of manuscripts and galleys that showed how editors and authors labored in the days when such close work was commonplace. Columbia's location in New York City was not only convenient for scholars, it was convenient also for the lawyers and litigants.

BookCrafters couldn't oppose the donation of my personal and professional papers that had nothing to do with Stein and Day,[2] but they opposed the transfer of Stein and Day's editorial and publicity files, not on any material ground and for no reason I could see except as a further means of putting pressure on me. Deryck Palmer, the lawyer representing BookCrafters, seemed not in the least embarrassed by the vapor of his unspecified objections.

---

2. Columbia was the third university to ask for my personal papers. A decade earlier the Hoover Library at Stanford had asked for them, and subsequently the University of Wyoming at Cheyenne, which was building an estimable collection of the papers and manuscripts of authors. I had a penchant for hoarding things, and had turned both universities down, but after my Chapter 11 experience I was ready to free myself of the past. My preference for Columbia came from strong personal reasons. Stein and Day as individuals were a "Columbia family," in that Patricia Day had gone to Barnard (the women's college associated with the university), both of us had done our graduate work at Columbia, and I had taught in the graduate school. In fact it was the then provost of Columbia, Jacques Barzun, who'd been our Cupid, and we were married in Saint Paul's Chapel on campus and feted at the faculty club through the courtesy of the vice president of the university. Even unto the next generation, our daughter Elizabeth was one of the first fifty women admitted to Columbia College when the barriers at last came down in 1983. That weight of personal sentiment involved Patricia Day in many weeks of full-time, uncompensated work in a hostile environment when BookCrafters took over Stein and Day's premises. It was to have a noxious outcome the reader will learn about before this chapter is over.

The simple matter of deeding the editorial files to Columbia was adjourned three times. It is a sine qua non of street fighters to find the short hairs of the CEO. And the most effective way of countering that is to find the enemy's short hairs. BookCrafters had a lot of those, but Stein and Day had long ago been prevented from hiring the lawyer who seemed to know how to keep the bad guys at bay.

These settlement conferences really meant that the Michigan Bank talked to BookCrafters and BookCrafters talked to the bank, and I, to whom all of these matters mattered most, was effectively left out of the loop on the grounds that the passive lawyer for Colophon was being kept informed. When pressed to do something, his excuse for not involving himself in anything but useless conversation was his need to maintain collegial amity.

The essence of the deal they came up with without my participation in the negotiations was that Michigan National Bank would get $500,000 from BookCrafters, the bank would release Patricia Day and me from our personal guarantee, and BookCrafters would get *all* of the remaining assets. These consisted of the twelve-hundred-title backlist that Royalty Capital had contracted to buy after winning an open auction; the forelist of manuscripts that BookCrafters and the bank had prevented us from publishing and had also prevented all but one author from publishing elsewhere; the inventory for which we had had a bona fide offer from a major customer for a long time; the receivables (including one six-figure check from Holt, long overdue and ready for delivery that BookCrafters kept from being delivered earlier), the furnishings of an office that had housed more than fifty employees, a Calder print that had hung over my mantelpiece for more than a quarter of a century, which an attorney had invited me to steal and that I instead made an offer to buy, and, of course, the Kable lawsuit that two years earlier had involved some $11.4 million for monies allegedly due and the direct damages caused by the allegedly improper withholding of funds.

There came a time on January 24, 1989, when the parties convened in the judge's chambers because I was being naughty. If BookCrafters got the Kable lawsuit along with the other spoils, I might be at risk for some $81 million of counterclaims that Kable News had directed at me personally. Those counterclaims, I was advised, were coextensive with our affirmative case against Kable. If we won that, the counterclaims vanished. Moreover, Howard Friedman, chairman of AMREP, which owned Kable News, had made statements in sworn testimony that invalidated Kable's counterclaims. Nevertheless, I was concerned about the Kable case being directed by Stein and Day's arch-enemy, BookCrafters. The judge suggested that Book-Crafters agree to keep on Solin & Breindel, which had acted as Stein and Day's counsel in the Kable case for years, and that I consent to cooperate.

It took very few minutes after that meeting to realize that I was being asked to devote what the lawyers estimated to be four months of my life to a case at a time when I desperately needed to restore my vitality and make a living. Moreover, the primary beneficiary of my efforts would be BookCrafters!

My head fuzzy from the antidepressant that had been prescribed for me to be taken especially before court appearances, I was led into a witness room to sign the global settlement that I hadn't seen before appearing at the courthouse.[3] I had read through the document hurriedly in the hallway. It was still full of false statements I had protested verbally and in writing over and over again. In addition, both the Michigan Bank's and BookCrafters' claims included large amounts of postpetition interest, which an undersecured creditor is not supposed to claim.

---

3. Michelle Coleman, a young lawyer waiting to pass the bar exam who worked at Weil Gotshal on BookCrafters' behalf in this case, told me in the hallway that there had been two *other* drafts that I had not seen of the document I was supposed to sign in more places than any other party.

But in my ears buzzed the words of my own lawyers, "If you don't sign, you will suffer a lot of pain and a great deal of cost you can't afford. Nobody is making you sign. It's your decision." But keep the pain in mind. And the cost.

I felt coerced. And there was reason to be.

When we first started doing business with Michigan National, the company was still in its post-Norton slump, suffering losses. Therefore, Patricia Day and I had to guarantee personally the company's line of credit, and the bank also took a formal mortgage on our home as security for the loan to Stein and Day. When the company returned to high profitability, the bank released the mortgage on our home and cut our personal guarantee to what was supposed to be half of the balance of the line. The paperwork, however, did not reflect that agreement, but made us responsible for half of the line's maximum rather than half the balance. Unfortunately we were not represented personally by counsel at the time, and my protests about the difference between the agreement and the paperwork fell on knowing but deaf ears. The wording made a great difference because it made us personally responsible for the last $375,000 owed to the bank, and once the principal and interest was paid down (including the postpetition interest to which they may not have been entitled), we would still be responsible for the bank's "collection" expenses, which, including their attorney's limousine, came pretty close to the amount of our guarantee.

Another cautionary observation is warranted here. After Stein and Day had returned to high profitability, the company's white-hat officer at Michigan National had misrepresented the purpose of the guarantee as being merely a way of seeing to it that we didn't hand him the keys and that we stuck around if assets had to be sold. He wasn't telling the truth, and neither would any bank officer who told you that. If they don't collect from the borrower, they can and will come after the guarantor, and if it's your home they have to take, they'll try to take it. Had we (or our numerous attorneys) known then what we know now

about lender's liability, we would have been less worried
about losing our home and more interested in suing the
bank and BookCrafters for their undue interference in
Stein and Day's business.

At the settlement conference, I looked around the table,
surrounded by lawyers. There was no principal from
Michigan National Bank, and the bank's signature was the
only one that meant anything to me. And the chairman of
the Creditors' Committee was not present to sign. (In fact,
the document was circulated to all creditors and shareholders with those two signatures missing.) Only Book-
Crafters, and a couple of lawyers, would sign. And this
misnegotiated agreement contained what in my view
were greatly inflated claims by BookCrafters. I had seen
no evidence to support the claims I was being told to
acknowledge in the stipulation, though Stein and Day was
entitled to receive such backup. The Michigan National
Bank had not supplied monthly statements since April of
1987. BookCrafters had not supplied an accounting, but we
were certain that its claims were vastly inflated. It had
been owed about $760,000 at the time of filing. They were
now claiming $1,700,000 and telling others that they were
owed $2 million.[4] In addition, this reprehensible docu-
ment put Stein and Day's authors at the mercy of their
greatest enemies, the folks who had barred the publication of their books. I felt great moral revulsion. Signing
this stipulation was wrong.[5]

I was told to initial the document wherever there had
been changes, and to sign in three places, as President of
Stein and Day, as President of The Colophon Corporation,

4. The last was reported to me by Robert Spencer, an attorney
engaged by BookCrafters to pursue the real estate claim that should
have been pursued by the attorneys of the estate.

5. I learned a couple of weeks later that the chairman of the Creditors' Committee had been loath to sign and did so only belatedly. As for
the Michigan Bank, they had not yet signed two weeks later.

and as just plain Sol Stein. When it came to the third signature, my moral revulsion won and I signed "Sol U. D. Stein," the "U.D." a signal to the judge that I was signing under duress. Previous testimony in court had shown that I had signed some of BookCrafters' prepetition documents under duress and had so indicated by signing my name Sol U. D. Stein. When BookCrafters made its motion to terminate the automatic stay and submitted their security agreements to the court, they craftily omitted the ones that I signed U.D.

A day or two later, Deryck Palmer, BookCrafters' lawyer, blew his cork. Though he had hovered over me during the signing, his glee at having his client walk off with the spoils apparently temporarily blinded him. He had belatedly discovered the U.D. in my signature. He more than anyone else deserved it, for in the early drafts of the same document he had given me a middle initial I didn't have, D. (for "duress"?), and he had probably helped my conscience make the last-minute decision to sign the document the way I did.

Palmer was the one lawyer on the case that I found I could not have a civil conversation with. In the ostensible privacy of phone conversations, most of the lawyers had said something about how much they regretted what Pat and I had lost in this man-made disaster. Palmer was an exception; he had lost even the pretense of compassion somewhere on the road to a partnership. Palmer seemed to get more rather than less hostile as the case dragged on.

A conference was scheduled in the judge's chambers. Palmer wanted to condemn my signature. Patricia Day and I wanted to have our say, since we had been denied our day in court on BookCrafters, motion to terminate the automatic stay. The conference was postponed several times. The judge's wife was sick. Then the judge was sick. Then some of the lawyers couldn't make it. Finally, on February 14, 1989, the St. Valentine's Day Massacre took place.

Before going up to our vigil outside the judge's chambers, Pat and I stopped in the clerk's office on the ground floor to file a claim for one of our two remaining loyal employees who hadn't been paid. The large room was decorated as if for a birthday party, with dozens of valentines hanging from crepe paper streamers that crisscrossed the room. Why was a bankruptcy office, where no love was ever at home, celebrating Valentine's Day in such a conspicuous manner? And was it at the taxpayers' expense?

After more than a half hour of waiting with all of the lawyers (figure one thousand dollars charged to somebody), we were invited into the judge's chambers for the conference.

A couple of the lawyers spoke briefly and then Patricia Day asked to speak. She spoke of Columbia's offer to set up an archive of Stein and Day's papers—that it had been a motion I had made weeks earlier and that kept being postponed without my consent.

The judge wanted to know if it was Columbia House. "No," said Patricia Day, "it was Columbia University."

Next came some hard matters. Ms. Day said it was her fiduciary responsibility to report that a bank deposit of $1,800 worth of checks had vanished from her desk, something that hadn't happened in twenty-six years. A Stein and Day employee had reported that a BookCrafters' employee had been going through the papers on Ms. Day's desk when she was out to lunch. The missing checks were reported to the police.

No comment from the judge.

Ms. Day told how BookCrafters had interfered with a $140,000 payment from Holt, for which the check had already been cut. The money was supposed to have been turned over to the bank. In the meantime, the interest charges were rolling up, presumably at the personal risk of Sol Stein and Patricia Day.

No comment from the judge.

Ms. Day pointed out that BookCrafters and others seemed to have interfered with a long overdue payment of $87,000 due the estate. The failure to receive this payment and the missing checks had prevented the company from completing its court-ordered January payroll as of February 14. Also, as a result of the missing checks and the interfered-with payments, the company had been unable to make two bank payments ordered by the court.

No comment from the judge.

As a result of BookCrafters' reneging on its payroll commitments to the four remaining employees, paying only two of them, Ms. Day said all four employees had fled the previous day and the offices were closed.

No comment from the judge.

BookCrafters was interfering with rights deals made long ago. BookCrafters' motion papers had grossly misleading figures. Mr. Kuckuck had given testimony that we were prepared to impeach.

No comment from the judge.

I was able to add just a few points I had prepared to make. I said the stipulation left me with the Scarsdale lawsuit on my hands, which was a suit that attempted to bypass the automatic stay and was for debts of the company. BookCrafters' attorney, Deryck Palmer, then asserted that the Steins had guaranteed the Scarsdale loans in question, although he knew this was being disputed on appeal. The Steins' attorney, whose firm represented them in the Scarsdale matter at considerable cost, said absolutely nothing. In fact, the judge asked him whether he was Scarsdale's attorney.

The theme song of the meeting seemed to be: Sign. Nobody is pressuring you to sign. Sign.

I explained that the duress I felt was from being told by attorneys that unless I signed I "would experience a great deal of additional pain and much cost I couldn't afford."

Sign.

I wanted to know why the Steins and Colophon were the only secured creditors not to get "adequate protection," and oft-mentioned function of the court in connection with the Michigan Bank and BookCrafters.

I didn't get very far. Judge Schwartzberg was angry. He

said that if I didn't put a proper signature on the settlement papers, he would have the case converted to a Chapter 7—in his words, "a real bankruptcy," as if Chapter 11 were not in fact treated by the press, the public, and the officers of the court as a bankruptcy. Presumably, it was intended to make Patricia Day and me feel that somehow the stigma would be worse if we didn't supply signatures.

That didn't seem to affect me, so the judge said that if he converted the case, my home would be at risk because the bank could come after me on the guarantee. The fact that the company had signed a contract with Royalty Capital for $400,000,[6] and that payment alone plus the sale of the attendant inventory would wipe out any claim the bank might have other than perhaps its excessive legal fees, mattered not in the least. The fact that Royalty Capital's offer was made a full five months earlier did not matter either. The judge made the choice clear. You are not being coerced. Sign the stipulation cleanly or I'll convert into a Chapter 7 and you'll lose your home.

In the military, if captured by the enemy, all I had to give was my name, rank, and serial number. Here the enemy wanted more—my signature on a set of falsehoods—and the judge was going to give it to them. Wasn't it Ambrose Bierce who described a litigant as "a person about to give up his skin for the hope of retaining his bones?" Okay, okay, I said, "I'll sign right now."

The judge refused to have me sign my name again. He demanded a totally new signature page with no vestige of my U.D. signal. And he added that even if I signed a new page he might still throw the case into Chapter 7 anyway

------

6. The contract, signed on November 15, 1988, sold the company's exclusive use of the copyrights on all previously published books to a Wall Street firm that agreed that after recoupment of its initial payment of $400,000, it would also pay 20 percent of profits from sales and licenses for a period of fifteen years. The Royalty Capital contract kept getting adjourned and was never heard. *Part of the game.*

and was ordering the U.S. Trustee to be in court on February 21 to make a motion to convert the case.

In case I changed my mind?

Nobody is forcing you to sign, the judge wanted to make clear. Besides, if you're opposing signing as a matter of principle, what's happened to your principles now that I mention you could lose your home? The judge said I might want to think about it and discuss it with my wife. But, in truth, the St. Valentine's Day Massacre was over. Not the pain and not the problems. There were the orchestrated horrors of February 21 to look forward to. You could tell by looking around the room at all the lawyers' faces. The judge, by throwing fear in my face, had frightened the bank and BookCrafters also. If the judge decided to convert the case to a Chapter 7, the bank wouldn't get its half a million dollars from BookCrafters, and BookCrafters wouldn't be able to walk off with the assets.

Pat says my face was very red. I remembered that the judge was a lawyer by training, too, and his objective was to clear his calendar of the case and move on. In the press of things, what did it matter if the Steins were devastated and seven hundred authors were flung into BookCrafters' limbo?

Two days later, Greg Borri, attorney for the Michigan National Bank, arrived at Scarborough House in a chauffeur-driven Cadillac. The chauffeur waited for three hours while Borri went over with us the various matters related to getting the stipulation approved. We were unrepresented by counsel, but that didn't seem to make a difference from the time when we *were* represented by counsel. Then Mr. Borri handed us a copy of the stipulation with a clean signature page so that I could sign it three times without the U.D.

In publishing, one's word is one's bond. In the world of banks, words that weren't on notarized paper were meaningless. Michigan National had proved that when it went against its own word on the purpose of the guarantee. As Sam Goldwyn said, "A verbal contract isn't worth the paper it's written on." Scarsdale National had reinforced the deception involved in bank guarantees. And in the nether regions of bankruptcy law, you were a fool to trust anybody.

I asked Mr. Borri whether he would agree to hold our signatures in escrow, as it were, until the stipulation was signed by everyone else, and if others refused to sign, would he return our signatures to us?

Mr. Borri declined. Angrily. He was here to get my signature, not to negotiate.

I asked Mr. Borri whether he would simply sign a receipt for our signature page.

Mr. Borri declined.

I went into another room to find a lawyer at Golenbock & Barell who might advise me since Stein and Day no longer had counsel and I felt unprotected. Mr. Silberberg was off till the following Tuesday. Mr. Solarsh was airborne on his way to Dallas and then heading directly into a courtroom. Mr. Meadvin was not in his office.

Mr. Borri went off in his chauffeur-driven car with our "uncoerced" signatures. If the stipulation was not approved, the Steins would be held accountable for the cost of the limousine as well as Mr. Borri's time. After all, wasn't it part of the collection process—of the whole charade in which the debtor pays?

On February 21, 1989, when the court approved the stipulation that turned all the remaining assets of Stein and Day over to its arch-enemy BookCrafters, it also approved the transmittal of the editorial and publicity files to Columbia University to set up the Stein and Day archive. Randy Kuckuck of BookCrafters said in court that he had been given the opportunity to go through the files and was satisfied that they contained nothing that BookCrafters needed to sell the assets. Deryck Palmer said that Book-Crafters was removing its objection. And so by order of the court Columbia University inherited the Stein and Day archives. Stein and Day and Columbia exchanged the court-ordered papers and the editorial files were now the property of Columbia. Or so we and they thought.

There were some fifty four-drawer file cabinets of material to be gone through page by page so that only historically relevant material would be transmitted to Columbia. This burdensome task fell largely to Patricia Day, who spent many weeks, including weekends, working (without pay, of course) to get the files ready for Columbia under circumstances previously described as horrendous. When Randy Kuckuck announced that Scarborough House, where the files were maintained, would be closed down at the end of April, Patricia Day did not see how she could possibly finish in time. But she did. I immediately telephoned Mr. Kenneth A. Lohf, Librarian for Rare Books and Manuscripts at Columbia, to say that the collection had been weeded down to some fifteen transfiles and seven cartons and to arrange for Columbia's truck to pick them up. I specifically asked that the pick-up not be on Monday, April 17, because BookCrafters was planning to move other contents of Scarborough House that day. I was subsequently advised that Columbia would pick up at precisely 1 P.M. on Wednesday, April 19. I called Mr. Kuckuck's office at once and advised his assistant of the pick-up time and said that either Patricia Day or I would be there before the appointed hour to make certain all went well. There is no question that all BookCrafters' employees on the premises knew that the marked boxes were Columbia's.

On Sunday, April 16, David Stein, one of our six adult sons, and Patricia Day drove to Scarborough House and affixed large yellow signs to the top and sides of each transfile and carton that belonged to the university. The signs, in oversize black letters, read, "FOR COLUMBIA, DO NOT TOUCH." The following morning, April 17, David Stein returned to Scarborough House to remind all concerned not to ship out the marked files.

The morning of the scheduled pick-up by Columbia Patricia Day drove to Scarborough House. At least eight of the editorial transfiles marked "FOR COLUMBIA, DO NOT TOUCH" were gone!

Kuckuck was not on the premises. She asked Benton Arnovitz, a former Stein and Day editor now working for BookCrafters, where the files were. Arnovitz at first said, "What files?" He then admitted that Columbia's files had been shipped by BookCrafters to Michigan.

When I learned that BookCrafters had taken Columbia's property, I phoned Kuckuck in Michigan. He readily admitted he'd taken the files (which he'd told the court he'd examined and found were of no use in the sale of the assets) and said he had taken them with Patricia Day's permission! Unbelievable!

That afternoon Mr. Lohf, Columbia's Rare Books and Manuscripts Librarian, called me to say that the shipment had arrived and did not contain the number of transfiles I had said would be ready. I told him that I was trying to do everything I could to get the files back.

Meanwhile I had phoned the court. Judge Schwartzberg had relieved Harvey Barr of his duties as counsel to Stein and Day as of late January. I was no longer employed by Stein and Day. I had resigned as an officer and director (as had the other directors) in March. I suppose I didn't have any standing in the matter except that the motion and the court order had specified that any subsequent matters relating to the documents were to be referred to Patricia Day or myself more or less in perpetuity.

On the fourth try I reached Denise Savage, clerk to Judge Schwartzberg, who had ordered the files given to Columbia. She said the court was powerless to do anything unless I brought on a motion. Based on experience that a motion would take weeks to be heard (only a motion put on by Weil Gotshal just before the Christmas weekend deserves a fast track in this game!), and concerned that Kuckuck could take anything he wanted out of these historically important archives that had not yet been catalogued by Columbia, I phoned the FBI.

I didn't know if a felony was involved in the interstate

transportation of someone else's property, but I hoped that the FBI would at least cause an agent in Michigan to seal the boxes forthwith until the court or others could deal with the matter. When at long last I connected with the agent who was assigned the case, he had trouble with the fact that the motion ordered by the court had stated that the documents had historical but no monetary value. I stressed that the files were invaluable and that it seemed to me that the relevant points were that the files had been deeded to Columbia by court order and that BookCrafters had taken them in defiance of that court order. When the agent asked, "How much money did Stein and Day owe BookCrafters?" I asked, "Why is that relevant?" He said, "It's relevant because I'm asking it." That's the precise point at which I gave up hope that the FBI would be of any help.

I called Weil Gotshal. Deryck Palmer was not there. I told his secretary what his client BookCrafters had done. The call was not returned. I phoned again the next morning early and got Palmer because he answered his own phone. Yes, he'd had a phone message from me, no he didn't know anything about the matter, so I told him. I also told him that as an officer of the court he had a responsibility to see that his client did not defy court orders. He said he would confer with his client and get back to me.

Later that morning Patricia Day received an overnight letter from Randy Kuckuck in which he wrote to confirm a conversation with her that never took place. She replied that very day, contradicting his lies, and sent copies to those whom it might concern: Judge Schwartzberg (who says he doesn't read letters but puts them in the file); Palmer's boss, Martin Bienenstock, who had received a copy of Kuckuck's letter; the managing partner of Weil Gotshal; William Nuffer, the president of BookCrafters; and the president of American Business Forms, the publicly traded company that owns BookCrafters. Of course if the shoe had been on the other foot, something would have happened fast. As it was, Stein and Day did not truly exist any more, and nobody to our knowledge was doing anything to recover the files that Patricia Day had labored over for months and that were then taken by BookCrafters, on orders of a member of the California bar, Randy Kuckuck. As for Patricia Day's letter to Kuckuck, perhaps it concerned no one in the justice system. Directing these copies to the world of law could be characterized in the vernacular as pissing into the wind. Which perhaps summarizes the entire effort of two years to preserve Stein and Day as a living entity.

And the attempt to stop BookCrafters from robbing the tomb.

CHAPTER 17

Dear Scarsdale National, or How Come They Sue You Personally for Money You Didn't Get?

> "Advertisements—especially bank ads—with asterisks followed by tiny print trouble us. They probably trouble you too! . . . What you see is what you get. As we promised—no asterisks and no small print!"
>
> —from an advertisement by the Scarsdale National Bank in the Gannett Westchester Newspapers, January 26, 1989

B ANKS can be liars, as witness the epigraph to this chapter, which is about the Scarsdale National Bank's "small print."

Some of the worst things that occur in Chapter 11 happen not to the company that sought protection but to the key individuals involved. The common reaction from executives is a declaration of surprise: Can this be happening to me? Can it be happening in the United States? Implicit in those questions is a shock to the individual's faith that in the United States the process of law is orderly and fair. Of course I was hearing this from white-collar executives, not from the economic underworld of working-class lawbreakers whose people know from long experience that the legal system is a jungle of abuse. Bankruptcy courts provide their white-collar debtors with sudden and startling views of the inequity that the denizens of inner cities expect and get.

When executives in other companies opened up to me about these things, their greatest concern usually was confidentiality, which is perfectly understandable; they were either still trapped in Chapter 11 or making a new life for themselves as people do in a witness protection program. Sometimes the problems of their companies affected their personal credit for years *after* those companies had come out of Chapter 11. There is no "adequate protection" for the individuals involved. Therefore, at this point I am taking the liberty that writers always resort to by disclosing what happened to me, my family, and my friends and associates, with the assurance that in many if not most respects the incidents that follow, with variations of course, have had their counterparts in the lives of others.

Despite my appalling ignorance of the process when Stein and Day was forced into Chapter 11, I did think that the company I fathered would be protected long enough to sort out its problems. I certainly didn't guess that I *as an individual* would be unprotected. Nor could I imagine that I would be offered up as a target for foxy lawyers, working for creditors with venom in their veins and deep pockets in their suits.

Here are just a few snowflakes from the blizzard of problems I thought the law protected me against.

I didn't think a bank could successfully bypass the automatic stay imposed on Chapter 11 creditors by suing the chief executive personally on a guarantee he didn't give.

The Scarsdale National Bank and Stein and Day had a minor relationship. When the company bought equipment such as a telephone system and an automobile, it financed these through Scarsdale as collateralized loans, secured by the equipment that was purchased. *No personal guarantee was asked for or given.*

When the company borrowed short-term cash in anticipation of a specific receivable, such unsecured short-term loans were personally guaranteed by Sol Stein and Patricia Day. That happened twice and the loans were repaid promptly. And the day the loan was repaid in full with interest, the personal guarantee was withdrawn in writing.

Stein and Day, despite its cash-flow problems, was pretty good about keeping up with all of its payments to its banks until Donnelley got a restraining order *making it illegal to pay anybody anything.*

The automatic stay was supposed to lift the restraining order, so the very first month after Stein and Day filed, it sent its monthly payments for the car and the phone system to the Scarsdale bank, payments that had been approved by the court as part of its cash collateral order.

Scarsdale sent the checks back. I should have been immediately suspicious. Or our attorney should have been. Scarsdale's excuse for returning the monthly payments was that the checks with which they were paid weren't debtor-in-possession checks. They were provably wrong. Those were legitimate DIP checks, a fact Scarsdale could have verified with a phone call, had they wanted to. Were the checks returned as part of a scheme to get around the protection that Chapter 11 was supposed to provide the company?

What Scarsdale did instead of taking the court-approved proffered payments was to file suit against Sol Stein and Patricia Day personally for the full amount of the two collateralized equipment purchases by the company, plus legal costs and interest on the money that Scarsdale had refused to accept from the company. They claimed that the guarantee the Steins gave *half a year later* for a short-term unsecured loan repaid in full in less than two months (and the guarantee withdrawn in writing) covered retroactively the two secured and collateralized car and phone system loans, though at the time those loans were made no guarantee was asked for or given.

How could Scarsdale possibly win on such specious

grounds? *By taking it to an entirely different court that had no knowledge of the facts in the Chapter 11 case.* New York State Supreme Court Judge Ferraro said he didn't want to examine intent or circumstances, only one piece of paper: the guarantee for that totally different loan. According to Judge Ferraro, that withdrawn guarantee had "small print" in it that made the guarantee apply to loans previously made.

Though two and a half years had passed and Scarsdale hadn't claimed at any time during that period that the two prior equipment-purchase loans by the company had been guaranteed personally by anybody, Judge Ferraro didn't want to look at the doctrine of laches (which is not unlike a statute of limitations). Incredibly, the Scarsdale bank won its "case" against the Steins personally for two loans that they had never asked Stein to guarantee!

Several weeks after Judge Ferraro refused to consider intent and examined only what he called the "four corners" of the irrelevant document, the good judge was indicted. That didn't help us because the indicted judge's previous decision stood.

In the meantime, before the Steins could post a bond and their lawyers file an appeal, unbeknownst to the Steins, Scarsdale, its judgment in hand, seized the Steins' personal checking account at the Chemical Bank and two Dreyfus accounts, stripping them of funds, and leaving the Steins without a checking account.

Moreover, Chemical, from which the Steins had borrowed and fully repaid over half a million dollars over time, didn't have someone pick up the phone and say, "What's going on?" or at least let us know quickly that Scarsdale had gotten a restraining order on our account, freezing it for over forty thousand dollars, though the outstanding balance on the two company loans was a total of about sixteen thousand dollars at the time. (That's how the law protects creditors, folks. The difference is supposed to cover interest as it accumulates, legal fees, collection fees, etc.) We didn't even know about the restraining order for three days because what Chemical did was to have a low-level clerical person send us a letter. The account had been opened twenty-five years earlier.

Caught by surprise, the Steins found their previously issued Chemical Bank checks bouncing all over the place—checks to the Food Emporium, checks we'd given to our Christmas charities, and the check with which I'd paid the annual care fees for my parents' graves.

Chemical closed the long-open account because there was no money in it. Dreyfus didn't even know who had seized the money from them; they told me it had been turned over to the IRS, which sometimes does this kind of thing.

The Steins found themselves suddenly unable to pay for anything with their own checks. How do you pay your electric bill, with a MasterCard? How do you deal with the bounced check at the place where you buy your weekly groceries? You can't tell them to redeposit the check because there's no money in the account. And you can't put money in the account because Scarsdale would seize it, if there was anything left after Chemical claimed its fees for all the bounced checks. *We had never borrowed a penny from Scarsdale National. The only money Stein and Day had borrowed from Scarsdale and that we had guaranteed was paid back in full.* We were suddenly trapped in a nightmare we couldn't awake from.

Though Patricia Day covered most of the checks immediately by volunteering replacement checks from a third party with a full explanation rendered and received, that didn't keep the manager of the local Food Emporium from excoriating her when, nearly a year later, she sought to pay a food bill by check as she had done in that same store almost every week for years.

Picture yourself in a situation where you've never in your life been unemployed and you suddenly can't cash a check to buy food. Actually, we were luckier than most executives would be in similar circumstances—if you can call anything that happens to you in Chapter 11 "lucky." One of my good friends was able to send us by overnight mail a check for $1,000 made out to a friendly corporation, which cashed it for us. Our local drug store, with which we had been dealing for many years, cashed an incoming check we received for a hundred dollars that we were now unable to deposit or cash in a bank. I felt suddenly back in the Great Depression of the 1930s, a world without money.

One thing all the executives I interviewed who'd been victims of Chapter 11 agreed on was the high level of stress. I, like others in the same situation, had been seeing a therapist over the profound reactive depression caused by the uncivilized Chapter 11 environment. Had one of the bounced checks been paid to the therapist?

No, the therapist's check had cleared before Scarsdale had seized the account. I turned the last check paid the therapist face down and saw the endorsement. The therapist had deposited the check in Scarsdale National! How could anyone in their right mind deal with a bank that did what Scarsdale had done to me?

Wait. When the Steins posted their bond for over twenty thousand dollars (remember, the amount owed by Stein and Day was sixteen thousand dollars), Scarsdale went to court to try to get the amount increased! At about the same time, the Steins learned that *Scarsdale could still keep the money they had seized out of the Steins' checking and saving accounts* pending the outcome of the appeal, which could take a year. It took more than half a year for us to learn in court that the money seized from our three accounts had been used by Scarsdale to pay down the company's phone system loan. Scarsdale didn't apply any of the money to the automobile because they were still trying to seize it and they knew the phone system wouldn't be worth a damn to anybody if it was ripped out. But this didn't keep them from filing a motion in bankruptcy court to do just that— rip out the phone system and prevent Stein and Day from communicating with the outside world.

That isn't all. At one point, one of Stein and Day's junior lawyers told the Steins that he had good news. Scarsdale wanted a "settlement conference." Those were his precise words. I insisted that the senior lawyer accompany me to the settlement discussion at the offices of Scarsdale's lawyer. That quite possibly saved the junior lawyer's life, for when the senior lawyer and I arrived at the offices of Scarsdale's lawyer on the Route 100 commercial strip that bisects southern Westchester, what I encountered were two public stenographers ready to take my testimony under oath. Scarsdale's lawyer, one Robert Cucinell, an unsmiling, dour, sullen, touchy grouch of a man, stood at the ready to depose me without proper legal notice.

After I was asked a couple of questions about the whereabouts of my other personal assets (those not yet seized by Scarsdale), I insisted on calling my personal lawyer, Michael Silberberg, who gave hell to both Cucinell and Stein and Day's lawyer and told Stein to tell the assemblage that this extralegal event was terminated.

I have two things to say. The Scarsdale case, on which I have won two motions in appellate court and, as this is being written, am still waiting for a decision that will get me my seized money back, *has cost me more in legal fees than the total amount claimed by Scarsdale when they first refused to accept the company's checks in payment.* Second, no one reading this should ever sign a guarantee with any bank that doesn't include the following words: "Anything in this document to the contrary notwithstanding, this guarantee applies to the one loan cited above (give the exact reference by paragraph and line) and no other loans of any kind, and shall be null and void when the above-named loan has been repaid." If a bank won't let you add words to that effect or permit you to remove words like "heretofore and hereafter," you've been warned. They can hold you accountable for loans you are not intending to guarantee.

As I've indicated, this hairy story, unfortunately, is not untypical of the bizarre punishments visited upon the officers of Chapter 11 companies. To take another instance, BookCrafters, a manufacturing company that depends on book publishers for its livelihood, has sued personally the chief executive officers of at least two of the companies they deal with. Among other things, they sued me for the $25,000 check taken by the first lawyer representing Stein and Day in the bankruptcy case as his retainer. In this book I call that lawyer Joe Doaks, though under my breath I have called him many other things. When BookCrafters' complaint was finally heard by federal Judge Griesa, he asked if Stein had received any of the money. BookCrafters' lawyer was obliged to say Stein hadn't. The judge then invited the defendant's attorney to submit a motion for summary judgment to get rid of the nuisance case. But do you know what it costs to file such a motion and have it heard?

Did Joe Doaks, the first lawyer, who had to be fired, ever account for the $25,000 he took and for which I got sued and had to defend myself at my own cost? Did Joe Doaks ever return one penny of the $25,000? He'd said it was okay for him to take, but when his replacement talked to him about getting the money back he said that Joe Doaks claimed he had already spent it! Can you imagine any defendant telling a judge that he couldn't return money he hadn't earned because he had already spent it?

Lawyers protect each other's income.

Judges are lawyers.

Why the harassment lawsuits against individuals? It's the equivalent of taking hostages. If they want you to do something down the line that you don't want to do, the personal lawsuit is used as a trading point. You sign, we'll release the hostage (drop the case). This is a clear abuse of process that is tolerated by the courts, where judges do not seem inclined to invoke Rule 11 sanctions against lawyers for deep-pocket clients who play harassment games with frivolous cases that are costly to defend.

Harassment lawsuits like the three I faced are not uncommon in Chapter 11 cases, even though they are costly to the creditors at a time when the head of the company is fighting for the company's life and to pay off the company's debts. In any other circumstance, purposely deflecting the attention of someone in charge of dealing with an emergency would be considered either irrational or perverse. Under the fishnet protection of Chapter 11, chief executives are even less protected from meritless lawsuits than the company itself. Harassment cases against the company are heard in bankruptcy court. Cases against the chief executive are brought in other forums where the judges don't want to hear about automatic stays or attempts to bypass them.

Actions against the chief executive that are really attempts to get around the automatic stay can sometimes be brought under the jurisdiction of the bankruptcy judge, which, if the judge is fair, can help diminish the obvious harassment of the executive and, at the very least, eliminate his expense of subsidizing battles in other courts out of his own pocket. They're known in the trade as the Otero Mills decisions (after the original case and its off-shoots). Some bankruptcy lawyers will volunteer to inform the executive of these cases and do something about them, but others will want to avoid the bother of getting a monkey off the CEO's back. After all, that's his problem, isn't it?

Can the all-powerful judge help? After all, one of the precepts of the bankruptcy laws is *equity*, meaning fairness to the parties. The problem is that the judge doesn't know much of what is going on, and it is apparently to the advantage of the lawyers to keep him in the dark as much as they can.

What does the citizen without a voice do—write a letter to the judge? Lawyers don't like that even if copies are sent to all the other participants. I wrote some letters to the judge anyhow, and though Judge Schwartzberg said he didn't read them and that he just put them in the file, they became part of the public record in the case. In an arena where satisfaction is scarce, that activity brought me a faint pleasure.

CHAPTER 18

What Your Lawyer May (or May Not) Tell You About Lender Liability

> "One should forgive one's enemies, but not before they are hanged."
>
> —Heinrich Heine

IF there is one subject that the general practitioners I talked to knew less about than bankruptcy it was lender liability, though a lawyer's knowledge of that subject could turn out to be of great value to any businessman. Even most members of the bankruptcy bar seem to know precious little about this important subject.

Sovereign nations that borrow money from banks can welsh on billions with impunity. Huge corporations often have major lending institutions competing for their business and are in a position to negotiate deals. But the people who run medium-sized and smaller companies often see banks as they do the government: The other side holds all the cards.

The good news is that is no longer true. In some recent and diverse cases banks have learned that they are lending institutions, not operators of businesses, and if they abuse their power they will suffer at law. A lender cannot seriously interfere with a borrower's business without risking an adverse court judgment. It also cannot with impunity mislead a borrower, and it has a fiduciary duty not only to the borrower but to all of the borrower's creditors. Turnaround consultant Malcolm Moses, who is also an attorney, puts it this way: "The lender has an obligation to deal fairly with a borrower. And if the lender deals unreasonably with a customer, puts a company out of business arbitrarily, or goes against its own practices, the injured borrower may be entitled to damages—even though the lender was entitled to take the actions it did under the loan agreement."[1]

If, like some of the lawyers I talked to, yours tells you that lender liability isn't an important issue, or that "there are only a couple of cases," or "the cases are only in California," steer him in the direction of the work of Helen Davis Chaitman, a partner in the firm of Ross & Hardies, which has offices in Chicago, Washington, New York, and Somerset, New Jersey—the last being the right place to inquire because that's where Ms. Chaitman hangs her hat.

Attorney Chaitman, a commercial litigator who knows bankruptcy law, is an expert's expert in the field of lender liability.[2] The business manager who hasn't the time to dig into the arsenal of technical material she's edited would do well to find a copy of her fifty-eight-page monograph, "The Ten Commandments for Avoiding Lender Liability," the November 1, 1988, version being the eighth edition of this priceless document. Ms. Chaitman's monograph seems directed to banks, telling them what to watch out for in the field of lender liability. Yet for the CEO who wants bargaining power to keep an aggressive bank in line, it is full of ideas. I wish I had come across it a year or two earlier. It is a first-rate primer of a legal rev-

---

1. Though I talked at some length with Malcolm Moses, this quote is from *Boardroom Reports*, November 1, 1988.

2. She is the editor of "The Lender Liability Law Report," published monthly by Warren Gorham & Lamont. Chaitman is also the editor of four volumes entitled *Emerging Theories of Lender Liability*, published by the American Bar Association. She is chairman of the Lender's Liability Subcommittee of the Commercial and Financial Services Committee of the American Bar Association Section of Business Law.

olution against the practices of some banks, and that "some" includes a few of the biggest banks in America.

In fact, the CEOs of healthy companies would do well to acquire a copy as a blueprint for dealing with banks in a way that, whatever their intended manners, will force them to behave in a businesslike mode.

As for the national relevance of Ms. Chaitman's research, she cites seventy-eight cases from Alaska to Florida, Arizona to Maine, Mississippi to Minnesota, Kansas to Wyoming, Texas to Canada, Wisconsin to Oklahoma, Arkansas to Tennessee and Maryland, and of course in New York, Illinois, and, naturally, California.

Perhaps the most important point for an executive to draw from Ms. Chaitman's advice to banks is "Thou Shalt Not Run Thy Borrower's Business." If a lender "exercises control" over business operations, it exposes itself to the risk of being held to the standards of a fiduciary. In *Security Pacific National Bank v. Williams,* the bank sued a car dealer on his guarantee and "he counterclaimed against the bank, alleging fraud, negligent misrepresentation, breach of contract, tortious interference with prospective economic advantage, and breach of the implied covenant of good faith and fair dealing." [3] A San Diego County Superior Court judge in 1986 awarded Williams $2.3 million in compensatory damages plus $2.5 million in punitive damages.

The outcome of a fair number of Chapter 11 cases depends on whether the owner or manager of the business has a personal guarantee hanging out. If he does, it is a weapon that can be used against him with great severity, either to tie him to the business or to cause him to lose whatever he's got left, including his home, to pay off the guarantee holder if the secured creditor can't get it out of the assets. Even in cases where the holder of the guarantee causes a drastic drop in the value of the assets, he holds the

---

3. All quotes that follow are from "The Ten Commandments for Avoiding Lender Liability," eighth edition, copyright by Helen Davis Chaitman.

guarantee as a killer club. It has been known to cause CEOs to sign false statements against their will and to turn over the keys to the business to the company's worst enemies. Nobody wants to lose his family's home.

The turnaround specialists have advice for CEOs who have not yet been called on to give guarantees. Daniel Morris says, "Avoid guarantees. The problem is that when clients come to me, most of them have already given guarantees. Sometimes a manager is so intertwined with his business that he'll guarantee more than he can possibly pay. Most banks use guarantees to make sure that the senior manager or owner hangs around. But homes are seized."

If you mention the word "guarantee" to Ken Glass, he comes back loud and clear: "Never ever." Then he gives a little: "Set a specific limit on a guarantee. Only what you can afford to lose. I've seen people who've given guarantees up to a hundred million and lose everything." And then he adds ominously, "If a company gets into a Chapter 11 situation, the holder of the guarantee will go after the difference between what he's collected and what he's owed in another court, not in the bankruptcy court. That's when a guy will lose his wife and children. The personal stress is scary."

Adam Radzik also counsels to avoid guarantees, "but if you have to give one make sure your home is excluded from the guarantee." Then he brings up a point most executives, even those who are good negotiators, often overlook. "If you're going to give a guarantee, make sure that what you get in exchange is worth it."

David Ferrari agrees. "Never give a guarantee unless you get something really worthwhile in return. If somebody threatens to pull the plug if you don't, let them pull it."

Chicago bankruptcy attorney Gerald F. Munitz's advice about guarantees is very direct: "If your guarantee is good, don't give it." Entrepreneurs give guarantees, Munitz points out, because they feel they can personally control the destiny of the company. Munitz believes that a guarantee should be considered only if you have nothing to lose.

Those who, like most of Daniel Morris's clients, have already given guarantees can take heart from lender liability authority Helen Davis Chaitman's cautions to lenders about starting suits to collect on personal guarantees. She tells of two cases in which the guarantors counterclaimed and *likely would never have sued the banks except as a result of the banks suing them in the first place.* In the Missouri case she cites, the bank spent a large amount of money and time getting a $7.5-million verdict against it overturned. In a Florida case, the jury came in with $3 million in compensatory damages and $9 million in punitive damages, where the bank had gone after a borrower and the guarantors for a mere $250,000 deficiency.

Ms. Chaitman maintains that the cases brought by guarantors on lender liability theories have forced lenders to become "much more sensitive to the rights of guarantors, which is good." She cautions, "If there is any question that the bank's actions may have contributed to the need to sue the guarantors, the lender would be well advised to write off the loan and move on to the next case."

Attorney Chaitman elsewhere notes that secured trade creditors could find themselves with risks similar to those of banks. "A trade creditor with a security interest in a customer's assets could subject itself to liability similar to that of a lender. There have been a few cases in which nonlender creditors have been sued for taking control of the customer's business."[4]

In an earlier case, a court "held that a lender who took control of a company in order to liquidate its assets and satisfy its

---

4. In Stein and Day's case, the company was not materially in default on payments to the Michigan National Bank prior to Donnelley's restraining order, yet the bank prevented the reorganization of the company by joining with BookCrafters in barring the manufacturing of books to fill orders, thus essentially excluding it from its only business, publishing. After reading Chaitman's document and other material, it is my opinion that Michigan National as well as BookCrafters might be liable, at minimum, for the many millions of dollars lost by other creditors and the shareholders.

own debt had breached its fiduciary duty to deal fairly and impartially with the debtor and with all of its creditors." The court's punishment was to subordinate the lender's $1.7-million claim to those of the unsecured creditors!

And listen to this: A bank that made a debtor's president take a 50 percent salary cut, replaced the debtor's accountant with its own, required bank approval of all payments, and even suggested that the landlord change the locks on the debtor's premises, got hit in court with a verdict for "tortious interference with a business."

In an interesting 1987 case *(Rubin Bros. Footwear, Inc. v. Chemical Bank)*, a major bank got into trouble because it misled a borrower into taking a course of action that benefited the lender at the borrower's expense.

Attorney Chaitman warns banks that, "In view of the seriousness of the jury verdicts that have been awarded against lenders in the past few years, workouts are serious business and they should be handled by people who specialize in handling troubled loans." Ms. Chaitman also points out the hazards at law of banks not keeping their internal memos objective, unemotional, and accurate. These memos, of course, are available to the borrower at discovery time if the borrower sues. We are reminded that jurors identify with borrowers, not with banks.

Ms. Chaitman's roll call of cases affecting lender liability has some very interesting items for executives to ponder.

Item: A lender must give a borrower a reasonable opportunity to seek alternate financing. Otherwise, it might be held that the lender has not dealt in good faith with the borrower, as required under the Uniform Commercial Code.

Item: A lender who precipitously terminated a line of credit lost the largest jury verdict in the history of the state of Maine.

Item: A "material breach," a phrase often found in bank agreements, strangely *means what it says.* Even under a workout agreement, a bank can't call a loan if the interest payment is, say, a day late.

Item: A Massachusetts bank destroyed a recently established business by foreclosing on real property over a small interest default that could have been cured by setoff against the borrower's account. Result: A judgment against the lender for more than half a million dollars.

Item: If a lender terminates workout negotiations without notice and joins other creditors in filing an involuntary bankruptcy petition, the lender could be liable for "malicious prosecution, abuse of process, and intentional interference with business relations."

Item: "The Alaska Supreme Court held that a borrower could recover actual and punitive damages from a lender" who seized collateral without notice, *even though the loan agreement permitted such seizure.* If a lender accepts late payments or negotiates with a borrower for an extension of a loan, it may be waiving its right to enforce a loan agreement strictly.

Item: When a bank supplies credit information in response to inquiries, it has a right to be silent, but if it talks at all, what it says must be truthful and *complete.*

Item: In a workout context, a bank that made threats it did not intend to carry out got itself clobbered with a verdict for $18.6 million after a Texas appellate court held that "the threat constituted a fraudulent misrepresentation."

Item: A lender can't refuse to honor a commitment for financing without subjecting itself to the possibility of compensatory damages. And if a bank officer verbally promises a borrower an extension of credit and then reneges without notice, causing damage, the bank could be held liable.

Item: If a business applies for a loan and the bank then

comes up with a smaller loan than "industry standards" would support, the bank could be incurring a liability.

Item: A Texas jury rendered a verdict of over $59 million against a bank that refused to honor the terms of its loan agreement.

Item: In one case a bank got itself into real trouble by injuring third parties (employees) while working out a bad loan.

In her coda, lawyer Chaitman cautions banks about their "traditional" arrogance. She says that they get that way because people richer than they are keep coming to them for money. She adds that the lawyers for banks become arrogant because they've usually been able to force borrowers' attorneys to eat whatever they draft. Because lenders are arrogant, they sometimes avoid negotiating settlements that, in their view, might set a precedent. Chaitman cautions, "It is often better to pay something to the borrower than to risk an adverse jury verdict. Almost without exception," she says, "all of the multimillion-dollar verdicts against lenders could have been avoided had the lenders been more compromising."

Sometimes problems arise because the actors are miscast. The bank officers who were personally involved in the litigation are not the right people to make the decision whether or not to settle the case. Settlement decisions, Chaitman maintains, should be made by more objective officers of the bank.

"Times are changing," cautions Chaitman. Banks "must ask themselves, with respect to whatever action they are contemplating, whether that action is fair to the borrower and whether any action which injures the borrower is absolutely necessary to protect the bank's interests."

The businessman's response to these developments can only be a long, loud, "Hallelujah!"

CHAPTER 19

Innocent Bystanders

WHEN the news tells us that in a shoot-out between Los Angeles street gangs or Washington drug dealers innocent bystanders have been hurt or killed, editorials express the sense of outrage we all feel. Yet I have never seen public comment about the literally tens of thousands of innocent bystanders who are severely hurt each year in the shoot-outs between lawyers in Chapter 11 cases.

When the Chapter 11 bus, loaded with attorneys, careens off the straight and narrow road and smashes into the people who ran the business, it also hits or sideswipes numerous innocent bystanders. These can be the small shopkeepers, merchants, and local suppliers, frequently much smaller businesses than the one in Chapter 11, many of whom may never have given a thought to the financial stability of their bigger customer until the crash. When they find out that their prepetition bills are stayed by the law—usually for years—and that they may never see their money, and if they do, it will be cents on the dollar, some of them are outraged; they have been betrayed by laws many of them didn't even know existed. Others, perhaps the more prosperous or mature, try to forget their loss, put it out of mind as a threat to their mental health, and get on with their businesses.

Turnaround specialist Gilbert Osnos points out that officers of a bank can also be "innocent bystanders." A bank is not a monolith; it is made up of individuals who are employees and who have their careers on the line. Since "nobody makes a bad loan," the workout banker has to prove that the loan wasn't a bad one by collecting every cent of it he can. Osnos's view doesn't necessarily sit well with CEOs who've had the "good-guy/bad-guy" routine played on them by bankers. If a person's going to play-act in order to trap you or persuade you into doing something you wouldn't otherwise do, he can hardly be called "innocent."

Osnos also sees public stockholders as innocent bystanders. Dan Morris says that is particularly true of small stockholders.

Ron Stengel, who's been consulting on other people's business crises for fourteen years, maintains that equity holders are "the least-informed group" of innocent bystanders. "Bond-holders," he maintains, "usually have adequate information, and trade creditors are not innocent."

David Ferrari expressed compassion for what he calls "good faith creditors who extended terms to the debtor. It's sad." The CEOs I interviewed felt the same way about the little guys, the ones who don't have sophisticated credit departments.

In the case of Stein and Day there was an unusual class of innocent victims that numbered seven hundred, most of them authors, a few widows of authors, or other proprietors of copyrights. Some of the authors, such as F. Lee Bailey and Elia Kazan, had income from alternate sources. Others were the authors of books that became steady backlist sellers, including a few that were considered classics; many of these books were suddenly unavailable, struck from their permanent niche because BookCrafters and the Michigan Bank would not allow sold-out books to be reprinted. The hardest hit authors were those whose books were counted on to provide income for their families. This special class of creditors included the survivors of now-dead authors, such as the widow of the historian of the Russian Revolution, Bertram D. Wolfe. A woman in her eighties, she wrote literally scores of postcards asking for money. Many authors found it beyond their comprehension that we were not allowed to pay royalties or reprint their books when they sold out. They were flummoxed by the bankruptcy laws that prevented them from getting their rights back so that they could place their books with other publishers. These circumstances made one Ph.D. author seem to go off his rocker: He sent us a postcard saying, "You are my Auschwitz." He telephoned my wife at home and said, "I hope you both die of brain cancer." And of course there were hundreds of authors from England, Australia, the United States hinterlands, and elsewhere who just didn't understand, and many of whom never learned how they became victims of the busload of lawyers who persisted in viewing authors as "nuisances," though they were easily the largest group of creditors and the ones most hurt by the tactics of the bank and BookCrafters.

The books by Stein and Day's authors have been read by many millions over the years—and some will continue to be read long after the Chapter 11 case is over. But some books that would have lived died because the buying practices of booksellers and librarians and schools are such that if a book is not available for a time—sometimes only for a few weeks—its place is taken by a similar book by another author. Though the authors suffered the depredations of the Chapter 11 process, it is to their everlasting credit that those who sought to understand what happened supported management's efforts with heart, soul, and in some cases personal sacrifice. There were a few exceptions, fewer than one percent of them, whose loyalty could be measured in a thimble. But the conduct of the 99 percent who stood by us stands in sharp contrast to that of, say, the book manufacturers like BookCrafters and R. R. Donnelley, whose enterprises depend on what the authors write, but who had their hands on the destruct button, and who did everything in their power to see that the books of the authors caught in this case were kept from the public.

On the afternoon of November 9, 1988, a squall erupted in the middle of a meeting of the unsecured creditors of

Stein and Day/Publishers. The speaker at the moment was a literary agent named Jane Gelfman, one of its more humane members.

Books, the press, and Hollywood have given agents a bad name by representing them in caricature. Actually, some of the most decent people I have met in three and a half decades of publishing have been agents, female and male alike, and several of them behaved with remarkable and recurrent decency while representing their authors well during the crisis. Gelfman, who heads the United States office of an important British literary agency, John Farquharson Ltd., was the only agent on the committee by virtue of the number of successful authors that firm had with Stein and Day, ranging from bestselling author Evan Hunter to such paperback espionage favorites as Clive Egleton. The more successful the authors, the more royalties they were likely to be owed at the time of filing. Presumably the agent who was owed the most got a place at the Creditors' Committee.

In previous meetings of the committee, at least those portions that Stein and Day's executives were permitted to attend, Ms. Gelfman was poised, attractive, and silent except for a rare question. But at the November 9 meeting she dared to raise a moral issue. Weren't authors really in a different class of creditors than, say, manufacturers? After all, professional authors relied on their income from books that continued to sell. Not only had Stein and Day been forbidden by its secured creditors from reprinting those books when they sold out, at the same time the authors weren't being permitted to move their books elsewhere. It was a crushing time for many authors. The average professional author in the United States is said to make about one-tenth of what a self-employed plumber or carpenter might make. With their books trapped in the Chapter 11 case, they weren't even being allowed to *buy* their own books back so that they could be placed with another publisher, if possible, and start earning money once again.

When Ms. Gelfman made her case, her emotion clearly

visible, she received from the lawyers the official word: Authors were to be treated no differently than other creditors, which meant their books, to which they owned the copyright but the publisher owned the exclusive publishing rights protected by the temporary stay, could be sold by the publisher to other publishers (or, as it happened, be taken over by BookCrafters) with the authors having no say in the matter.[1]

While the lawyers read Ms. Gelfman the rather cruel law, I tried to assuage her obvious pain by saying that in each of the perhaps fifty licenses that I had granted so far, I had consulted with the agents involved and had succeeded in steering the books to publishers approved of by the authors. Those practices presumably went by the board when BookCrafters seized the remaining assets.

Not all manufacturers were villains in the case, and some might well be called innocent bystanders, hurt by the actions of their manufacturing colleagues, BookCrafters and R. R. Donnelley. For instance, Arcata, a large manufacturer, seemed sympathetic and understanding during the early days, and discussed means of getting books produced, perhaps on a cash-in-front basis. The committee's chairman,[2] Ian Richardson, seemed friendly enough throughout. Richardson was executive vice president of the Offset Paperback Company of Dallas, Pennsylvania, which manufactured almost all of Stein and Day's mass-market books. Offset Paperback is owned by Bertelsmann, the world's largest media company; it is the same German company that owns the American publishing giants Ban-

---

1. An exception should be made for the Writers Union that represented five out of seven hundred Stein and Day authors. The established professional writers' organizations in the United States are the Authors League and the Writers Guild of America. The Writers Union, for motives best known to itself, allied itself with the authors' number one enemy, BookCrafters, which had led the attack on the publishing of authors' works and reprinting their books as they sold out.

2. The real chairman of the Creditors' Committee, of course, was its attorney, Henry Swergold.

tam, Doubleday, and Dell. It was Richardson who had alerted Stein and Day to the fact that when we were obeying the suggestions of the chairman of Kable News to greatly increase the size of type in our books and fatten them up for market, we were actually handicapping our sales, because dealers were reluctant to put two or three overfat books into rack pockets that could accommodate five normal-sized paperback books. We were grateful for Richardson's advice, though it came after we had already expended hundreds of thousands of dollars uselessly. Richardson's firm, after all, would have been making more money out of the artificially fattened books than out of normal-sized books if the whole mass-market operation hadn't come tumbling down on our heads. He is a decent man, an innocent bystander who nearly lost his job because he was the one who had extended credit to Stein and Day to print its mass-market books.

Among the innocent bystanders on the Creditors' Committee, one would have to acknowledge a remarkable man named Glenn Corlett, who with his wife runs a literate typesetting operation in Massachusetts called Comp House, which deserves to be first on any publisher's priority list of typesetters to use. By "literate" I mean the Corletts actually read and proofread well what they typeset, and Mrs. Corlett was never averse to rendering a favorable opinion of a book-to-be that really excited her. Her opinions proved reliable and gave us an early clue to the public acceptance of a book. The people at Comp House were the kind of professionals whom you cannot avoid developing an affection for. We liked working with them so much we nearly were their undoing; our production manager kept steering more and more typesetting work their way until we represented more than three-quarters of their business. When cash-rich Donnelley prevented us from publishing or paying anyone, including the people at Comp House, the Corletts very nearly went under themselves. Glenn Corlett became a member of the Creditors' Committee because of the size of Stein and Day's obligation to his firm.

The Creditors' Committee's cast of characters in this drama, nine of them when they attended in force, covered the spectrum from bad guys to saints. Actually the one "bad guy" wasn't a guy at all but Barbara Kelly, the lawyer from Skadden Arps who had threatened to have me thrown in jail if I dared to publish books when her client R. R. Donnelley, the largest printer in America, pulled the plug on Stein and Day. Most of the members of the committee were characterized by others as "friendly to the debtor." Though they represented a thousand other innocent bystanders, they seemed to have little if any influence on the case, though one of the primary missions of the court is to protect them. The only way they could recoup would be by Stein and Day producing books to fill orders. And blocking that doorway to recovery were two secured creditors, BookCrafters and Michigan National, whose motivation remains a puzzle to this day to all who would have explanations judged by a rational standard.

All of the turnaround specialists I talked to, as well as the CEOs, sympathized with the second largest group of innocent bystanders, the loyal employees who get shafted in Chapter 11. Ken Glass says that "employees are the number one sufferers. They go through the mental anguish of not knowing if they're going to be working the next day." And that torturing uncertainty can go on, of course, for days, weeks, months, and even years.

Crisis manager Dan Morris was concerned about the employees who lose whatever job security they had, and the job itself, sometimes without the severance pay they'd have gotten without the Chapter 11 filing.

In the six weeks before filing for protection, Stein and Day, then under R. R. Donnelley's restraining order, was prevented from paying its employees because to do so without Donnelley's permission would have been a criminal offense. Finally, after some negotiation, the company was permitted a small part of its payroll. At the same time, some of the employees were terminated. Donnelley did

278	A FEAST FOR LAWYERS

not even allow enough for all of the terminated employees to be paid. Some continuing employees volunteered to forego their pay so that those who had been terminated could receive their checks. They were advised that once the company filed, their lost pay, or up to two thousand dollars of it, would become "a priority administrative expense" that would eventually be paid. But the secured creditors with deep pockets took what there was to get. If anything was left over, these self-sacrificing employees learned, the "administrative expenses" of the enormous legal fees being claimed would probably step in front of their long-overdue paychecks, and they might never be paid.

It has been said that many members of the bankruptcy bar find their work heady and intoxicating. If in their drive to pocket as much cash as they can from other people's misfortunes they routinely run over innocent bystanders, who will haul them up on DWI charges? Surely not the courts that are run largely by former bankruptcy lawyers.

CHAPTER 20

Some of My Best Friends Are Lawyers

> "Had an accident? Dial 1-800-CRIPPLED. If you've lost a limb, dial 1. If your physician has removed a vital organ during a routine examination, dial 2. If you're in a coma, please hold."
> —Debby Reiser, a personal injury lawyer, quoted in *The New York Times*, February 17, 1989.

SOME of my friends who are lawyers seemed apprehensive about the birth of this book. Perhaps the title did it. Or knowing what I lived through and that I would try to report the events accurately.

Lawyers in the United States are getting gun-shy about the declining reputation of their profession. Even the Chief Justice of the United States Supreme Court has lamented publicly the transformation of the law into a business. I prefer that my view of the profession not be misunderstood.

The way many law firms are run today, the client is not really hiring the lawyer of his choice but taking pot luck. In many instances you hire a particular firm because of one person in the firm, a lawyer who has impressed you, or that you know from some other circumstance, or who has been recommended by someone you trust. You think you're hiring that lawyer, but if you study your bills, you will soon learn that much of the work is being done by other lawyers in the firm, usually associates because they are the biggest profit centers for the partners, though you are usually told that it is for your benefit because less per hour is charged for their services. This practice is based on the obvious fallacy that all lawyers do the same quality of work at the same speed. Some of the subordinate lawyers I've encountered think and talk at about one-third of a normal pace, which would mean that one should triple their hourly charge to determine the real cost.

In other circumstances, the work is not being done by the partner you hired but by another in the firm with alleged expertise in the matter at hand. The fellow or woman you thought you hired remains the shill, fronting for the firm in his relationship with you. In fact, if there's a problem, you'll often find that you're on the phone with two lawyers, the one you hired and the "expert" on that issue or the lower-ranking person who's doing the work. You are paying for both of them. The partner who is your contact person may be just "keeping his oar in," or learning more about some specialty at your expense, or reinforcing the advice the other person is giving you, or lending his imprimatur to the strategy already decided on before you were included in the phone call.

You may also find that a court appearance is being made on your behalf by yet another lawyer you never heard of. It is all part of the machinery of law as a business. The person-to-professional relationship that once existed between client and lawyer is still there, but like a bouncing ball, less and less, to the detriment of the client and the enrichment of the firm. This is a particular problem in the field of bankruptcy because, as previously declared, most lawyers don't know the field, and your friend and counsel may put you into the hands of a specialist who makes a fine first impression but in the close-quarter combat of bankruptcy may prove to be useless in achieving your goals.

This pattern of delegation can be particularly harmful in Chapter 11 proceedings because so much of the process is negotiation rather than knowledge of the code. As most business people know, negotiation is a skill that some people master and some don't. Law school is not much help if you didn't inherit the genes, develop the personality, or learn the maneuvers.

Before I am wrongfully accused of prejudice against lawyers, I want to make it as clear as a pane of glass that I take the same view of members of other professions, including my own. Since most readers have no experience of doctors of manuscripts and at least some experience of the medical variety, I will refer to the latter: Of the physicians I know, some are remarkable diagnosticians; two are estimable human beings, men of high moral character whose personal care for their patients is exceptional; and one of them might not recognize a fracture unless it was compound and the bone was sticking out. If I've got something, I've got to be damn sure to pick the right doctor to go to, and if I need his or her diagnosis I don't want it from the nurse.

My experience with the bar has covered an equally wide spectrum. I'd worked with Edward Bennett Williams, whom some consider to have been the premier trial lawyer of his era. It was on a matter that was important enough to make a four-column headline on the front page of *The New York Times*.[1] Williams's associate on the matter was Michael Tiger, a bright young man whose advocacy eventually earned for him some national celebrity, including a photo in *Time* magazine. Williams, unlike some of the slow-moving lawyers I've met, agreed to see me and

---

1. It involved the successful publication of *The Complete Bolivian Diaries of Ché Guevara*, which revealed, among other things, that four of the thirteen "campesinos" who accompanied Ché to Bolivia were members of the Central Committee of the Cuban Communist Party. Castro attempted to abort our coup by publishing an expurgated version of two of the five diaries ahead of time. Our competitor for the diaries was McGraw-Hill, backed by Bantam's paperback money; they went down to Bolivia waving $100,000 and hoping to attract the right attention. I sent Tom Lipscomb down armed only with his credit card and we got the book.

Daniel James, the expert editor of the book, on very short notice, and did a superb job quickly. He sent us a bill for four thousand dollars and before we could pay it, told me to tear it up, that the work was "pro bono" because it involved a matter of national security.

Samuel Lane of Casey, Lane & Mittendorf, a Wall Street firm, was a gentleman of the old school, including the kind of starched collar unseen for decades. He represented me well, and when I invented something in the 1950s, joined forces with us as a principal. One day, Sam, a yachtsman as well as a gentleman lawyer, sailed off into the Atlantic and, alas, was never seen again.

Also of Wall Street is C. Dickerman Williams, a conservative lawyer who was a member of the board of the American Civil Liberties Union. We worked together for several years in a group that successfully brought together influential intellectuals of right, left, and center. He impressed me as a lawyer who used his verbal skills not for adversarial purposes, but for bringing feuding folks together for a common purpose.

Morris Ernst, whose efforts on behalf of James Joyce's *Ulysses* made the fountainhead of twentieth-century literature available to Americans, represented me. So did Charles Rembar, whose skill with language often outrivals the writers he represents. I was embarrassed to have that brilliant lawyer sitting at my side for several hours of excruciatingly boring deposition in a case that was later deemed by a judge to have been frivolous.

I admire also Rembar's partner, Frank Curtis, the absolute best of the several libel lawyers I have worked with on "controversial" manuscripts. It's a field an independent publisher had better know well.[2]

No, I don't "hate lawyers."

---

2. The American Bar Association invited me to join Dan Rather and several experts on its panel on libel for their August 1986 convention. I had to respectfully withdraw when I learned that Judge Pierre Leval, who was then sitting on the Kable case, was also on the panel.

I was once represented by Bertram Mayers, a brilliant negotiator, who'd asked me what dollar amount I was looking for in a matter in which I'd been wronged. Listening to Mayers twisting the opposing counsel's tail on the phone was a great spectator sport. In short order, just after my marriage to Patricia Day, he reported a settlement that was four thousand dollars higher than the amount I'd asked for. "What's the four thousand dollars for?" I asked Mayers. "It's a wedding present," he said.

His longtime partner, H. William Fitelson, is also a remarkable individual. Fitelson, in addition to heading a law firm, was managing director of the Theater Guild—a very busy man who sometimes dictated to his secretary while walking down Fifth Avenue between his two offices. One day in the early 1950s he phoned me and learned I was downhearted. He canceled his next appointments and insisted on taking me to his club for a workout, a steam bath, and a restorative ice-cold shower, hardly the act of a man counting hours. Once, when I was soliciting funds for a worthy organization, Fitelson took me up to Billy Rose's office atop the Ziegfeld Theater and hit Rose for a one-thousand dollar-check. As we were at the elevator, Billy Rose wagged his finger at Fitelson and asked him for a one-thousand-dollar donation for one of Rose's charities.

The point is that both of these law partners were interesting as people, and while both became wealthy, neither to my knowledge ever gave money priority over human decency.

One of the present-day partners in that firm is Clifford Forster, a lawyer whose quick trip to Washington once saved Stein and Day from a takeover. In the Chapter 11 case, representing one of Stein and Day's most important authors, he seemed to be one of the very few general practitioners who came to understand the Bankruptcy Code.

Once, in the early 1970s, long before hostile takeover moves became a popular financial sport, Stein and Day became a target in a sudden attack that made it necessary to get expert legal advice quickly. We were referred to what was known in the trade as Judge Pollack's firm, where I and several of my directors got the ear of Sam Greenspoon of Tennessee, a lawyer who impressed us immediately because of his ability to spear the essence of a case. He also had a phenomenal memory that enabled him to direct associates to case law by chapter and verse nonstop. If memory serves me, we were there well into the night, but by the next morning the Tennessee mastermind had formulated for our enemies a "Here's what we're going to sue you for" approach that blasted the opposition to a standstill before twenty-four hours had passed. That's what I call impressive lawyering. Time-servers please take note.

In a litigator I admire toughness and a determination to win. Arnold Stream fits that description and was at my side when I was being deposed in a suit that involved a successful yet cranky author whose biggest financial triumphs were the two books of his that I published. For an hour, Stream didn't let opposing counsel finish a single sentence. As I sat at Stream's side my heart went out to the opposing lawyer, who was no match for Stream in a winning mood, and I wanted to tug at Stream's sleeve and say "Leave the poor guy alone, he's bleeding to death." Within an hour opposing counsel had his client in the hallway and was back in minutes to settle the matter. Stream was being efficient in getting rid of a problem and not looking for a way to stretch out and milk the case.

Stream also acted for Stein and Day in what proved to be a case that made law. He seemed so carried away with enthusiasm that in the break I asked him, "Arnold, what are you doing?" and he said, "I'm laying the ground for an appeal, just in case." He didn't have to appeal. We won hands down. Stream's hourly rate was the highest I ever encountered, but in those days I considered him cheap because he was efficient. I remember when he once handled an emergency, someone going for a temporary restraining order that another lawyer didn't feel he could deal with successfully. Perhaps because he hadn't been called in from the start, Stream for the first time insisted on a $7,500 retainer. He went down to court, won whatever there was to win, and returned half the money. And as I've mentioned, when Stein and Day's Chapter 11 case was thwarting every effort to return to publishing, Stream offered to do anything he could without fee because he was so mad at the bastards.

It is public knowledge from the acknowledgment pages of my many novels since *The Magician* that Charles L. Brieant, the Chief Judge of the Southern District, and I have been close friends. When it comes to my fiction about the law, he has been my law school for nearly twenty years (though not for this book). And the three lawyers in his immediate family have also gathered around whenever I exposed a first draft out of my imagination to the chill of their combined experience. If my lawyer-protagonist George Thomassy seems to critics to be real in a way that Perry Mason does not, and if his in-and-out-of-courtroom tactics teem with tough practice that seems authentic, much of it has to be credited to Judge Brieant and his clan of lawyers, sitting in a semicircle around my living room fireplace making point after point to George Thomassy's author.

Clearly I am dependent on lawyers.

Stein and Day's board of directors was for many years graced by the presence of two members of the bar whom I considered friends, Robert Mitchell, a high-seas yachtsman whose choice of books was more reliable than that of most editors, and Preston Searle, whose precision with grammar exceeded that of any editor of my acquaintance. And therein lies a clue.

A writer schools himself to perceive the actual—that is, to observe what is true rather than what is supposed. The difference between writers and most lawyers can be detected in a common tool they both must use: language. Seneca said, "The language of truth is simple." To this one is tempted to add, "Some lawyers practice obfuscation, for it gives them something to fight about while it is being disentangled. And some provide us with mangled thought because they presumably learned to practice law without also learning to master the language that it is practiced in." Readers of Orwell know that the corruption of language is a serious political offense. Readers of legal briefs know how much the legal profession has tumbled in this century. Hence the high praise earned by those few members of the bar who understand the moral necessity of using language well.

One summer before the Chapter 11 filing, we had a succession of overnight guests in the Hamptons. Of the four couples, three of the men were lawyers. (Their occupations didn't occur to me until the very moment of writing this.) Is it a coincidence that all three were known for their writing skills?

It should be clear by now that I am not prejudiced against lawyers, just critical of the incompetents and those who abuse process. You have met some of each in this book. Let's take a closer look at two examples of the latter, one who worked for the government as a prosecutor and another who worked for a private company.

One of Morris Ernst's colleagues, a former prosecutor, accompanied me to the front-page trial of Leslie Fiedler [3] and his wife in Buffalo, where I had been subpoenaed by the prosecution to testify. Fiedler was accused of "maintaining a premise" where marijuana was used (presumably by a friend of one of his children). The premise he was accused of "maintaining" was his own home. The real reason the authorities went after Fiedler was that as a civil lib-

---

3. For the uninitiated, Fiedler has generally been regarded as the dean of American literary critics since the death of Edmund Wilson. I published his first remarkable book, *An End To Innocence*, in 1955, long before there was a Stein and Day. His best-known work is *Love and Death in the American Novel*. It is the only case I know of where an author of an established classic did a drastic revision of it years after its first publication.

ertarian he had agreed to serve as the faculty advisor to
any student organization that couldn't get a faculty
advisor, and so he was co-opted by Lemar, a student organization that favored the legalization of marijuana.

During a recess in Fiedler's trial, the young assistant district attorney who prosecuted Fiedler apologized for yelling at me when I was in the witness box. He said, "In law
school they taught us that if we didn't have much of a case,
we should yell a lot. We don't have much of a case against
Professor Fiedler." Fiedler was sentenced to six months in
jail. He had to expend many tens of thousands of dollars
taking the trumped-up case all the way to the Supreme
Court, and finally saw it dismissed at the highest level of
the New York State judiciary, the court deciding that not
only had Fiedler not been properly convicted, but that he
had not even been accused of a crime since "maintaining
a premise" had to involve a nuisance or the making of a
profit.

In his play-acting, the young prosecutor of Leslie Fiedler
who "didn't have much of a case" was merely following
orders. But "following orders" has acquired a special taint
in this century, and many have been held to account for
their actions in "following orders." It was his job to pros-
ecute Fiedler, so he did, despite knowing that he "didn't
have much of a case." It wasn't only his lack of objectively
verifiable evidence; it was a case [4] prosecuted in bad faith
by a lackey of the system.

"My client right or wrong" remains the excuse for
much wrongdoing by lawyers in our time. It is absurd to
consider them "officers of the court" when they are at the
service of their clients with the same blind allegiance that
is expected of rank-and-file soldiers.

In criminal law the lawyer deals with the amoral, the
psychopathic, and the viciously criminal, who when

---

4. That doesn't need elucidation here. A book was devoted to it:
Being Busted, by Leslie Fiedler, Stein and Day, 1969. My copy bears the
inscription, "To my 'collaborator,' from darkest Buffalo, Leslie."

caught is now dependent on the lawyer's skill for his future. And in civil law there is, among other fields, bankruptcy. Criminal law attracts those who can comfortably consort with criminals. Civil law in our time has drawn those whose primary comfort is money; the field of bankruptcy has enticed some who, in addition to money, enjoy the whip.

Which leads me to what is in my opinion the bottom of the legal barrel, a California lawyer who did more than any other person to bring down the house of Stein and Day.

One of the earliest guidelines I was taught, I suspect by my parents, was that a person's character had an external giveaway. If a person's face improved when he smiled, that was a good sign. If a person's face disimproved when he tried to smile, that was a bad sign. I have known people with not particularly attractive faces out of whose expressions shone the light of intelligence and vitality, a radiance that simply overwhelmed any deficiency in physical attractiveness. And when they smiled, they were transformed and beautiful. Randy Kuckuck's face when at rest cannot be said to be handsome; it is offputting, as if a higher power had mixed genes badly on this particular palette. He seems to have an inability to smile convincingly. When he tries to smile, and I have actually seen him try to do so on several occasions, the impression one gets is not of joy or pleasure but of an unsuccessful attempt to deal with constipation. It is a visage entirely suitable for the man who months before the filing told Patricia Day of his determination to liquidate the company.

Randy Kuckuck's letters were the only ones ever to threaten Stein and Day with involuntary bankruptcy long before the Chapter 11 filing. BookCrafters is in the business of manufacturing books. What did Kuckuck accomplish for BookCrafters by his years-long campaign to destroy rather than help rehabilitate a customer that was in trouble because of its venture into the strange territory of mass-market distribution of paperback books? If

Kuckuck accomplished little for his employer, what did he accomplish for himself? Trying to understand the motivations of a lawyer like Randy Kuckuck is an exercise that leads to despair.

To anyone who studies human nature, as a writer must, *Homo sapiens* is, of course, a misnomer. It took the critter eons to emerge from the slime. There are always a few throwbacks jumping back in. Not even God can do more than give them Hell.

While we cannot see into a man's soul, we can test his brain. During the decisive meeting in the witness room outside the bankruptcy courtroom on January 24, 1989, about a dozen people were seated about the table. The occasion: Randy Kuckuck and BookCrafters were moving to take over the assets of Stein and Day/Publishers from the hands of its founders. In a pause as the papers of surrender were being signed, Laurence Solarsh, one of the lawyers present, asked, "What's the most successful book you ever published?"

Patricia Day replied, *"The Arrangement."*

Randy Kuckuck asked, "Who wrote it?"

It was, of course, written by Elia Kazan, winner of two Academy Awards and director of five Pulitzer prize plays, and was the most successful hardcover book of its decade. And Randy Kuckuck, who had proposed himself as publisher of Stein and Day to the Michigan Bank in the spring of 1987 and now, after successfully blocking the company's return to publishing for a year and a half, was about to take over the remains, unapologetically wanted to know who wrote the company's most successful book. The reign of ignorance was now complete.

CHAPTER 21

Turnarounds: How to Avoid Chapter 11 if It's Humanly Possible

> Razors pain you
> Rivers are damp;
> Acids stain you;
> And drugs cause cramp.
> Guns aren't lawful;
> Nooses give;
> Gas smells awful;
> You might as well live.
>   —Dorothy Parker

ONE day, quite late in my company's chapter 11 case, I received a phone call from Washington, D.C., from Barbara Benham, then editor of a publication called *Turnarounds & Workouts: News for People Tracking Distressed Businesses.* She'd read in the *Wall Street Journal* about Stein and Day's Chapter 11 case and was following up with a few questions that would interest her readers. That call was the first time I learned about an occupation of skilled people who specialize in keeping companies out of Chapter 11 if at all possible.

I read several issues of that publication. I learned that turnaround specialists don't necessarily go by that name. Most call themselves "business consultants," which doesn't say much. Others call themselves "crisis managers," which says more. One that does business all over the

United States and in several foreign countries called itself a "crisis and workout specialist" firm.

I talked to more than half a dozen of these turnaround people and decided they deserved a special place in this cautionary tale. They are the emergency room physicians for troubled companies. They stand between troubled companies and their creditors in a way that the Chapter 11 law, in practice, doesn't.

And, unlike the semicompetent unbusinesslike waddlers who populate much of the bankruptcy bar, these crisis managers work to get their client companies back on their economic perches, ready to compete and produce value in the world of business once more. Moreover, if a client company of a turnaround specialist finds that it cannot avoid Chapter 11 (usually because it sought help too late), it couldn't ask for a more knowledgeable ally to help it find one of the small number of efficient bankruptcy lawyers with class and clout.

Some of the turnaround managers can come on strong in a first meeting with the head of a company in trouble. They'll say something like, "I'm here to solve the problems. If I find out that the problem is you, will I be able to fire you?" If the CEO can't agree to that condition, several of the consultants won't take on the assignment.

Who are these people? What are their backgrounds? How do they function? Of the seven I spoke to,[1] two were lawyers by training, another a CPA, one had degrees in engineering and economics, and one, astonishingly, was an ordained rabbi whose working motto is "It's never too late." Another was actually a kind of temporary CEO who takes charge of the business for a delimited time when its CEO cannot function constructively. All of them—and this is a key to understanding their occupation—are businessmen with special experience in helping to turn troubled companies around.

---

1. Thanks to Christopher Beard, publisher of *Turnarounds & Workouts*.

These turnaround specialists get referrals from bankers, attorneys, accounting firms, venture capitalists, and from their speaking engagements and articles they have written for publication. How is it then that no banker, lawyer, accountant, or venture capitalist of the dozens I was in contact with ever referred us to—or even mentioned—a turnaround specialist? I am convinced that had we been put in touch with any of the ones I interviewed, the outcome of our case would have been different. These people are interested in saving businesses, not milking them. In fact, one of their duties, as they see it, is to protect a company from those who would scavenge it.

As in any occupation, there are exceptions. In 1982 a family-owned business that was in the red, Contempo Metal Furniture Company, applied for a loan of $250,000 from Union Bank in Los Angeles. The owner of the business, Robert Schuster, was required by the bank to hire consultants. The consultants, according to Schuster, took control of the production and accounting departments and installed new methods that were leading to $100,000 of red ink a month.

The Union Bank insisted that Contempo give the consultants an equity interest in the business or the bank would call the loan. By the time the business went down the tubes, "the consultants owned 50 percent of the firm and 25 percent of the company's building, and Contempo was $3 million in debt." Schuster, the original owner of the business, reported that "to say it was a nightmare is putting it mildly." He sued Union Bank and won a judgment for $12 million. The jury was still out on the issue of punitive damages when "the bank settled with Contempo for an undisclosed amount."[2]

The Contempo case would suggest two cautions: Who refers the consultant to the company matters, and it would make sense for a CEO to find his own consultant, if possi-

---

2. Reported in *Newsweek*, May 8, 1989.

ble, and to check the consultant's reputation and track record carefully.

All the turnaround people I talked to said they prefer to work with companies that may be in serious financial trouble but that are still savable short of Chapter 11. Routinely, however, they admit that most companies come to them late in the game, when the trapdoor of insolvency is already open.

While the techniques of turnaround specialists vary as much as their personalities, there are certain striking similarities in what they do. Kenneth Glass of Canton, Ohio, a take-charge person, puts it this way: "I've got four categories of people to deal with: secured creditors, unsecured creditors, employees, and shareholders. First I meet with the ones that are yelling loudest. I organize trade payables by priority, meaning the ones the company needs most to keep swimming. I also have to keep an eye out for any creditors who might get together to file an involuntary. I always meet with the parties individually, not in groups. I tell them I need sixty days of breathing space. To build confidence, I give them my references, successes I've had in restoring companies. I also remind them of the cost of litigation. And the specter of costs in a Chapter 11, where the chances of recovery are far less because the costs are so much higher. I cue them about the proliferation of characters that crop up in an eleven—the accountants, lawyers, the exacerbation of the problems by attorneys seizing on the frustration of creditors who find opportunities to sue directors and officers . . . if they get the point, they give me the time to turn things around."

David Ferrari, president of the Argus Management Corporation in Natick, Massachusetts, has a different starting point. About a quarter of his clients are already in an eleven or in the countdown stage when they get to him. "The typical case," he says, "involves a severe shortage of cash. I've got to find ways of cutting costs that management doesn't see or is avoiding, and at the same time I've got to lay plans for getting more cash either from an alternative lender or by selling off some assets. To the CEO every part of his business is like one of his kids. I tell him that if he's got four kids and can only feed three, he's got to put one in an orphanage. Very often a divestiture of some asset or some part of the company makes business sense but the CEO is holding on to it because of some social relationship. As a turnaround specialist, I don't have those ties." You also get the feeling that Ferrari doesn't have to listen to the CEO's wife. He can be the objective element at a time when executives flounder because of the stress they've been under. "I get vendors to defer payments." One has the impression from all of the turnaround specialists that as the "new boy on the block" they can get the ear of creditors in situations where the man who's been running the business can't.

Adam Radzik, president of R & E Business Consultants in West Orange, New Jersey, is a networker who once wrote a column of advice for a major New York City newspaper. His approach is to talk to the bank, the usual maximum source of pressure, and present himself as the man who's done this before successfully and can do it again. He stresses the candor he establishes, especially important where the relationships of the CEO have deteriorated. He becomes the expert on the scene, the buffer, and the morale restorer. "In many instances," Radzik says, "the fellow who's been running the business has tried various solutions but too often they are the wrong solutions to the problem. As a result, his credibility isn't what it should be." Like Kenneth Glass, he knows that banks don't like Chapter 11 and uses that.

But Radzik's most apparent gift is networking. I've watched him in action. He calls up a gung ho lawyer, young enough for combat. He calls a banker who knows another consultant who happens to know the CEO of the troubled company. Radzik once scored a success in a certain midwestern city. There's a lawyer there whose wife knows the wife of someone way up in the hierarchy of the bank that's giving a particular debtor a very hard time. He makes the call. He puts the people in touch. His biggest immediate effect is to draw the CEO out of isolation, out of his sense of despair into a frame of mind to fight because now, with Radzik's help, he's got allies.

The range within which turnaround specialists work varies greatly. Ken Glass has worked with companies doing "as little as ten million in sales and as much as two and a half billion." Radzik seems to have cottoned onto some smaller businesses that needed saving. If he likes a company or its people, its size doesn't seem to matter.

Another turnaround consultant who takes on the smaller firms is Malcolm Moses, who prefers client firms in the $5-million to $35-million annual revenue range. Moses is an impressive executive who learned the ropes when, some decades back, he was the man in charge of General Electric Credit's asset-based lending operation. He knows what the fellows on the other side of the table think and feel, which makes him an ideal guide for the CEO of a troubled company. Malcolm Moses is a lawyer who doesn't practice bankruptcy law but knows some of the best ones who do. He works with them, with banks, with investors, and with the company in need of help in a hurry. He works *out* of Merrick, New York, "out" because he is always on the go. On the day I first met him face to face, he was trouble-shooting situations in West-chester, Long Island City, and Binghamton, New York, involving two airplane rides and a lot of mileage in a car. Even in the car he's working and networking on the car phone. Unlike some of the bankruptcy lawyers I met, he *always* calls back.

How do these people get paid short of heaven? Without exception, by the hour. Some require a retainer equivalent to one month's work, some don't. And some are attracted to bonus arrangements for success; if they turn the trou-bled company around, they get a cash bonus from the board or an option for equity. But unlike the bankruptcy lawyers, they are looking for the short pull, the quick rescue if it's possible, the reeducation of management—not the indeterminate sentence of Chapter 11. If they're needed again, they come back.

When is the right time to call in a turnaround specialist? "Ideally," says Radzik, "when the manager of a business sees a weakness that is part of a pattern. Typically, I see people who run out of cash and who can't run out of the business. They are embarrassed. They are losing their self-esteem. They have to overcome a lot of reticence to make a comeback."

When is it too late? Daniel Morris, president of Morris Anderson Associates in Glenview, Illinois, says, "It's never too late." Radzik agrees. Ferrari says, "It may be too late if they can't make payroll. But it's never too late to look." Ken Glass thinks it's too late "if the core business has fallen below a critical mass." Gilbert C. Osnos, head of a firm that's been around for forty years, thinks it's too late if a company "has been in Chapter 11 too long and the creditors' positions have hardened." He'd much prefer to get involved before a filing and put together a plan before a company files, if it has to.

It was from Osnos that I first heard that excellent metaphor of an emergency ward that leads to an intensive care unit. "We are doctors, not undertakers," he says pointedly to an executive whose lawyers have acted as morticians. "We are temporary," he emphasizes. "Typically, we're involved for six to nine months. If we're involved as long as two years, that's too long. When we leave it's a good sign."

Osnos sees himself as the crisis manager who must stabilize the business (again the medical metaphor). It's not just the cash crisis that requires first aid, it's "the deep-rooted problems," but first he's got "to stop the hemorrhaging."

Osnos—one is tempted to say Dr. Osnos—sees himself as the alter ego of the CEO, or, if the CEO can't handle it, as the interim CEO. When he comes into a situation, he usually finds the people demoralized and tries to provide them with even small gains on their problems because "success is contagious." He tries to understand why the company is in trouble and gets a feel for the people. Osnos says he has to find the best out of the 90 percent who are constructive (and presumably bypass or get rid of the other 10 percent, the resistant ones). He gets everybody involved in providing cash flow monitoring tools and looking at receivables, inventory, and of course the expense side.

Meanwhile, he's working out short-term strategies. Creditor claims have to be satisfied in order of their priority. You deal first with the people you need most. His end goal is "to get the ownership of the solution within the management group."

With the increase in business bankruptcies[3] and a backlog in the courts, a greater need has developed for alternative ways of dealing with corporate financial difficulties, quite apart from the expense and other hazards of Chapter 11. If the debtor has a good relationship with his creditors, an out-of-court workout is possible. The creditors do nothing. In a "composition," "creditors agree to stretch out the debt or take a discount. Compositions only work when there are a small number of creditors."[4] In simple cases there is also an extreme solution that can be arrived at outside of court, a kind of liquidation under state law in which the debtor assigns his property or his equity to the creditors. Even with a credible debtor, a mediator is needed for an out-of-court resolution, and the National Association of Credit Management has acted as a go-between in such cases. The advantage to the creditor is

---

3. Personal bankruptcies, which are not the subject of this book, rose from less than 9,000 for the entire year 1946 to very nearly 9,000 as a weekly average. While there has been much speculation about the cause of the increase, I agree with Charles A. Luckett, author of a *Federal Reserve Bulletin* issued in September 1988, that the expansion of consumer debt is chiefly to blame.

4. Stacy Soltis in *Turnarounds & Workouts*, January 15, 1989.

that he doesn't have to worry about the debtor "taking care" of one or another creditor to the disadvantage of others. The Association helps resolve disputes, works on a plan, and sees to it that creditors are paid pro-rata. Debtors should be aware of an important "compliance tool." Once a deal is struck with creditors and a first check is sent out with a restrictive endorsement binding them to the deal, it is very rare for a creditor to renege, or return a check.

If a few creditors won't agree to an out-of-court solution there's a section of the Bankruptcy Code, 1126(b), that lets a debtor work out a plan of reorganization before filing under Chapter 11 and then try to get confirmation of the plan from the bankruptcy court. There a majority of creditors holding at least two-thirds of the debt can back a plan and see it approved.[5] In 1985 a company then known as Brock Hotel Corporation in Texas had attorneys who shaped what might be called a "pseudo Chapter 11" without filing. Larry Robinson of Stinson, Mag & Fizzell in Dallas says, "Brock probably saved $4 million to $5 million by staying out of Chapter 11."[6]

Clearly, if Chapter 11 can be avoided there is much to be gained besides the saving of treasure. With chief executives almost without exception facing a drastic assault on their health in Chapter 11, much can be gained from exploring alternatives. Sad to say, the percentage of cases that can manage to stay out of court remains small.

While turnaround specialists work hard to keep their clients out of Chapter 11, they do not all agree on what happens when a company must file. Ken Glass has found bankruptcy courts to deal on the basis of equity or fairness

---

5. Soltis, Ibid. Attorney David B. Post, executive director of the Turnaround Management Association, called my attention to this relatively obscure section of the Code. Under ideal conditions it enables a company to go in and out of Chapter 11 in record time, which upsets the time-servers.

6. Quoted by Soltis, Ibid.

rather than tight interpretations of the law. Daniel Morris disagrees, saying, "The procedures tend to distort the real business significance of the parties. There is a lot of procedural nonsense by after-the-filing stakeholders intended to bring the bar and others an annuity income for substantial periods." David Ferrari says that in New England it depends on the judge.

It's got to be a bit like rolling dice, which isn't what one thinks of when coming under the umbrella of the law. By and large the turnaround specialists I interviewed were motivated to keep client companies out of Chapter 11 because of the things that can go wrong under the present system. When I asked for their suggestions for improvement, I got an earful.

David Ferrari has us recall what he tells his clients: "You are paying for all the lawyers in this courtroom." Something the bankruptcy judges could do "is to impose a cap on all legal fees that will be paid for by the debtor, directly or indirectly, as a percentage of the assets of the debtor when they are finally determined. That might constrain attorneys from destroying assets wantonly. It might encourage attorneys to counsel their clients to prevent actions that destroy assets. And it might actually discourage some attorneys from dragging out a case instead of getting it over with efficiently."

Ferrari adds, "The forms used in filing a Chapter 11 petition are archaic, something out of the dark ages. They should reflect current conditions." He also points out that there aren't enough bankruptcy judges to go around and they ought to be paid the same as district judges, presumably to attract or keep a higher-quality judge on the bench if he doesn't have an independent income.

Kenneth Glass believes priority should be given to reducing the bureaucracy in procedures. There should be more rapid response—the process needs to be accelerated. Companies spend too long in Chapter 11. The minority that come out of Chapter 11 alive could exit a lot sooner if the procedures were streamlined. He also believes the role of the U.S. Trustee should be clarified.

Daniel Morris comes to this conclusion: "If at best thirty percent of the companies that go in come out, the system obviously could stand some serious improvements. First, the system should be geared toward dealing with equity, fairness, and good business rather than statutes." His second point is a corollary of the first. "What the bankruptcy courts need badly is a streamlining so that they can deal more with substantive business issues and a lot less with procedural matters. Third, everyone has to realize that if the company is going to emerge from Chapter 11, it has to come out *as a business*, which means the process needs to be geared to business rather than legal business or one-time restructuring. Chapter 11 is expensive, and the only way it's going to become less expensive is if it becomes less procedural."

Ron Stengel thinks that what needs to be done is to separate the cases by size. His demarcation point would be between $20 and $25 million in revenue. "If the companies are smaller," he says, "they stand a good chance of being liquidated. The vast majority of companies that file for Chapter 11," he points out, "are tiny, under $10 million of assets."

Bankruptcy judges, as I've said, have a lot more leeway than other judges. A good many of these suggestions could be implemented by them without changes in the law. But it has to be understood that we sometimes are where we come from; that is, if our impulse is to spend our lives as lawyers, and as we come to know the practices of law we choose bankruptcy as a specialty, and if as a result of those preferences we then become bankruptcy judges, how likely are we to view the field we've come from with clear objectivity? A baseball player who becomes a coach is not the likeliest candidate for reforming the rules of the game.

Crisis manager Gil Osnos asks some rhetorical questions. "Who are you representing? Whose crisis are you managing? Who is the company?"

You can hear a sigh out of long experience as he delivers a definition of a company worth paying attention to. "The shareholders have the most to gain and the most to lose. But the company is also its employees, its customers who are dependent on it, its suppliers who have depended on a long-term relationship, and how about the communities in which the company is embedded? They are all the company. And they are all worth saving."

Should those words be inscribed on a plaque nailed to the courtroom door so that they would be seen by everyone entering, lawyers, debtors, and creditors alike?

You'd need two plaques because the judge enters the courtroom from another door.

CHAPTER 22

Sanctuary or Pillory?

> "In time, all balloons that keep expanding will burst."
>
> —George Thomassy, Esq.

L ET us recognize that Chapter 11 as it is practiced now is not a saving law. It demonstrably does not work for the vast majority of companies that enter it. It discriminates in practice against smaller companies and those without easily salable assets. Chapter 11 as an instrument for retrieving money that is owed is pathetically inefficient for companies of any size. It is a refuge for a few opportunists and a feast for many lawyers. For the leaders of businesses trapped in it, Chapter 11 is the twentieth-century equivalent of the eighteenth-century pillory, a dehumanizing, inefficient public spectacle. What can be done about it?

Let us for a moment be playful. Let us suppose this is a perfect world and that the court is really intent on administering justice. The court *knows* without a shadow of a reasonable doubt that the CEOs carrying their companies like wounded friends into the Chapter 11 hospital are bewildered, confused, frightened. Let us suppose that the court wants to play fair. The court could require that when each filing is made, the clerk immediately send directly to the debtor a printed instruction card that would say something like this:

To the Debtor and its Management

1. The purpose of the Chapter 11 law is to reorganize your company, not to liquidate it. To reorganize it, you must have a plan. If you do not already have such a plan and funding for it, discuss the matter with your attorney as soon as possible. You have the exclusive right to submit such a plan for only 120 days. After that, unless the right to exclusivity has been extended by order of the court, any party in interest including any creditor may propose a plan, including a plan to liquidate the assets of the company.

2. The debtor company is the client. The purpose of the attorney is to advise the client as to the law and the legal alternatives. The role of the client is to make the decisions.

3. Do not sign anything that is untruthful or with which you do not agree. If you are being coerced into signing anything, inform the U.S. Trustee in writing. The Trustee has been instructed to advise the court immediately of any such complaint and to investigate it promptly. The Trustee must pass on the complaint to the court even while it is being investigated. It is not necessary that a complaint be seen by an attorney before it is submitted.

4. You are not on trial as an individual. If any party attempts to humiliate, harass, or intimidate you, please advise the U.S. Trustee in writing.

5. You have a fiduciary responsibility to *all* the creditors. If you believe that any creditor is taking an action that will harm other creditors irreparably, it is your duty to inform the court through your attorney. If your attorney won't do so, you have the right to do so directly.

The other side of the instruction card would say "April Fool."

Courts do hand small instruction pamphlets to prospective jurors. But in bankruptcy court debtors are not provided with any "objective" information as to their rights though they are given a page or two about their obligations with regard to accounting and reporting to—and fees, of course for—the U.S. Trustee. Nobody provides you with the information I've put on that nonexistent instruction card. Many debtors learn it in due course, as I did, but not in time to save their companies.

A court cannot offer advice—even a statement of the law—to a principal in an environment where the protocol is total dependence on the advice of counsel. It cannot offer the most elementary information about the bankruptcy laws to debtors even when that information *is being purposely withheld* from debtors by lawyers whose practice it is to keep debtors in the dark about their rights in order to avoid interference with the attorneys' main aim of milking a case.

In school the debtor might have gotten reading lists. But in court, where knowledge might be more urgent, the court couldn't even presume to offer debtors a short bibliography listing such worthy texts as Mr. Martin Bienenstock's,[1] for no other reason than that Mr. Bienenstock's law firm might be representing someone in that case, as he himself was in ours. The real reason for the withholding of information, of course, is the same as the one that motivates the bar to come down hard on anyone who tries to criticize or reform it and isn't a member of the union. That includes the authors of books such as this.

Once, during a Sunday rehearsal of a play of mine that was being readied for Broadway, the work light, a high-wattage bulb that illuminates the entire stage, went out.

---

1. *Bankruptcy Reorganization*, Practising Law Institute, 1987.

Union rules provided that only an electrician could change the bulb. It being Sunday, the electrician wasn't available. The actors stood around restlessly, chafing to get on with their work. The director wanted to know, couldn't anything be done? The stage manager had the electrician's home number and telephoned. He wasn't home. But, ah, his son was, and as happens in tightly held unions, the son was also an electrician, and he came down in an hour or so and changed the bulb.

A lawyer hearing this anecdote might well sense the absurdity of certain types of union constraints. Some unions aren't called unions, of course. They are professional organizations, but the effect of their work rules is the same: to benefit the paychecks of the members no matter how ludicrous the work rules sometimes seem.[2] The law, not just in bankruptcy, has become a caricature of make-work government procedures. The profession is almost universally criticized for its high hourly rates that can only be paid by deep pockets and therefore, in practice, defeat the objective of "Equal Justice for All."

The intrusive outsider cannot stop with an examination of the practices of the bankruptcy bar alone. It is a small splinter carrying an infection. If the body of the law as a whole were healthy, it would have long ago sealed off the splinter, extracted it, put on some disinfectant, and all would be well. But the body of the law has been delinquent in sealing off or healing its infected splinters. Therefore we have to step back and look at that body of present-

---

2. When a lawyer phones a lawyer, they are both running up time charges. Conference calls are even more beneficial to the trade. But in bankruptcy, where every lawyer on the line intends for his fee to be paid by the debtor, that conscious piling up of time charges is an unstated but widely practiced conspiracy to run up costs. That example is trivial compared to the more sophisticated way of ballooning billings, the filing of overlong and frequently pointless legal motions and memoranda that must be read by the lawyers for all the parties or—as has been observed here by a senior member of the bankruptcy bar—at least charged for even if not read.

day lawyering. We know where it has come from, a justifiably prideful profession. What is it now and where is it headed?

The American Bar Association, like every professional group of its kind, would of course prefer to superintend its own reform. If a man who represents himself has a fool for a client, what are we to call those who would be their own doctors, as the American Bar Association insists? That would probably be as effective as having prisoners supervise their own rehabilitation. The exceptional cases of self-reform get books and movies written about them, but they are rare. Self-reform, let us recognize, is particularly difficult during a period when the compensation of lawyers, especially in major cities, has reached elephantine proportions and when there are many influential figures in the bar who don't want that music to stop just yet.[3]

The law suffers from the practices of its morally weakest members. As a subspecies, some of those who practice bankruptcy law cannot resist temptations to deprecate the humanity of others, as if decency were a finite quantity to be observed only in losers.

They are by no means the worst. In California, an attorney named Paul Ian Mostman "paid a hit man to have [a] former client murdered."[4] What is morally as shocking as the solicitation of a murder is that a California bar panel and a majority of the State Supreme Court said the crime "should not cost Mr. Mostman his license to practice law."[5] The bar panel found that Mr. Mostman had not committed

---

3. On the day that *The New York Times* reported the serious defections from the law discussed later in this chapter, I learned for the first time what the hourly charges had been for me *personally* during the turmoil of surrendering the assets of Stein and Day to its arch-enemy. Whenever the lawyer I hired was on the phone with me together with the bankruptcy lawyer in his firm, or if they were only discussing our case in his office, it was costing me $500 an hour. On that same day I learned that unemployment insurance paid $180 a week.

4. *The New York Times*, February 24, 1989, page B5.

5. Ibid.

moral turpitude because he had been acting under duress. It imposed three years of supervised probation. A dissent, written by Justice David N. Eagleson and concurred to by Chief Justice Malcolm M. Lucas, argued that lawyer Mostman should be disbarred on the ground that he "intended to commit murder and paid money to guarantee that result." The degree to which lawyers are incapable of policing themselves is apparent in the fact that the view that a murderer should be disbarred *was a minority opinion.*

There are so many morally decent lawyers that the profession flinches at being judged by its delinquents, corrupt judges, and child killers.[6] There is much disapproval in the profession, for instance, of the lawyers who hang around courthouses like pigeons looking for an opportunity to launch a nuisance case that will be bought off by a quick settlement just to escape the cost of defense. To be fair, let us then judge the profession by those who are thought of as its most worthy practitioners.

During the heat of the early 1950s, the indecent behavior of a lawyer-turned-senator, Joseph McCarthy of Wisconsin, focused worldwide attention on what came to be called the Army-McCarthy hearings. On one side was the senator and his acolyte, attorney Roy Cohn, clearly perceived by civil people as the bad guys. On the other side, in defense of the army, was Joseph Welch, an attorney from the respected Boston law firm of Hale and Dorr.

At one point in the proceedings that capped what could only be termed the McCarthy madness, the senator accused a young attorney in Welch's firm of having been a member of the National Lawyers Guild, a Communist front. True or not (it was true), the point perceived by the public was that it was irrelevant. McCarthy seemed to be accusing Joseph Welch of somehow being tainted secondhand because of the prior association of a young colleague.

---

6. This reference is to attorney Joel Steinberg, whose conviction for manslaughter in the death of his daughter Lisa was a television melodrama of early 1989.

When McCarthy launched his accusation of the young lawyer in front of the TV cameras with millions watching, Welch drew universal respect for declaiming to Senator Joseph McCarthy, "Have you no sense of decency?"

It was a remark that went down in history. For, having delivered an untoppable rhetorical line, lawyer Welch left the chamber with tears in his eyes, but not before winking as he passed from the hall. Was he admitting, as one must assume, that *he was merely acting?* If the best-known proponent of decency of his time could do this, what does it say about the profession? Does the adversary system promote dissembling as a courtroom skill?

The point should now be clear. If the law has at bottom its ambulance chasers and courthouse pigeons and at top its distinguished dissemblers, perhaps it is an inappropriate profession to control Chapter 11 proceedings, as it now does, because Chapter 11 was intended by law to be a sanctuary and not a pillory.

The public has come to recognize that those who are trained for combat are inappropriate peace-makers. If Chapter 11 is to perform as its legislators intended, as a place of reconstruction, if the profession were to clean house tomorrow, if it saw to it that its rules of conduct and codes of ethics were followed in practice on pain of real punishment for violations, the bar associations would still be stuck with human nature. Any group 700,000 strong trained in adversarial conduct, to score points, to work around the law, will have large pockets of resistance to reform.

In recent years Americans have come to recognize that the country has spawned far too many lawyers for its own good. The public understands that lawyers manufacture more trouble than they cure. Seldom, however, has attention been directed to the cause except in jokes. It is a very old saw indeed that with one lawyer in town, he may not find much to do. With two lawyers in town, both will find lots of work.

But the racket of making work for each other has been

opened to public view. It is no longer a joke because it is no longer an exaggeration.

That doesn't mean that a great lawyer who can save a corporation from catastrophe by an overnight demonstration of genius, as one of Stein and Day's once did, doesn't deserve elevated compensation, just as a great surgeon who has the power to save a life because of a skill that other surgeons lack should be fairly compensated. But when the semiskilled hacks of the law claim large hourly fees, and apprentices at the bar are billed out for more than their recent teachers are paid, the conditions for an economic revolution are in place.

An increasing number of lawyers are now as disgusted as the public is with the practices of the fraternity. The failure of bar associations to clean up their own effluent is resulting in massive individual defections. *The New York Times* tells us that despite spectacular pay and perks, "the mood in the legal profession is oddly grim."[7] The Bar Association of the State of Maryland released a survey of one thousand attorneys picked at random from thirty-nine law firms and discovered that "a lot of lawyers do not like their work."[8] Ninety-four percent "said they were concerned that law was becoming less of a profession and more of a business than it used to be." The lawyers surveyed reported that they worked an average of sixty to seventy hours a week and "felt overloaded," though their 1,800 to 2,000 billable hours was less than many attorneys in major city law firms are required to work. A spokesperson for the Maryland Bar Association, Janet S. Eveleth, said the lawyers reported "very high levels of stress in both their personal and professional lives. Many of them said they didn't have a personal life," or time to continue the

---

7. January 27, 1989, p. B5.

8. Ibid. The survey was designed by a Philadelphia polling firm called PsyCor Inc., and the interviews were conducted in the summer of 1988 by graduate students from the University of Maryland. The sample reportedly covered law firms of all sizes, largely in urban areas.

tradition in the profession of legal work for the public at no charge. A third of the lawyers weren't even sure they would continue to practice.

There would seem to be a higher percentage of "I don't want to work like this" than "I don't want to be a part of this," but both elements are there. And as we have learned from observation of the international arena, a little change does not act as a pacifier; it invites more change.

The wind is also blowing from another direction. According to *The New York Times*, lawyers "have been devalued in the corporate marketplace."[9] Personnel executives and business school administrators were reported as saying "a job seeker's legal training is as likely to be seen now as a liability as an asset, and lawyers trying to switch careers say they are often typecast as narrow-minded, confrontational and unimaginative."

Judging by the reports in America's leading newspaper on a single day, much of the legal profession is hiding behind a high dam. A soaring proportion of lawyers can see the cracks. The crisis is already here.[10]

Usually if there is a surplus in any profession, students divert themselves away from that overstaffed field. Why is that true of, say, teachers and engineers and not of lawyers? Because law, especially in the largest firms, has become a business *where the highest profits are made from recruiting new soldiers* called associates, at salaries astronomically high compared to those with equal periods of training in other professions. Though these young lawyers are paid very well, the firms double, triple, and quadruple that amount when they charge for the services of these relative newcomers. That percentage of profit is

---

9. January 27, 1989, p. B5. This story had no apparent connection to the Maryland story except for its appearance on the same page of the same newspaper.

10. When I was editing Lionel Trilling's *Freud and the Crisis of our Culture*, Trilling asked me if "crisis" was not an overdramatic word. I suggested that a crisis was not a crisis until it was named, and the title stayed unchanged.

hard to come by in most businesses. If you can net several times the salary of every associate, especially if you work them fifty, sixty, seventy billable hours a week, you have to develop ways of keeping these newcomers busy.

There need be no fear that the overstocked bar will be diminished by those who are leaving its ranks for cause. The news in March of 1989 was that for the second year in a row law school applications were on a sharp upswing. For these youngsters, the honey is irresistible. Trained for adversarial combat, deficient in moral education, they will march like lemmings.

Why should the rest of society find that appalling? The single most important ingredient in democracy is the existence of countervailing forces, each with enough power to effect a balance of interests. Yet an asp has secreted itself in the democratic fabric. A single occupation has come to dominate all three branches of government. The law is most often the degree that leads to a political career and Congress. The executive branch also has a predominance of lawyers, and in its department that administers justice it is difficult to find anyone of authority who is not a lawyer. And of course in the third branch of government, the judiciary, there are only lawyers.

What is wrong with the predominance of lawyers in all three branches of ostensibly countervailing forces is their prior training in adversary relationships. They have learned to use threats to improve their bargaining strength, to go at the truth selectively, to press precedent when the facts do not sustain a case. Among people so trained, it is only a small minority that are equipped to work to produce a sense of community and common purpose. There is such a purpose at the root of each Chapter 11 case, for wherever there is a debtor and there are creditors and a body from which they are to derive what they can, it is almost always the successful reorganization of the business that produces the greatest good for the greatest number.

There is another alarming point to consider. The one

factor that most distinguishes totalitarian societies from our own is that in the former people do not have much control over their own existence. The most significant lure of democracy is the control over one's own life. *That is what is lost by the individuals whose companies are trapped in the economic quicksand of Chapter 11.* They have been convicted of no crime, yet they are forced to forego the most essential aspect of freedom. And their out-of-control lives are now saturated with fear.

One day in 1988, in the spring of *glasnost* and *perestroika*, the articulate Russian poet, Yevgeny Yevtushenko, was interviewed by Robert McNeil of the *McNeil-Lehrer News Hour*. When questioned about what it was really like in the Soviet Union at that time, Yevtushenko talked of the "red" and "white" corpuscles as they still exist in the Soviet Union, and mingling with them, "the gray corpuscles of fear." Patricia Day and I turned to each other in recognition. For a year we had floated in a perfidious, deceitful, conniving, and manipulative world in which the rules aren't known in time, where some of the lawyers who are supposed to be on your side are playing their own game while you and your company are destroyed irremediably. What the bankruptcy process in the United States has created is an underworld of inequity for the benefit of a special breed of lawyers, who know just how to administer "the corpuscles of fear" in order to get their way.

It should not surprise us. Plato warned us in *The Republic* that all societies we know of are governed by the selfish interests of the ruling class. Each Chapter 11 case creates a micro-society. Its particular junta of lawyers becomes its ruling class.

Who is it that these lawyers rule? Who is the debtor and how did he get where he is?

There would seem to be three main causes of a company or an individual ending up in bankruptcy.

First, there is simply bad economic management of the corporate or family enterprise.

Second, there is just plain hard luck. The farmer who loses his crop to drought cannot be faulted for bad management. The rainmaker did not give good rain.

Third, there is what I call "the nefarious other," the actions of a third party that force a sudden and involuntary "election" of Chapter 11 as the only means of survival.

The cause of filing may be in all three, or in some combination of bad economic management, bad luck, or the activity of another party. The result is the same: Imprisonment in the Chapter 11 environment for a period likely to exceed the term visited upon most burglars.

As the witnesses in this book have testified, the majority of those who out of desperation or hope elected the cover of Chapter 11 find themselves subjected to cruel and unusual punishment. That cannot have been the intent of the law, for such punishment is unconstitutional. If the torture were physical, there would be a national outcry. Because it is psychological, and therefore sometimes more intolerably painful, it is ignored even if it is in contravention of the law.

This punishment, including the deprivation of one's control of one's own life, is, of course, superintended by the court *in a way that no other court in the land functions.* The judge has the power to bring all sorts of other actions under his tent. His decisions are appealed less successfully than those of other judges. If a ruling by a bankruptcy judge is appealed to a federal district judge, we learn that the district judge usually doesn't know enough about bankruptcy and has to refer the case back to the bankruptcy court from which the appeal was made. That subverts the process of appeal. And by the time this ritual passing of decisions up and down the line gives birth to a conclusion, it may be too late to have any practical effect.

The latitude with which a bankruptcy judge governs the economies and conduct of the participants is very great. The danger involved in the near-absolute power of

the judge in bankruptcy cases is obvious. One error—
either of judgment or perception—can prevent reorganization, as in Stein and Day's case.[11]

Bankruptcy judges, many of whom were once bankruptcy attorneys who elected lower pay for more power,
should consider using that power in five ways:

First, judges should see that secured creditors do not
continue to abuse process as if it were their right.

Second, they should make sure that companies that cannot afford or cannot get competent bankruptcy counsel,
particularly smaller companies, receive equal protection
under the law by having the bench control the conduct of
the churners, milkers, time-servers, and professionally
incompetent members of the bankruptcy bar. Judges duck
their responsibility by saying that is not their job; but
their job is precisely to see that justice is done, and justice
cannot be done if judges continue to blink the conduct
described in this book.

Third, bankruptcy judges should see that false claimants, secured or unsecured, are punished as the law provides; the printed claim forms say that the claims are
being made truthfully under penalty of perjury. Yet, as
we have heard, the bankruptcy industry devotes an
appreciable amount of its costly resources to the process of
weeding out false claims, which are endemic and by and
large go unpunished.

Fourth, if judges want to stop disgraceful lying in the
courtroom, perjury should not go unnoticed and unpun-

---

11. It is unclear whether Judge Schwartzberg denied Stein and Day's
urgent request to use $97,000 of cash collateral to manufacture books to
fill bona fide, profitable orders because he meant to do so, or as Patricia
Day believes, he couldn't figure out what the request was and didn't
ask amidst the bedlam of that first cash collateral hearing. The request,
had it been approved, would have permitted reorganization to begin.
The fact that he did award that precise amount, $97,000, for overhead
is either ironic or an indication of the chaotic conditions that can obtain
in the bankruptcy court environment. Whatever the circumstances,
the ruling was a nail in the coffin.

ished. There are no juries to tell the court who is lying. The judge has to have his lie detector turned on all the time.

And fifth, while the courts do threaten sanctions against members of the bar who disgrace the profession, I have yet to see sanctions imposed in any way that would be an effective deterrent to future conduct.

There is a sixth way that judges could try to ensure a fair outcome to Chapter 11 cases. Since bankruptcy judges have power that is so very nearly absolute, it is their responsibility to know what's going on. They can't know if they don't read briefs or get an accurate summary from their clerks. They can't know if they rely only on what goes on in court and then hear motions and not opposition to such motions. The black robe carries with it not only authority but responsibility for the lives and economies in the court's control.

Bankruptcy judges are referees in serious matters that have come to be played as games: by creditors' lawyers who, as part of the process of their own dehumanization, have lost sight of the harm they cause to human beings in blind pursuit of a single goal, bolstering their client's position; by debtors' lawyers who are milking a case in ways that must be obvious to the experienced court; by the largely useless though costly rituals of the U.S. Trustee and his minions.

Your Honors, you are referees but also *judges*. The players who are lawyers, most of whom have become inured to suffering, will simply go on to the next game. The principals, who are also players, will have to live with the decisions you make; to them what you are governing for better or worse is not a game.

There are certain positive measures that bankruptcy judges could put in place quickly. For instance, as David Ferrari suggests, they could impose a cap on all legal fees that will be paid for by the debtor, directly or indirectly, as a percentage of the assets of the debtor when they are finally determined. That might constrain attorneys from destroying assets wantonly. It might encourage attorneys for creditors to counsel their clients to prevent actions that destroy assets. And it might actually discourage some attorneys from churning a case instead of getting it over with efficiently.

Could such a cap be enforced? Of course. It is already being done partially, informally, haphazardly, and in the end unsatisfactorily by judges who slice down padded or undeserved bills. But that's giving cough syrup in a pneumonia case. The goal is to *prevent* the machinations by creditors, debtors, or attorneys that deplete the assets and prolong the case.

However, even powerful bankruptcy judges can be rendered relatively powerless when faced with an advocate who seems too dumb or too inexperienced to do what he's supposed to do to prove his case. I have seen judges teach lawyers by direction, indirection, and even by mockery. It is better to instruct than to blink a miscarriage of justice.

There are other palliatives to consider. The ethical members of the bankruptcy bar could bring themselves to be less cooperative with those who prolong cases and destroy assets belonging to others. No profession has ever benefited from tolerating shady practitioners in its midst.

Such suggestions are Band-Aids.

If medicine as it is practiced produces illness in more than one in four cases, think of the amount of social illness that is produced by lawyers. Is it possible that in certain fields—marital matters, custody, and bankruptcy, for instance—what is called for is the advice and assistance of professionals trained in rehabilitation rather than adversarial advocacy? If a turnaround is more constructive than a liquidation for everyone concerned, shouldn't the first life raft sought in the storm be that of the trained crisis manager?

Bankruptcy courts, which were legislated into existence to provide shelter for the revival of a troubled business or, at worst, the redistribution of the assets of a company for the benefit of its creditors, have become a kind of supervised ritual for exacting economic revenge. That has been testified to in this book. The turnaround specialists who try to keep their client companies away from the expensive, retributive arena of Chapter 11 have testified in this book. And members of that small and honorable cadre of bankruptcy lawyers who understand the process as the reconstruction of a business and not as a carcass to feed on have also testified in this book. As the lawyers say, in this book the questions have been "asked and answered."

Implicit in those answers is a road map for entrepreneurs and business managers: whom to turn to to stay out of the Chapter 11 wilderness, how to prepare for the trip if it becomes necessary, and how to survive in it provided the businessman has picked the right lawyer to take along for what could be the most important trip he's ever taken.

In the larger view, one can hope that the conditions described in this book could lead to a tripartite coalition:

1. of businessmen whose companies have survived the Chapter 11 process;

2. of the ethical leaders of the bankruptcy bar who would like to see the failed process converted to one that is efficient for all sizes of companies, with lawyers conducting themselves for the maximum good to the greatest number in a manner that will help regain respect for the law and lawyers;

3. of the crisis managers, consultants, and turnaround specialists whose experience is in the particular art of saving businesses rather than dismembering them.

Those three groups, working together, could bring Chapter 11 back from where it is now into civil process, a sanctuary for rehabilitation.

In the meantime, while we raise hope for the coalition, there is this book.

Appendix A

Barr and Faerber

ATTORNEYS AND COUNSELORS AT LAW

664 SOUTH MAIN STREET

POST OFFICE BOX 664

SPRING VALLEY, NEW YORK 10977

(914) 352-4080   (914) 356-2500

TELECOPIER (914) 352-6777

HARVEY S. BARR
JOSEPH FAERBER*
ELIZABETH A. HAAS

BARRY A. STURTZ
MINDY R. ZLOTOGURA**
JOSEPH J. HASPEL*
LEWIS E. LOVE, JR.

*MEMBER OF N.Y. AND FLA. BARS
**MEMBER OF N.Y. AND N.J. BARS

WESTCHESTER OFFICE
199 MAIN STREET
WHITE PLAINS, NEW YORK 10601
(914) 997-7707

FLORIDA OFFICE
14031 BARRETT ROAD N W
NORTH FORT MYERS, FLORIDA 33903
(813) 995-8885

November 19, 1987   PLEASE REPLY TO SPRING VALLEY OFFICE

By Telecopier and Regular Mail

Deryck Palmer, Esq.
Weil Gotshal & Manges
767 Fifth Avenue
New York, NY 10153

Gregg Borri, Esq.
Drinker Biddle & Reath
405 Park Avenue
New York, NY 10022

Henry G. Swergold, Esq.
Platzer Feinberg & Swergold
150 East 52nd Street
New York, NY

Re: Stein and Day, Our File No. 9056

Dear Messrs. Palmer, Swergold and Borri:

I have just hung up the telephone from calling the
Court and moving the adjourned hearing date from this
morning to Monday at 11:00 a.m.. If you will recall I was
charged with the duty last weekend of adjourning the hearing
on Monday, November 16th. Judge Schwartzberg refused to
adjourn it without date, and he adjourned the hearing to
this morning.

I am writing this letter to advise of my utter frustration as to what has occurred. In September, when we
spent many hours drafting a thirty day stipulation, and I
complained about the amount of time it took to arrive at an
agreement, I was comforted by the statement that this would
be a format for the future, and that all we would have to
do was to make simple amendments. I have been rudely
awakened.

This is not the first Chapter 11 debtor that I have represented, and in all modesty, I must admit that my firm is reasonably familiar with Chapter 11 and what is expected of a debtor in possession. When I first assumed representation of Stein and Day, I believed that my predecessor may not have devoted the time necessary to put the case in its proper perspective on an on-going basis. I now see that it was not my predecessor, and in all candor, I must now acknowledge my client's repeated statements that the secured creditors do not wish to see this debtor survive, but are deliberately and improperly motivated to dismantle the debtor and extinguish its existence. Your actions have undermined the debtor's staff so that they are no longer optimistic about the future. More importantly, working under the "cloud of doom" does not encourage enthusiasim in anyone. Your actions and delay are depreciating the debtor's assets daily. The end result will be a warehouse full of pulp and an empty structure in Scarborough. If this is your intention, why the charade?

What has transpired over the last two months is unconscionable and obscene. I will not participate any longer. Ten days ago I told you that I would not attend any more meetings. On your assurance that we would finally reduce our agreement to a writing I gave up another Sunday and attended yet another meeting. What purpose was served? Why should I bother consenting to terms of an agreement that change as frequently as the second hand on a clock.

It is my intention to go forward on Monday of next week with the cash collateral hearing and to fully inform the Court as to the abuse of process orchestrated by the secured creditors in this case.

Very truly yours,

BARR AND FAERBER

Harvey S. Barr

HSB/sg

Appendix B

FIRING THE CANONS

The following canons are excerpted from *The Lawyer's Code of Professional Responsibility*, adopted by the New York State Bar Association, effective January 1, 1970, as amended through April 29, 1978. The Bar Association publishes the canons in a pamphlet that I carried with me into court on many occasions during the Stein and Day Chapter 11 case as an observer of the differences between reality and illusion.

Canon 1.

A lawyer should assist in maintaining the integrity and competence of the legal profession.

Canon 2.

A lawyer should assist the legal profession in fulfilling its duty to make legal counsel available.

Canon 6.

A lawyer should represent a client competently.

Canon 7.

A lawyer should represent a client zealously within the bounds of the law.

Canon 8.

A lawyer should assist in improving the legal system.

Canon 9.

A lawyer should avoid even the appearance of professional impropriety.

Each of the canons is followed by ethical considerations and disciplinary rules. It is no secret to the bar that the breach of the canons is full of shot.

Appendix C

Stein and Day is proud to have been the originating publisher of works by:

F. Lee Bailey • Claude Brown • Joseph Buloff • Mary Cheever • Robert Conquest • John Crosby
Leslie Fiedler • David Frost • Jack Higgins • Sidney Hook • Barbara Howar • Elia Kazan
James Kirkwood • Derek Lambert • Wanda Landowska • Robert Lewis • Shari Lewis
Sinclair Lewis • Herbert London • Jerry Lucas • Malachi Martin • Marilyn Monroe • Leonard Mosley
Robert Payne • William Phillips • Jill Robinson • Selden Rodman • Anthony Sampson
Dore Schary • Budd Schulberg • John Simon • Neil Solomon, M.D. • Arianna Stassinopoulos
Reay Tannahill • Dylan Thomas • Gordon Thomas and Max Morgan Witts • Hannah Tillich
Ernest van den Haag • Bertram D. Wolfe

We are also pleased to have been the American publisher of works by:

Sarah Bradford • Brigid Brophy • Elias Canetti • John Creasey • R. F. Delderfield
Maurice Edelman, M.P. • Lord George-Brown • Maxim Gorky • Ché Guevera • L. P. Hartley
The Right Honorable Edward Heath • Arthur Koestler • J. J. Marric • Elaine Morgan
Desmond Morris • Eric Partridge • J. B. Priestley • Peter Quennell • Peter Shaffer • Idries Shah
George Bernard Shaw • A. J. P. Taylor • Piotr Ilyich Tchaikovsky • Leon Trotsky
Colin Wilson • Barbara Woodhouse

STEIN AND DAY/*Publishers*, Scarborough House, Briarcliff Manor, N.Y. 10510

The back cover of Stein and Day's last catalogue, Fall 1987, listing some of its notable authors. The company was forbidden to publish all of the books in this catalogue by two of its secured creditors.

Appendix D

Stein and Day: A CHRONOLOGY

1983 and 1984   Respectively the third and first best fiscal years in the company's history.

1978–1983   Stein and Day publishes its first rack-sized mass-market paperback line, called Day Books, which achieves a successful sell-through rate.

December 1983   The Kable News Company starts distributing Stein and Day mass-market books through the independent distributor trade with a sales force of thirty-two men. At Kable's insistence, Day Books has ceased distribution. Kable contract to run three years.

Spring 1984   Stein and Day completes payment in full on $565,000 note held by R. R. Donnelley and begins regular monthly payments on a $889,000 non-interest-bearing Donnelley note.

Spring 1984   Kable stops making payments to Stein and Day (except for those that flow to the printer) on the grounds that it projects "poor" sell-through of the mass-market books. Meanwhile, Stein and Day's own sales of the same books at the same time to bookstores and book chains and jobbers shows an excellent sell-through rate.

June 1984   Stein and Day became suspicious that
                     Kable was shipping books to independ-
                     ent wholesalers who hadn't ordered
                     them, producing an artificial 100 percent
                     return rate to mix with the regular
                     returns.

September 1984 Some months after cut-off of cash flow
                     from Kable, Stein and Day is unable to
                     keep up payments on the second Don-
                     nelley note.

July 1985   Stein and Day files suit in federal court
                     against Kable News and three of its offi-
                     cers under the federal racketeering act
                     and common-law fraud.

June 1986   Donnelley files suit on the balance of its
                     note. Stein and Day files counterclaims of
                     $3.5 million.

October 1986   A mini-trial of Stein and Day's lawsuit vs.
                     Kable is held before Magistrate Francis in
                     the Southern District. Subsequently, after
                     months-long delaying tactics, Kable
                     offers unsatisfactory settlement that
                     would have left authors and others out in
                     the cold. Settlement offer rejected.

February 28,   Damages caused by the domino effect of
1987   Kable's withheld monies come to $11.4
                     million.

April 1, 1987   Discovery completed in the Kable case.

April 9, 1987   Donnelley states to Stein and Day's coun-
                     sel that it doesn't want to damage or
                     destroy the company, asks company to
                     stipulate to amount owed on the note.
                     Stein and Day on advice of counsel does
                     so.

May 13, 1987   Donnelley obtains a judgment on the note
                     in the amount of $1,011,733.96, which
                     includes interest, legal fees, etc.

May 15, 1987	Black Friday. Donnelley gets a restraining order paralyzing Stein and Day and preventing all publishing and related activities. Donnelley's counsel tells Stein and Day counsel that it will ask the judge to throw Sol Stein in jail if he attempts to publish. Motivation for Donnelley's action unknown.
June 1, 1987	Stein and Day files a motion for summary judgment on the amount of money that Kable's auditors say Kable owes.
June 25, 1987	Restrained from publishing, selling, or distributing books, Stein and Day files for protection under Chapter 11 in the hope of resuming publishing activities immediately.
July 14–15, 1987	First hearing for the use of cash collateral requests, among other things, $97,000 for production of books for which orders are on hand. $97,000 is awarded for payroll, minimal housekeeping, and zero for production.
September 1, 1987	Stein and Day reaches agreement in principle with new investor for funding of production and reorganization of its sales force. The business plan forecasts net profits of over $1 million by June 30, 1988. This plan stymied by the Creditors' Committee, though authors and other creditors would be chief beneficiaries of restored production. Motivation for Creditors' Committee action unknown.

September 10, 1987	Stein and Day concludes newsmaking deal with Barnes & Noble to license fifty titles for hardcover reprint for $100,000 advance against royalties with the intention of going into full production with Barnes & Noble's further assistance. Bank takes $70,000, production still blocked. Stein and Day's management protests treatment of authors and other unsecured creditors; company is still barred from manufacturing backlist or forelist books to fill orders. Two of five secured creditors opting to dismember company rather than allow it to resume profitable publishing.
November 2, 5, 1987	Experts testify in court to value of Stein and Day's backlist, forthcoming books, receivables, inventory, and real estate.
November 5, 1987	Attorneys and principals agree on terms of a cash collateral consensual order that would fund an ongoing business plan for Christmas sales to bring in over half a million dollars. Attorney for BookCrafters says he will draft overnight.
November 6, 1987	Stein and Day signs contract to sell real estate for $2.6 million. Has great advance reviews for forthcoming books and thousands of orders that it is still not being allowed to fill.
November 1987	Briarcliff Manor Planning Board hostile to proposal of developer who bought Stein and Day's real estate. Developer withdraws.

December 8, 1987	"Overnight" drafting, turned into a weeks-long renegotiation. Purposeful delay by lawyers termed by counsel for Stein and Day as "objectionable and obscene." Document is finally signed this date, too late for plan to take effect. Last chance for resumption of publishing activities destroyed.
Spring 1988	Two successive buyers of real estate default on closing. Bank interest on mortgage and bank "legal costs" zoom.
August 1, 1988	Stein and Day's exclusive publishing rights offered to over 200 publishers, with deadline of September 15.
August 8, 1988	Real estate finally sold to Judelson Development for $1.5 million cash, $1.1 million less than appraised value. Contract, however, calls for $129,000 additional for each unit above ten approved by Village Planning Board and Trustees of Briarcliff Manor. Lawyers for company and Creditors' Committee get carve-out of fees at the Steins' sole risk.
September 15, 1988	Offers from some fifty bidders do not equal Royalty Capital's offer of $400,000 plus 20 percent of profits for fifteen years for entire Stein and Day backlist.
November 15, 1988	Stein and Day signs contract with Royalty Capital. Delaying actions by various parties hostile to Stein and Day.
November 17, 1988	The kiss of death on the real estate. Briarcliff Board of Trustees, in direct conflict with own Master Plan Update, turns down Judelson and Stein and Day petition to rezone property to R-30, which would bring in $774,000 and pay off the Michigan Bank.

December 29, 1988	BookCrafters, after two and a half months of planning, brings on a motion to terminate the automatic stay, presents its case, and when Stein and Day is ready immediately to present its strong rebuttal of BookCrafters' figures and testimony, the parties convene to negotiate a global settlement of the case.
January–February 1989	Sol Stein's motion to accept Columbia University's offer to set up a Stein and Day archive alongside that of Random House, Harper & Row, Simon & Schuster, etc. is blocked by BookCrafters in order to pressure Steins to become the only creditors to forego all claims and to turn over the remaining assets, including the publishing rights, to BookCrafters.
February 14, 1989	The St. Valentine's Day Massacre. It is made clear by judge and attorneys that unless the Steins sign, the case will be converted to a Chapter 7 and the Steins will lose their home.
February 21, 1989	Judge approves "global stipulation." Randy Kuckuck realizes his determination announced to Patricia Day two months before the Chapter 11 filing: the liquidation of Stein and Day. Motivation unknown. Kuckuck confirms in court that he has personally examined files to be donated to Columbia University and that they are not needed for the sale of remaining assets. Judge orders Stein and Day archives having no monetary value donated to Columbia University.

February 22– April 14, 1989	Patricia Day completes the task of weeding down more than fifty four-drawer file cabinets of Stein and Day papers to some fifteen transfiles of historical interest.
April 16, 1989	Patricia Day and David Day Stein place large yellow tags stating in large black letters "FOR COLUMBIA, DO NOT TOUCH" on three sides of each file belonging to Columbia.
April 19, 1989	At 1 P.M. Columbia University's truck arrives to pick up the transfiles, finds that the majority were shipped to Book-Crafters in Chelsea, Michigan, on April 17, 1989 under instructions from Randy Kuckuck. Kuckuck acknowledges to Sol Stein that BookCrafters has the files. Motivation unknown.

Index